MEMORY AND UTOPIA
THE POETRY OF JOSÉ ÁNGEL VALENTE

LEGENDA

LEGENDA is the Modern Humanities Research Association's book imprint for new research in the Humanities. Founded in 1995 by Malcolm Bowie and others within the University of Oxford, Legenda has always been a collaborative publishing enterprise, directly governed by scholars. The Modern Humanities Research Association (MHRA) joined this collaboration in 1998, became half-owner in 2004, in partnership with Maney Publishing and then Routledge, and has since 2016 been sole owner. Titles range from medieval texts to contemporary cinema and form a widely comparative view of the modern humanities, including works on Arabic, Catalan, English, French, German, Greek, Italian, Portuguese, Russian, Spanish, and Yiddish literature. Editorial boards and committees of more than 60 leading academic specialists work in collaboration with bodies such as the Society for French Studies, the British Comparative Literature Association and the Association of Hispanists of Great Britain & Ireland.

The MHRA encourages and promotes advanced study and research in the field of the modern humanities, especially modern European languages and literature, including English, and also cinema. It aims to break down the barriers between scholars working in different disciplines and to maintain the unity of humanistic scholarship. The Association fulfils this purpose through the publication of journals, bibliographies, monographs, critical editions, and the MHRA Style Guide, and by making grants in support of research. Membership is open to all who work in the Humanities, whether independent or in a University post, and the participation of younger colleagues entering the field is especially welcomed.

ALSO PUBLISHED BY THE ASSOCIATION

Critical Texts
Tudor and Stuart Translations • *New Translations* • *European Translations*
MHRA Library of Medieval Welsh Literature

MHRA Bibliographies
Publications of the Modern Humanities Research Association

The Annual Bibliography of English Language & Literature
Austrian Studies
Modern Language Review
Portuguese Studies
The Slavonic and East European Review
Working Papers in the Humanities
The Yearbook of English Studies

www.mhra.org.uk
www.legendabooks.com

STUDIES IN HISPANIC AND LUSOPHONE CULTURES

Studies in Hispanic and Lusophone Cultures are selected and edited by the Association of Hispanists of Great Britain & Ireland. The series seeks to publish the best new research in all areas of the literature, thought, history, culture, film, and languages of Spain, Spanish America, and the Portuguese-speaking world.

The Association of Hispanists of Great Britain & Ireland is a professional association which represents a very diverse discipline, in terms of both geographical coverage and objects of study. Its website showcases new work by members, and publicises jobs, conferences and grants in the field.

Founding Editor
Professor Trevor Dadson

Editorial Committee
Professor Catherine Davies (University of Nottingham)
Professor Sally Faulkner (University of Exeter)
Professor Andrew Ginger (University of Bristol)
Professor James Mandrell (Brandeis University, USA)
Professor Hilary Owen (University of Manchester)
Professor Christopher Perriam (University of Manchester)
Professor Philip Swanson (University of Sheffield)

Managing Editor
Dr Graham Nelson
41 Wellington Square, Oxford OX1 2JF, UK

www.legendabooks.com/series/shlc

STUDIES IN HISPANIC AND LUSOPHONE CULTURES

1. *Unamuno's Theory of the Novel*, by C. A. Longhurst
2. *Pessoa's Geometry of the Abyss: Modernity and the* Book of Disquiet, by Paulo de Medeiros
3. *Artifice and Invention in the Spanish Golden Age*, edited by Stephen Boyd and Terence O'Reilly
4. *The Latin American Short Story at its Limits: Fragmentation, Hybridity and Intermediality*, by Lucy Bell
5. *Spanish New York Narratives 1898–1936: Modernisation, Otherness and Nation*, by David Miranda-Barreiro
6. *The Art of Ana Clavel: Ghosts, Urinals, Dolls, Shadows and Outlaw Desires*, by Jane Elizabeth Lavery
7. *Alejo Carpentier and the Musical Text*, by Katia Chornik
8. *Britain, Spain and the Treaty of Utrecht 1713-2013*, edited by Trevor J. Dadson and J. H. Elliott
9. *Books and Periodicals in Brazil 1768-1930: A Transatlantic Perspective*, edited by Ana Cláudia Suriani da Silva and Sandra Guardini Vasconcelos
10. *Lisbon Revisited: Urban Masculinities in Twentieth-Century Portuguese Fiction*, by Rhian Atkin
11. *Urban Space, Identity and Postmodernity in 1980s Spain: Rethinking the Movida*, by Maite Usoz de la Fuente
12. *Santería, Vodou and Resistance in Caribbean Literature: Daughters of the Spirits*, by Paul Humphrey
13. *Reprojecting the City: Urban Space and Dissident Sexualities in Recent Latin American Cinema*, by Benedict Hoff
14. *Rethinking Juan Rulfo's Creative World: Prose, Photography, Film*, edited by Dylan Brennan and Nuala Finnegan
15. *The Last Days of Humanism: A Reappraisal of Quevedo's Thought*, by Alfonso Rey
16. *Catalan Narrative 1875-2015*, edited by Jordi Larios and Montserrat Lunati
17. *Islamic Culture in Spain to 1614: Essays and Studies*, by L. P. Harvey
18. *Film Festivals: Cinema and Cultural Exchange*, by Mar Diestro-Dópido
19. *St Teresa of Avila: Her Writings and Life*, edited by Terence O'Reilly, Colin Thompson and Lesley Twomey
20. *(Un)veiling Bodies: A Trajectory of Chilean Post-Dictatorship Documentary*, by Elizabeth Ramírez-Soto

Memory and Utopia

The Poetry of José Ángel Valente

Manus O'Dwyer

Studies in Hispanic and Lusophone Cultures 44
Modern Humanities Research Association
2020

Published by Legenda
an imprint of the Modern Humanities Research Association
Salisbury House, Station Road, Cambridge CB1 2LA

ISBN 978-1-78188-365-5 (HB)
ISBN 978-1-78188-368-6 (PB)

First published 2020

All rights reserved. No part of this publication may be reproduced or disseminated or transmitted in any form or by any means, electronic, mechanical, photocopying, recording or otherwise, or stored in any retrieval system, or otherwise used in any manner whatsoever without written permission of the copyright owner, except in accordance with the provisions of the Copyright, Designs and Patents Act 1988, or under the terms of a licence permitting restricted copying issued in the UK by the Copyright Licensing Agency Ltd, Saffron House, 6–10 Kirby Street, London EC1N 8TS, *England, or in the USA by the Copyright Clearance Center, 222 Rosewood Drive, Danvers MA 01923. Application for the written permission of the copyright owner to reproduce any part of this publication must be made by email to legenda@mhra.org.uk.*

Disclaimer: Statements of fact and opinion contained in this book are those of the author and not of the editors or the Modern Humanities Research Association. The publisher makes no representation, express or implied, in respect of the accuracy of the material in this book and cannot accept any legal responsibility or liability for any errors or omissions that may be made.

Trademark notice: Product or corporate names may be trademarks or registered trademarks, and are used only for identification and explanation without intent to infringe.

© *Modern Humanities Research Association 2020*

Poetry by José Ángel Valente quoted in this volume is
© *Herederos de José Ángel Valente 2020*

Copy-Editor: Dr Ellen Jones

CONTENTS

	Acknowledgements	ix
	List of Abbreviations	x
	Introduction: Romans and Carthaginians	1
1	Valente's Poetics	11
2	Memory and Signs	27
3	Poetry and Community	55
4	Valente and Jabès	73
5	Valente and Celan	93
	Conclusion	115
	Bibliography	119
	Index	127

*To my mother,
who always told me one more story*

ACKNOWLEDGEMENTS

This book derives from a PhD dissertation undertaken at the University of Santiago de Compostela with the support of the *María Barbeito* doctoral funding program of the *Xunta de Galicia*. At Santiago de Compostela, I benefited from the support and encouragement of my thesis director, Fernando Cabo Aseguinolaza, who was exemplary in his patience and breadth of knowledge. I also benefited greatly from the brilliance of teachers and colleagues, especially those that I have worked with most closely: María do Cebreiro Rabade, César Domínguez, and Margarita Candeira García. Claudio Rodríguez Fer facilitated my access to the *Cátedra Valente* and provided many insights into the life and work of Valente. Francisco Xavier Redondo Aval and the library staff at the *Facultade de Filoloxía* were extremely helpful and professional. I spent the first of two doctoral *estancias* at the Department of Spanish, Portuguese, and Latin American Studies at University College Cork, where I gained valuable insights into the tradition of Spanish poetry with Stephan Boyd. At Trinity College Dublin, where I spent the second of my *estancias*, I would especially like to thank Caitriona Leahy, for her exceptional generosity and encouragement, and also my postgraduate colleagues at the Long Room Hub, with whom I had many enriching conversations. Thanks also go to Jonathan Mayhew, Osvaldo Silvestre, and Martín Veiga, the external readers of my thesis, as well as the members of the defence jury, Diana Cullell, José Manuel Cuesta Abad, and Claudio Rodríguez Fer, whose comments and advice on my work were invaluable. At the University of Liverpool, I learnt much in my discussions of Iberian Jewish culture with Şizen Yiacoup. At Durham University, I enjoyed many enlightening discussions with Manuel Hijano and Francisco Hernández Adrián. My conversations with Mike Gonzalez and Feargus Denman, both brilliant and generous minds, were of immense help in developing my ideas. Permission to use the cover photo was granted by the Fundación Manuel Falces; the poems cited are reproduced courtesy of the Estate of José Ángel Valente. My editors at Legenda, Graham Nelson and Ellen Jones, were always professional and helpful. I have been supported throughout by friends, both longstanding and those I met along the way — Danny Barreto, Mairead McGrath, Isabela Figueiredo, Sara Ludovico, Gonçalo Duarte — and family. None of this would have been possible without Ana Bela, who was always *a mi lado, y más próxima a mí que mis sentidos*.

M.O'D, February 2020

LIST OF ABBREVIATIONS

I   Valente, José Ángel. 2006. *Obras Completas*, ed. by Andrés Sánchez Robayna, vol. I (Barcelona: Galaxia Gutenberg)

II   Valente, José Ángel. 2008. *Obras Completas*, ed. by Andrés Sánchez Robayna, comp. by Claudio Rodríguez Fer, vol. II (Barcelona: Galaxia Gutenberg)

DA   Valente, José Ángel. 2011. *Diario Anónimo: 1959–2000*, ed. by Andrés Sánchez Robayna (Barcelona: Galaxia Gutenberg)

INTRODUCTION

Romans and Carthaginians

In an article written in 1994, the Spanish poet José Ángel Valente (1929–2000) recounts an episode from his childhood in 1940s Galicia:

> Cuando yo era niño, muy niño, en la escuela de los reverendos padres de la Compañía, solían dividir la clase en dos grupos: los romanos y los cartagineses. El profesor, con un providencial sentido de la Historia, solía poner a los menos avispados en el grupo cartaginés, para que al oponerse en docta contienda un grupo al otro, el triunfo de 'los romanos' diese razón de la absoluta verdad de la Historia misma. (II: 1498)

Valente, who was academically gifted, would be placed on the side of the Romans, so as to guarantee the classroom rehearsal of Rome's historical triumph. But the future poet rebelled against this celebration of Rome's might. He recalls how he would change sides and join his less gifted classmates: 'solía infiltrarme en el grupo cartaginés y, aunque conseguía a veces que peligrara el triunfo cierto de Roma, quedaba siempre en el bando de los derrotados' (II: 1498). Taking the part of the doomed 'Carthaginians', Valente placed himself firmly on the side of the defeated.

To better understand this story in the context of late 1930s and 1940s Spain, we might turn to British historian Michael Richards's (2013) description of a post-war Francoist 'liturgy' of memory, propagated through education, ritual, and public monuments, which had the aim of creating cultural consensus with regard to Spain's past. According to this vision of Spanish history, the victorious Nationalist forces of the recent civil war were heroic defenders of a homogenously Castilian and Catholic Spain. Republicans and regional nationalists, on the other hand, were painted as foreign interlopers bent on destroying an imagined national purity. This was the period during which Francoist forces enthusiastically adhered to the values of European fascism, which in some of its manifestations had taken on motifs and symbols from ancient Rome.[1] It was common during this period for the children of leftists to suffer various forms of humiliation in their schooling. Being placed on the side of the Carthaginians could serve to remind these pupils of their place in the post-war social order.[2] By taking the side of the Carthaginians, then, the young Valente was allying himself with the defeated side of the Civil War, subverting a vision of history favourable to the victors, and foreshadowing what would become his adult rejection of the tenets of Spanish national Catholicism.

Valente's childhood gesture echoes an important moment in the history of Spanish literature. It recalls the famous 'Soneto a Boscán', a poem in which the founder of modern Spanish poetry, Garcilaso de la Vega, also takes the side of Rome's defeated enemies. Written on the occasion of Carlos V's successful campaign against Turkish-backed forces in North Africa, and the sack of the town of Goleta near the site of ancient Carthage, Garcilaso's sonnet employs motifs from Virgil's *Aeneid* to portray Charles's Spain as a reincarnation of the ancient Roman Empire:

> Boscán, las armas y el furor de Marte,
> que con su propia fuerza el africano
> suelo regando, hacen que el romano
> imperio reverdezca en esta parte,
>
> han reducido a la memoria el arte
> y el antiguo valor italïano,
> por cuya fuerza y valerosa mano
> África se aterró de parte a parte.
>
> Aquí donde el romano encendimiento,
> donde el fuego y la llama licenciosa
> sólo el nombre dejaron a Cartago,
>
> vuelve y revuelve amor mi pensamiento,
> hiere y enciende el alma temerosa,
> y en llanto y en ceniza me deshago. (2006: 34)

However, as Richard Helgerson (2007) and others have noted, what should be an unambiguous celebration of imperial might ends on a melancholic note: the epic description of martial fury of the octet is followed in the final tercet by a lyrical expression of unrequited love. As in Virgil's *Aeneid*, the tale of epic conquest is interrupted by the tears of the lover. In Virgil's tale, these are the tears of Dido, abandoned by Aeneas; in the sonnet, the tears are of Garcilaso, the spurned lover. Taking into account the historical and intertextual resonances of the poem, Helgerson claims that Garcilaso, despite fighting as a soldier of Charles's conquering army, 'ends by identifying with the victims of that army and even more particularly with the victims of that army's ancient Roman predecessor' (2007: 49).

Garcilaso's sonnet suggests a complex intertwining of history, memory, and poetry. Past and present are superimposed within the poem, with Charles and Spain embodying the former might of the Scipios and the Roman Empire. More specifically, Garcilaso's evocation of the ancient ruins of Carthage seems to presage what, in a modern context, becomes a fascination with ruins as sites of nostalgia, but also as sites that inspire desires for alternative social and political conditions. As Peter Fritzsche has shown, in the nineteenth century ruins become a focus for utopian thought, where 'the ruins of the past were taken to be foundations for an alternative present' (2004: 96). It is, perhaps, not too much of a leap for us to imagine that Garcilaso, closely related to the leaders of the *Comunero* rebellion of 1521, could look upon the sacked city of Goleta and not only identify with the defeated, but also intuit the contingency of Charles's victory. If, in the *Aeneid*, Dido's self-immolation confirms a future Carthaginian challenge to Rome's might, so the lover's undoing in the sonnet implies the possible undoing of Charles's empire. The sonnet points to the ways that poetry, and especially a poetry, like Valente's, written in a moment of political defeat and disillusionment, can enter into dialogical relationship with literary sources and historical events, allowing us to read the past into the present and to understand contemporary predicaments in novel and sometimes subversive ways.³

This capacity to trace dialogical relationships between past and present is a central aspect of Valente's work. Significantly, his childhood anecdote forms part of a short text dedicated to the work of the Jewish writer, Elias Canetti. Valente notes that Canetti, the descendant of Sephardic Jews, is one of the Iberian Peninsula's 'vencidos o echados' (II: 1499), victims of a destructive imperialism that Canetti, in his *The Human Province*, traces back to the expansion of Rome. Valente links Canetti's ideas to Walter Benjamin's well-known description of Paul Klee's Angel in his 'Theses on the Philosophy of History' of 1940, according to which Klee's portrait represents the hidden destruction wrought by the forces we call progress. Valente claims that Benjamin's ethical commitment to the defeated, his understanding of what Canetti calls the legacy of Rome — a vision of linear historical progress destructive of difference — has allowed him (Valente) to 'comprender mejor mi vida personal, la convivencia, y conmoriencia con los otros, mi vida colectiva' (II: 1499). As Garcilaso can see in the ruins of the sacked city of Goleta the outlines of Carthage, so Valente can see the cruelty, triumphalism, and destruction of difference in post-war Spain as part of a historical pattern of imperial violence, framing this synchronous vision in terms of the work of two twentieth-century Jewish writers, Benjamin and Canetti.

The themes invoked in Valente's short text lead us, I believe, towards fundamental aspects of his poetry and thought, pointing to the ways in which his writings reveal an ethical commitment to the outsiders or losers of Spanish history, to the absences that mark the Spanish and wider European post-war period. Valente's desire to remember the marginalized is evident in his remarks on the five hundredth anniversary of the key date in Spanish history, 1492:

> El 31 de marzo de 1492 empieza en la historia peninsular y, en términos generales, la historia de la Europa moderna, el ciclo de las grandes diásporas con la expulsión de los españoles judíos. La península ibérica había sido hasta entonces tierra de recepción, de acogida, de mezcla, de impura y germinal diversidad. Ese signo de incorporación y de cruce se invierte para dar paso a una estructura político-social caracterizada por el cierre y la exclusión. La ideología y la estirpe, la Inquisición y la limpieza de sangre imponen su ley. No hay cabida para protestantes, erasmistas, alumbrados, judíos, moriscos o — más tarde, pero como fenómeno de igual naturaleza — para afrancesados, masones, republicanos. Se inicia así un prolongado y tenaz proceso de aplastamiento de la diferencia en un país que había nacido y se había conformado en la diversidad. (II: 681)

Here Valente proposes a perhaps idealized vision of a multicultural pre-reconquest Iberia, a time and place which, as Richard Fletcher notes, has become subject to modern liberal fantasies of medieval cultural tolerance (2000: 84). In the context of Valente's writing, however, the idealization of the past allows him to articulate a critical vision of Spain's national history that is informed by an ethical commitment to diversity, a discourse that stands as a corrective to the triumphalist narratives of the chauvinistic nationalisms that, paradoxically, were consolidated in the liberal democracies of the post-war era.⁴ As we will see, in his poetry, Valente defends everything that the stultifying, fascist culture of his youth despised: where the culture of national Catholicism celebrates purity, heroic masculinity, and military triumph, Valente's work defends difference, passivity, and the victims of violence. If the dictatorship sought to create what Jan Assmann (1995: 128) terms a common 'cultural memory' informed by Catholic and Castilian triumphalism, Valente's poetry is informed by a historical vision attentive to Spain's marginalized political, ethnic, and religious others.

Central to the understanding of Spanish and European history and memory that informs Valente's thought are a series of Jewish writers and thinkers — Gershom Scholem, Walter Benjamin, Ernst Bloch, Emmanuel Levinas, Edmond Jabès, Paul Celan. It is, I believe, necessary to understand the importance of Valente's ethical and literary engagements with these writers to fully understand the development and significance of his poetry in the panorama of twentieth-century Spanish and European literature. In this work, I describe how Valente's increasing interest in Jewish culture from the 1960s on is reflective of wider intellectual and political developments within Europe that have brought about the preoccupation with memory and difference that characterizes contemporary cultures. From this point of view, my reading of Valente's poetry contributes to the growing body of academic work on the theme of historical memory in Spain, a discourse that has tended to ignore poetry.⁵ To begin this task, it is important to trace Valente's life and career as well as his reception within the Spanish cultural field.

Placing Valente

Valente occupies a singular position in the history of twentieth-century Spanish poetry. Born to a lower-middle class family in the provincial Galician town of Ourense in 1929, Valente's academic gifts were recognized from an early age and he benefited from the friendship and tutelage of local luminaries such as Vicente Risco. He also had access to the personal library of a family friend, a priest and Republican sympathizer, which allowed him to freely develop his literary interests. His university years were spent in Madrid, where he enjoyed the intellectual stimulus of the recently founded university residences, the *Colegios Mayores*, which, despite their national Catholic ethos, were at the heart of a slow post-war *aperturismo*. It was there he came into contact with some of the leading poets of the time, forming a particularly close bond with the poet who was a mentor for many young writers of the time, Vicente Aleixandre. From the mid-1950s onwards, he lived outside Spain, first in Oxford, where he held the position of Spanish *lector*, and then in Switzerland, where he was a translator at the World Health Organization. Valente would only return to live in Spain in the late 1980s, spending his final years in Almeria.⁶

Valente's literary career covers a fifty-year period, from the early 1950s to his death in the year 2000. His poetry develops from early collections marked by the social realism and existentialism of the mid-century, through a more experimental middle phase during the 1960s, to a fragmentary, minimalist, and conceptually complex later poetry that Jonathan Mayhew (2012: 77) regards as a quintessential example of 'late modernism'. Such a trajectory makes it difficult to place Valente within a narrative of Spanish literary history that typically describes poetry as moving from the social realism of the 1940s and 1950s to the more detached 'critical realism' of the *generación del 50*, the linguistic exuberance of the *novísimo* poets of the 1970s, and on to the more straightforward confessional *poesía de la experiencia* of the 1980s and 1990s. Valente's singular path is reflected in his resistance to his inclusion as a member of the so-called *generación del 50*, a term Spanish literary historiography employs to describe poets born between 1924 and 1938.[7] Paradoxically, Valente participated in the creation of this historiographical demarcation through his compilation of 'Once poetas', an anthology published in the *Índice* journal in 1955. This project had the explicit aim of publicizing the work of a new generation of poets under the age of thirty through the publication of a short introduction to their work and number of their poems. In fact, Valente only managed to publish the work of seven authors: Lorenzo Gomis, Alberto Costafreda, José Manuel Caballero Bonald, Claudio Rodríguez, Jaime Ferrán, Ángel Gonzalez, and José Agustín Goytisolo. Despite his involvement in preparing the anthology, Valente would later resist the positioning of his work within a generational context, and refute the very notion of 'generation', claiming in 1976: '[...] ni la noción de generación ni la de grupo servirían realmente para apresar, desde un punto de vista crítico, la obra del escritor individual' (II: 1219).

Valente's self-proclaimed marginality with regard to his contemporaries is belied, however, by the archival material held at the University of Santiago de Compostela, which includes correspondence with some of the greatest literary figures of his time: Vicente Aleixandre, José Lezama Lima, Octavio Paz, María Zambrano, among many others. As Marcela Romano writes, for all the rhetoric of marginality, Valente is:

> Considerado, hoy, uno de los mayores poetas dentro del campo intelectual español, y precisamente se encuentra en el centro (no en los márgenes) de muchas discusiones. Desde ya hace más de una década ha sido varias veces premiado, su poesía fue objeto de diversos encuentros y jornadas, y existen libros y revistas monográficas dedicadas con exclusividad a su producción. La extensa bibliografía circulante en torno a su obra y aquí citada da clara cuenta de ello. Por otra parte, muchas casas centrales dentro del mercado editorial español han publicado y publican su obra: Seix-Barral, Tusquets, Alianza, Cátedra, Círculo de Lectores. (2002: 141)

Valente's self-perception as a solitary voice has to do both with the length of time he spent outside of Spain as well as with his uncompromising stances with regard to the work of other Spanish poets, most vigorously expressed in his polemical engagements with what is termed the *poesía de la experiencia*, the predominant poetic tendency of the 1980s and 1990s. In his introduction to an anthology of Spanish poetry from 1968 to 1998, Luis García Montero, the leading figure of this school, alludes implicitly to the work of Valente, and to the complex philosophical and theological grounding of his poetics:

> El tradicionalismo se disfraza de odios diferentes según los tesoros que vigila. [...] Concibo la poesía como un oficio, un género de ficción que necesita el conocimiento técnico y muchas horas de trabajo. [...] Frente a la cursilería decimonónica del silencio lírico y las esencias ocultas, prefiero aceptar que la poesía es una cuestión de palabras. (qtd. in García Montero, 1998: 569)

Valente, for his part, refers witheringly to the *poesía de la experiencia* in one of his final interviews. Responding to the question as to whether literary or everyday experience is more important for poetic creation, Valente replies: 'Sería, ciertamente, muy de agradecer que los poetas o grupos epigonales en quienes encuentra origen esta falsa cuestión empezasen a ir a la escuela' (II:1614).[8] Valente's physical absence from Spain as well as the sheer ferocity of the polemics of the 1980s and 1990s made it easy for him to cast himself as an outsider, a position that coincided with a vision of Spanish history that pays special attention to Spain's marginalized others. But while it is true that the difficulty of Valente's work has meant that he has not gained the broader public recognition of poets such as Luis García Montero, it is also true that his poetry and theoretical essays have attracted the attention of numerous academics and literary theorists, provoking what Julián Jiménez Heffernan describes as an 'industria (a veces comparsa) exegética montada en torno al poeta' (2004b: 199).

We can trace the development of this 'industry' from the late 1970s, with Ellen Engleson Marson's short study of the *Poesía y poética de José Ángel Valente* (1978), through the 1980s, with Milagros Polo's (1983) study of Valente's poetry and thought, in which she emphasizes Valente's position as a poetic and political outsider; Santiago Daydí-Tolson's (1984) analysis of the intertextual resonances in the poems, which he combines with a concern for the development of distinctive enunciative positions in Valente's poetry; Miguel Mas's short study (1989), which offers a unifying vision of Valente's career as a search for the Word that underlies language; to, at the end of the 1980s, Eva Valcárcel's (1989) exploration of the central symbols in Valente's poetry.

At the beginning of the following decade, the Galician poet and scholar Claudio Rodríguez Fer edited two significant collections of essays (1992 and 1994) on Valente's work, with the first of these gathering important reviews and essays on the poet, allowing us to track the development of his critical reception in the readings of critics, fellow poets, and academics from the 1950s until the late 1980s. The 1990s also saw two other important collections of essays dedicated to the Galician poet: *El silencio y la escucha* (1995), edited by Teresa Hernández Fernández, and *En torno a la obra de Valente* (Ancet and others 1996), the result of a colloquium on Valente's work held at the *Residencia de Estudiantes* in Madrid. At the start of the new century, Nuria Fernández Quesada's anthology, which is accompanied by short texts by philosophers, literary scholars, and poets, *Anatomía de la palabra* (2000), reflects the sustained attention paid to Valente's writings, despite the prevailing *poesía de la experiencia* of the time.

In the 1990s, Valente's work also attracted approaches that could be framed within a more generally deconstructive perspective. Jiménez Heffernan's 1998 study of the links between English metaphysical poetry and the Spanish tradition,

La palabra emplazada: Meditación y contemplación de Herbert a Valente, culminates in a chapter dedicated to Valente's poetry, in which the author claims that 'lo que precede no ha sido más que una larga excusa para poder hablar de Valente' (1998: 327), and combines an erudite investigation of the Galician poet's approximations to metaphysical poetry with theoretical reflections that owe much both to the work of Harold Bloom, but also, if in a critical vein, to the legacy of the work of Paul de Man, and in the more specific context of the study of Spanish poetry, Philip Silver. Jiménez Heffernan also devotes various essays collected in his *Los papeles rotos* (2004b) to Valente. José Manuel Cuesta Abad (1999) concludes his exploration of the rhetoric of the enigma, which includes essays on literary figures that are of central importance for Valente — Mallarmé, Celan, Zambrano — with a discussion of the Galician poet's conception of a foundational *antepalabra*. Cuesta Abad had previously participated in the collection curated by Teresa Hernández Fernández, with an essay that identifies a tendency in Valente's poetry towards a dissolution of the poetic self in the indeterminacy of the corporal. He also contributes an important essay on the negative categories — *silencio, vacío, nada* — in Valente's poetry in the more recent collection dedicated to his work edited by Jordi Doce and Marta Agudo, *Pájaros raíces en torno a la obra de José Ángel Valente* (2010b). Also taking an approach indebted to aspects of the deconstructive moment, the American scholar Jonathan Mayhew dedicated a chapter of his *Poetry of Self-Consciousness* to the 'logocentrism' of Valente's late work (1994: 66–79).

In the first decade of the twenty first century, Valente's work was the focus of a number of doctoral studies: Manuel Fernández Rodríguez (2001) provides a thorough reading of Valente's prose writings in his *Análisis integral de la narrativa de José Ángel Valente*; Carlos Peinado Elliot's *Unidad y transcendencia: estudio sobre la obra de José Ángel Valente* (2002) unifies the dialectic of immanence and transcendence in Valente's work under the rubric of an *eros* for the Levinasian category of the Other; and David Conte Imbert's *La palabra de lo singular: figuraciones del origen entre lírica y filosofía (Martin Heidegger, Claudio Rodríguez, José Ángel Valente)* contains important reflections on Valente's theorization of the material in terms of Heidegger's later philosophy. Conte Imbert's approach is summarized in his contribution to the collection of essays *Referentes europeas en la obra de Valente,* which also includes texts by Manuel Fernández Rodríguez, Jonathan Mayhew, María Lopo, and Rosa Marta Gómez Pato. The year 2008 marks a veritable cascade of academic theses centred on the Valente's work. José A. de Ramos Abreu provides in his *La fascinación del enigma. La poética de José Ángel Valente en sus ensayos* a full account of Valente's poetic theories and the contexts in which they were devised; José Luis Fernández Castillo studies the convergences between the work of Valente and Octavio Paz in his *El ídolo y el vacío: La crisis de la divinidad en la tradición poética moderna: Octavio Paz y José Ángel Valente* (2008); while Fatiha Benlabbah advances a fascinating reading of Valente's engagement with the traditions of Sufi mysticism, and touches on aspects of Valente's reading of Jewish tradition that I will explore in depth below, in her *En el espacio de la mediación. José Ángel Valente y el discurso místico* (2008). For her part, Ioana Ruxandra Gruia explores the centrality of the work of T. S. Eliot for both Valente and Jaime Gil de Biedma in *Escribir el tiempo: Huellas de la obra de T.S. Eliot en la obra de José Ángel Valente y Jaime Gil de Biedma* (2008). The following year saw the publication of Jorge Machín Lucas's *José Ángel Valente y la intertexualidad posmoderna mística*, which reads Valente's poetry and thought in terms of a postmodern 'religious turn'. More recently, in 2018, Stefano Pradel published his *Vértigo de las cenizas,* a study of the aesthetic of the fragment in Valente's work.

Recent years have also seen the publication of a three-volume biography on the poet, *Valente Vital* (Rodríguez Fer, Agudo Ramírez, and Fernández Rodríguez 2012; Lopo, Blanco de Saracho and Rodríguez Fer 2014; and Fernández Rodríguez, García Lara, and Rodríguez Fer 2017). Valente's diary, edited by Andrés Sánchez Robayna, was published in 2011 as his *Diario anónimo* (Valente 2011). A number of autobiographical short prose pieces, collected in the appendix of the *Obras completas II*, under the title *Palais de justice*, were republished in 2014. Valente's correspondence with Lezama Lima is collected in 2012's *Maestro cantor*; his correspondence with several of his contemporaries from the so-called *generación del 50* is collected in Saturnino Valladares's *Retrato de una figura ausente*, which was published in 2017.

This enumeration of the critical attention paid to Valente's writings reflects the impact that his poetry, as well as his philosophically inflected theories of language, have had in Spanish literary and academic circles. The ever-increasing academic production is a challenge to anyone attempting to create new readings of Valente's work. The question arises as to whether it is possible to say anything new with regard to a poet who has had so many expert readers. Perhaps one of the openings for new readings of Valente's work might have to do with the very expertise of his interpreters. Valente's complex poetics and the theories of language on which they are based invite academic speculation, and readers such as Cuesta Abad, Jiménez Heffernan, and Mayhew elaborate upon them brilliantly, drawing out a poetics of immanence that is an essential part of Valente's work. There is a tendency, however, as Jiménez Heffernan (2004b) himself notes, to allow Valente's sophisticated theoretical armature to over-determine readings of the poems, and with that a tendency to neglect the social and political context in which this poetry was written.[9] The poet and critic Miguel Casado, in a particularly insightful essay on Valente's work, also identifies this critical tendency:

> La necesidad de totalizar que impulsa a la crítica y comparte el propio autor en su proyección extratextual (ver sus entrevistas, por ejemplo) choca con el carácter conflictivo de su práctica y la defensa que siempre realizó de lo fragmentario. Quizá su lectura requiera en este momento recordarlo, reemprender el camino desde los poemas sin grandes pretensiones: solo hacer pie, recuperar un terreno abierto, incluso a costa de que parezca que se rebajan los objetivos. (2012: 154)

The powerful theoretical apparatuses which many critics feel necessary to approach Valente's work might in fact elide the complexity and range of an oeuvre that comprises almost fifty years of writing.

On the other hand, and again to cite Casado, while Valente's poetry and thought is of considerable range and complexity, it can be argued that it maintains 'siempre una forma similar de moverse, de relacionarse consigo misma' (2012: 157). For Casado, this constancy within a poetry that is fragmentary and varied has to do with its fundamental concern with lack or absence: 'El corazón, la pérdida, el vacío y la palabra componen, con la fuerza imprevisible de las formaciones irracionales, un grumo originario en que la privación alimenta el vínculo entre identidad y escritura' (2012: 152). Similarly, Jiménez Heffernan claims that 'en ningún poeta como en Valente es tan letal la conciencia de una imposeción existencial' (2004a: 448). Any attentive reader of Valente's work will concur with Casado and Jiménez Heffernan's comments. Valente's poetry is profoundly elegiac, often defined by address to that which is unavailable: a distant or inexistent God, an unknowable body, a total but unpronounceable word, a lost child, and, ultimately, the absent dead.

Neither critic, however, draws out fully the social context in which Valente writes. As brilliant as their readings are, there is no detailed consideration of the ways in which Valente's work constitutes an intervention within the Spanish public sphere, or how the absences referred to in his work can take on particular resonance in the post war political context. Jonathan Mayhew compounds this tendency when he argues that Valente's

> poetic achievement resides in a kind of distillation, or *translation*, of a Heideggerian tradition of poetic modernity, in a specifically Spanish context. [...] Valente is not the originator of the modern tradition: he is, rather, the quintessential *late* modernist, putting the pieces together in a brilliant but belated fashion. (2009: 86)

Mayhew's discussion of Valente's modernist poetics, while pertinent to his work, understates the variety, and also the social, political, and ethical relevance of Valente's poetry. In this study, I discuss Valente's complex writings on poetic language, identifying central questions that are common to them, while also pointing to the ways in which his poetry and poetics imply a specific political stance. Beginning with an examination of Valente's theories of poetic language and the contexts in which they arise, I argue that they describe a poetry that serves both to commemorate the dead but also to awaken utopian desires. In the second chapter, I discuss the first half of Valente's career in terms of Walter Benjamin's conception of melancholy and explore the ways in which his poetry mourns the defeat of Republican Spain but also reveals disillusionment with what he sees as the totalitarian aspects of contemporary Communism, while maintaining hope in the possibility of revolutionary change. In the third chapter, I address the ideas of community in Valente's work, and challenge notions of a slackening of political engagement in Valente's later poetry. The fourth chapter discusses Valente's construction of a poetics of exile in the context of his reading of the work of Edmond Jabès. My fifth chapter discusses Valente's reading and translations of Paul Celan in terms of witnessing, testimony, and cultural memory. I conclude with a consideration of the centrality of death in the Valente's final collection and point to the political and ethical implications of a poetry, such as his, that addresses itself to absence. In each case, I will attempt to show the social and political stakes at play in the development of one of the most significant bodies of work in twentieth century Spanish literature.

Notes to the Introduction

1. For a discussion of the symbolic use of *Romanità* in Italian fascism see Jan Nelis (2011). It is significant that, in a poem — 'Las légiones romanas' — written in the late 1960s and included in the collection *Breve Son*, Valente links the then current American military campaign in Vietnam to the exploits of the Roman army: 'Las légiones romanas aún se baten | desde hace dos mil años | en los pantanos y los arrozales' (I: 261).
2. For a description of schooling in the immediate post-war, see Guichot Reina (2010).
3. Jaime Gil de Biedma's reference (2017: 95) to Rodrigo Caro's 'A las ruinas de Itálica' in his consideration of the 'ruins' of 1950s Barcelona in 'Barcelona ja no es bona, o mi paseo solitario en primavera' would mirror the relations between literary and historical past and present I trace here.
4. Tony Judt (2005) describes the period after the second world war as one in which the cosmopolitanism that had once characterized many parts of Europe is replaced by a network of 'hermetic national enclaves where surviving religious or ethnic minorities — the Jews in France, for example — represented a tiny percentage of the population at large and were thoroughly integrated into its political and cultural mainstream' (8).
5. The majority of scholars working with the tools of memory studies to describe the cultural production of post-war and contemporary Spain — Sebastiaan Faber (2018), Joan Resina (2000, 2017), Alison Ribeiro de Menezes (2014), Jo Labanyi (2007) — ignore the role of poetry in the construction of collective memory.
6. Valente's life has been described in detail in the three-volume biography *Valente Vital*, which charts his childhood in Galicia, his university years in Madrid, his teaching post in Oxford in the mid-1950s, his professional life in Switzerland and Paris, and his final years in Almeria. Marta Agudo gives a detailed account of Valente's time in Madrid in *Valente Vital: Galicia, Madrid, Oxford* (2012: 169–310). Juan Goytisolo, a friend and contemporary of the poet, offers a vivid description of university life in the Madrid of the early 1950s in his autobiographical *Coto Vedado*.
7. For a critical perspective on the formation and perpetuation of the *generación de los 50* see Miguel Casado (2005: 29–48) and Juan José Lanz (2009: 9–65).
8. Jonathan Mayhew (1999) describes the *poesía de la experiencia* defence of an imagined poetic 'normality' as opposed to an avant-garde experimentation. For Mayhew, and for the author, the stance of poets like García Montero with regard to the modernist tradition, and to Valente, betrays a fundamental misunderstanding of both.
9. Jiménez Heffernan (2004b: 193–99) urges us to resist Valente's sophisticated theoretical self-presentation and to remember that his work exists within a tradition of Spanish lyric poetry. For Jiménez Heffernan what is needed is less theory and 'más Valente'.

CHAPTER 1

Valente's Poetics

Poetics of the 1950s

Valente's critical and theoretical essays are profound, wide-ranging, and influential. They include *Las palabras de la tribu* (II: 37–265), a collection of programmatic texts and literary criticism written between 1955 and 1970 and published as an anthology in 1971; two collections of essays pertaining to the mystic tradition, *La piedra y el centro* (II: 271–364), first published in 1982 and *Variaciones sobre el pájaro y la red* (II: 367–447), first published in 1991; and copious contributions to journals, newspapers, and anthologies, a catalogue that runs from his earliest writings in 1948 to his final interview in the year 2000. There is undoubted range and complexity in Valente's theorization of poetry — Miguel Casado identifies 'por lo menos dos poéticas' (2012: 157) in Valente's work — reflecting the broad sweep of his literary, philosophical, and theological knowledge. In this chapter, however, I will argue that it is possible to identify a common thread running throughout Valente's essays: a constant concern for the relationship between poetry, political change, and cultural memory that takes on a special resonance in the context of the aftermath of the Spanish civil war.

Valente's best-known writings on poetry are those essays which contribute to the literary polemics of the Spain of the 1950s and 1960s. These debates turned on the possible social functions of poetry, and took place within the context of the exhaustion of the Spanish social realism of the 1940s and 50s, as well as wider European debates as to the relationship between poetry and politics.[1] A key text here is Jean Paul Sartre's 1948 essay, *Qu'est-ce que la littérature?* (Sartre 1964), in which the French philosopher argued that lyric poetry favours form over content and is therefore essentially autotelic and politically unengaged. In Spain, these ideas were to inform the poetics of social realism, which includes the work of poets of the generation prior to Valente such as Gabriel Celaya, Blas de Otero, and José Hierro, writers who championed a social realist poetry that would be relevant to the experiences of the 'inmensa mayoría'.[2] This stance was elaborated theoretically in the work of the Madrid-based critic Carlos Bousoño, and confirmed in Vicente Aleixandre's 1955 apology for poetry, in which the Sevillian poet defended the idea, in accordance with the work of Bousoño, that the primary function of poetry should be to communicate a given emotion or state of affairs.[3] Though Valente's early collections show much of the *compromiso* of the social-realist poets, and though he shares with them a commitment to the fight against Francoism and a belief that literary activity has a role in this struggle, a commitment consolidated in his participation in the twenty-year commemoration of the death of Antonio Machado at Collioure in 1959, Valente also displays a critical attitude with regard to what he would come to see as the overly simplistic theoretical bases of social realism. In a rich and multi-layered text, 'Comunicación y conocimiento' (I: 39–46), written in 1957 but first published in 1963, Valente argues that poetry's value lies not in its communicative function, but in its capacity to provide knowledge of the singular and unrepeatable aspects of experience that are elided in other forms of discourse.[4] Here, Valente corroborates the approach of Carlos Barral, the Barcelona based poet and critic whose polemical article, published in the journal *Laye* in 1953, 'Poesía no es comunicación', had forcefully argued against the poetics of social realism. Rather than reflecting a given state of affairs, a preordained reality open to direct representation, according to Valente: 'Todo poema es [...] una exploración del material de experiencia no previamente conocido que constituye su objeto. El conocimiento más o menos pleno del objeto del poema supone la existencia más o menos pleno del poema en cuestión' (II: 42). Valente derives this terminology from a section of the literary theorist Eliseo Vivas's *Creation and Discovery*, according to which the poet's gift lies in revealing a pre-existent but heretofore unarticulated 'object' of the poem (1955: 138). Vivas's ideas themselves derive from T. S. Eliot's conception of the 'objective correlative', which the American poet describes in his essay on Hamlet from 1919 (Eliot 1948: 145) as the capacity of the poem to creatively embody experiential states that would otherwise remain inarticulate.

Valente's account of the epistemological capacities of poetic language in 'Conocimiento y comunicación' betrays the influence on his thought from this period of Eliot's essays and the wider Eliot-informed critical environment to which he was exposed during his spell in Oxford as a Spanish lecturer.[5] Valente taught at Oxford from 1955 to 1958, during which time he researched the influence of Spanish, and especially Catholic devotional, literature on English letters in the sixteenth and seventeenth centuries. Reminiscing on this period of his life in 1993, Valente emphasizes the importance for his intellectual development of these early experiences outside of Spain:

> El estar fuera de España, y concretamente en Inglaterra, en mis primeros tiempos de poeta, fue determinante para que yo no me sumara a la mera copia — que es lo que abunda — de Cernuda. [...] Allí entré en contacto, en su propia lengua, con poetas inglesas que para mí fueron muy decisivos: en la generación mayor, Eliot, y en la siguiente, Auden. Leo intensamente a Eliot en poesía y en prosa y el ensayista me lleva de la mano a la poesía metafísica, que el mismo trajo a la poesía moderna. Por esa vía, Eliot me acercó a Cernuda, quien realizó una trayectoria similar a la de él. (qtd. in Gruia 2008: 8)

Inspired by Eliot's literary criticism and the comparative work of Louis J. Martz, Valente found a way to re-read literary tradition, placing Spanish baroque poetry and devotional texts at the base of a pan-European 'poetry of meditation' that would have inflected modern poetry since the Romantics, and which would only return to Spain in the work of Unamuno and Cernuda.[6]

Alongside the essays of Eliot, while at Oxford Valente read the Anglo-American 'New Criticism' of the time. The articulation of the relations between the social and the poetic in the work of the leading New Critic, Cambridge lecturer F. R. Leavis, leave a clear mark on Valente's writings of the late 1950s and early 1960s. This is visible in Valente's approving references to Leavis's influential *New Bearings in English Poetry* in his short text, 'Oxford, 1956' (II: 1023–29), published in the *Índice de artes y letras* of the same year. Valente's diary entry for March 1961 — 'Conocimiento y communicación — F.R. Leavis p.13' (DA: 60) — shows that he drew directly from the arguments of *New Bearings* for his polemical essay. In *New Bearings*, Leavis had claimed that Romantic poetry, which he defined as the 'direct expression of simple emotions' (1954: 9), had, by the end of the nineteenth century, become a pretentious poetastry, a dream language removed from the realities of twentieth-century mass society. Overcoming Romantic diction, the modern poet (the paradigm here is Eliot) should be 'unusually sensitive, unusually aware, more sincere and more himself than the ordinary man can be' (1954:13), and therefore capable of combining his unique insight with expressive means that would be adequate to the social conditions of modernity. It is important to note that this adequacy is not merely thematic; paraphrasing Eliot, Leavis quips that if the motor car enters poetry it will do so because the 'modern's perception of rhythm has been affected by the internal combustion engine' (1954: 24). Poetry, then, is the privileged discourse that in the totality of its rhythm and organization can be the 'objective correlative' to the affective life of the twentieth century city-dweller. The capacity to suggest and discover emotions that are adequate to the age will determine the quality of the poem.

These ideas, if inflected by progressive political positions, inform Valente's readings of Spanish literary figures in his essays from the 1960s. In an essay dedicated to the work of Rafael Alberti, 'La necesidad y la musa', first published in *Ínsula* in 1963, Valente follows the critical presuppositions of Eliot and Leavis to the letter, defining one of the central problems of the modern age as the 'quiebra entre la experiencia personal y la experiencia colectiva' (II:159). The disintegration and atomization of modern societies is expressed in the work of the modern writers — he lists Kafka, Musil, Faulkner, Camus, and Beckett — who convey:

> formas exasperadas de la subjetividad, de lo patológico, del absurdo, de la inmovilidad de la condición humana, en la sustitución de un universo de seres próximos o prójimos por un universo de individuos adyacentes o contiguos clausurados en su experiencia personal y en la mitificación, por último, de la incomunicabilidad de esa experiencia. (II: 159)

The contemporary writer should move beyond these myths of corrosion towards a new mythology of the collective.[7] It is in this sense that Valente reads the significance of Alberti's turn away from the neo-popular and neo-baroque fashionings of his earlier collections towards the anti-rhetoricism of the poems from the 1930s, as in his *El poeta en la calle* (1966) and *De un momento a otro* (1937). This turn marks Alberti's attempt to arrive at a 'mitificación de lo nuevo' (II: 163), in which the means of poetic expression would be adequate to the social conditions within which the poetry is written. Alberti's subsequent return to Gongorism presents, in this context, a self-acknowledged failure, in which the poet admits to his incapacity to marry form and content. Valente's reading of the career of Miguel Hernández, also included in *Las palabras de la tribu*, mirrors in many ways his understanding of Alberti's trajectory. For Valente, the neo-baroque virtuosity of Hernández's Góngora-inspired first collections hides a more profound voice that comes to the fore in the civil war poems, which in their simplicity better convey the brutality of war.

Critical Marxism and Linguistic Freedom

Valente's absorption of the poetics of Eliot and Leavis, which includes their problematic reliance on conservative notions of collective mythologies, is tempered from the early 1960s onwards by his reading of a critical Marxist tradition that includes figures such as Walter Benjamin, Berthold Brecht, Georg Lukacs, Theodor Adorno and Henri Lefebvre. Valente's reading of these thinkers gives him the conceptual tools to criticize the poetics of social realism from a leftist perspective. Such an approach is evident in 'Literatura e ideología. Un ejemplo de Berthold Brecht', an essay, first published in the *Revista de Occidente* in 1969, that criticizes the mediocrity of poets who write strictly in accordance with the tenets of the social realism of the 1940s and 50s. Here, Valente claims that poets who slavishly follow the strictures of the social realism of the post-war era write according to an 'a-priori ideológico' (II: 48) that determines the thematic content of their work. In the Lukacsian terms Valente borrows, these poets follow a *tendencia* instead of developing a unique style that would allow for the creative discovery of the real.[8] From this perspective, the literary social realism of post-war Spain would have exhausted its usefulness, becoming the 'fruto de un fenómeno de cristalización ideológico del pensamiento marxista que, operando en contra de sus propios enunciados, vino a coartar gravemente las posibilidades de acceso del escritor a la realidad' (II: 61–62). As clichéd, over-determined form, social realism fails to achieve what the Adorno of 'Lyric poetry and society' defines as poetry's revelatory function, its 'giving voice to what ideology hides' (1991: 39).

The struggle between poetry perceived as communicating a given state of affairs and poetry as discovery of reality is represented for Valente in Sophocles's *Antigone*, which he discusses in his essay, published in *Ínsula* in 1968, 'Ideología y lenguaje' (II: 76–81). Here, Valente claims that the character of Creonte in the tragedy stands for the order of the city and the revealed God, whereas Antigone represents the realm of possibility, the possibility of new mythologies and an alternative social order: 'Antígona existe para forzar una nueva manifestación de lo divino que, en última instancia [...], consiste en la sanción de una nueva órbita de humana libertad' (II: 76). Significantly, Antigone's resistance to the law of the city also implies a resistance to its language. If language under totalitarian regimes becomes corrupt, a public language that 'es necesario preservar de toda grieta, de toda fisura, de todo cambio' (II: 77), what Henri Lefebvre (1966) terms *discours*, poetry has the potential to create new linguistic uses and help us to overcome restricted mental horizons. It is in this sense that Antigone restores 'la palabra de raíz poética, creadora y, por eso mismo, denunciadora de un lenguaje público que reducido a la inmovilidad impositiva del discurso ha perdido validez, es decir, se corrompe, está corrupto' (II: 77).

It is important to contextualize these claims within the context of Valente's political self-positioning during the 1960s. Valente was a committed leftist, a contributor to the anti-Francoist *Cuadernos de Rueda Ibérico* and a member of the *Frente de Liberación Popular*, a clandestine organization that attempted to carry out its anti-fascist activities at a critical distance from the Communist Party.[9] Valente's alignment with the FLP meant that his commitment to anti-fascist activities did not preclude him from criticizing the totalitarian aspects of Communist regimes. Valente's experiences in Cuba in 1967, detailed in personal notes published in his *Diario anónimo*, reflect his ambivalence regarding a historical event he saw as having genuinely revolutionary potential but that was developing oppressive tendencies. In Cuba, Valente met with the writers José Rodríguez Feo and José Lezama Lima, both of whom were to suffer at the hands of the Castro regime, as did Valente's close friend, the homosexual Cuban writer Calvert Casey, who was to commit suicide in 1969. These friendships deepened his concern about the violation of human rights on the Caribbean island. This critical attitude towards Cuba was to reach its apogee with Valente's signing of a collective open letter, published in *Le Monde* in April 1971, and signed by a number of major progressive intellectuals including Jean Paul Sartre and Simone de Beauvoir, criticizing the Castro regime for the treatment of the writer Heberto Padilla (Alegria and others 1971). Valente responded to the playwright Alfonso Sastre's criticism of the *Le Monde* letter with the publication of 'Cuba: Dogma y ritual' in the literary magazine *Triunfo* in June 1971, in which he condemns the 'vulgaridad del modelo represivo' (II: 1174–77) that forced Padilla's humiliating public retractions.

Valente's response to the Cuban situation reveals a fundamental political orientation that, though leftist, could never accept the authoritarian aspects of contemporary Communist regimes and the overdetermined language of Party officialdom. In this he has much in common with the generation of 1968, as well as with many of the Spanish intellectuals of his time — Jorge Semprún, Juan Goytisolo — who, disillusioned with the Soviet Union and the Communist Party, searched for alternative models of liberation more attentive to difference and singularity. It is in this context that we can understand the centrality of freedom in Valente's writings on poetic language of the late sixties, and the importance for him of finding creative means of expression that would be capable of denouncing the capitalist status quo, yet at the same time free from the stifling strictures of the party line.

It is this potentially liberatory aspect of poetry that Valente describes in his 1971 essay on Vicente Aleixandre, 'El poder de la serpiente'. Valente claims that Aleixandre's surrealist-influenced works — *Pasión de la tierra*, first published in 1935 (1987), *Espadas como labios*, first published in 1932 (1993) and *La destrucción y el amor*, first published in 1935 (1993) — are defined by an 'unconditioned' (Valente will later use the word *sobreintencional*) poetic language. With this term, Valente means that the surrealist language of these collections is not wholly governed by conscious subjective intention. The images in the poems attempt to describe a world that has not been limited by the categories of logical understanding, that 'todavía es pura posibilidad de proyección en formas múltiples, no sujeto aún a los condicionamientos de su natural desarrollo en una obra larga, continua [...]' (II: 165). This is precisely a work that does not constitute an 'Obra' with a capital 'O', but expresses 'la nostalgia infinita de la obra posible' and the 'proteica apertura a la posibilidad' (II: 166) in which 'lo que existe en verdad no es la forma, sino la transforma o la meta-forma, la metamorfosis o la transformación (II: 170). For Valente, the symbol that represents this semantic instability in Aleixandre's earlier works is the serpent — the serpent stands for metamorphosis and processes of emergence and destruction, a poetry in which non-subjective impulses and drives emerge in a concatenation of irrational images.

The trope of metamorphosis, in Valente's understanding, links Aleixandre's early collections to the *Chants* of Lautréamont (1967).[10] As Valente comments in an essay from the same collection, 'Lautréamont o la experiencia de la anterioridad', Maldoror's capacity for metamorphosis in his struggle against the Demiurge can only take place in a world that is '[...]anterior al mundo, donde la palabra queda a la vez dicha y negada, y el lenguaje en un estado de disponibilidad infinita, como el vuelo del milano real cuando ya el ave vuela sin finalidad o objeto' (II: 253). Both the serpent and the 'milano real' here stand for a poetic language that exists for itself, words that have an aesthetic value beyond the meanings that might be attached to them. The unlimited animal metamorphoses that the *Cantos* describe would, from this perspective, represent both the inhuman creativity of nature as well as the creativity and freedom of a poetry that exceeds subjective intention or *a priori* ideological constraints. For Valente, this excess constitutes poetry's political potential, its capacity to allow for new ways of seeing, understanding, and being.

Utopia and The Philosophy of Symbolic Forms

Valente's essays of the 1950s and 1960s respond to the difficulty of maintaining the political and social relevance of poetry while at the same time guarding against its reduction to pamphleteering or propaganda. Squaring the circle, so to speak, Valente brings together his vast arsenal of literary and philosophical resources — the conservative poetics of anglophone writers like Eliot and Leavis; the writings of Sartre and the theorization of the *nouveau roman*; the critical Marxism of Adorno, Brecht, Benjamin, and Lefebvre; the writings of the Early German Romantics; and the poetry of Lautréamont and the Surrealists — to construct a poetics that argues for the specificity of a poetic language that is different from the everyday but that can also speak for social ideals and become a repository for personal and communal memory. Central to this vision is a belief in the capacity of poetic language to prefigure a world transformed. It is in this context that we can understand Valente's engagement with what for him is a vital tradition in European aesthetics: the philosophy of symbolic forms.

In 'Conocimiento y comunicación', Valente identifies one of the principal sources for his conception of poetry as knowledge in the Romantic philosophy of the symbol, which, according to him, develops along a 'linea trazada entre pensadores como Vico, Herder, o Humboldt por Cassirer en sus dos obras mayores, *Philosophie der Symbolischen Formen* (publicada en Alemania de 1923 a 1929) y *An Essay on Man*' (II: 43). Literary theorist Hazard Adams identifies the roots of this tradition in the writings of J. G. Herder and Wilhelm von Humboldt, and in their idea that 'language is constitutive of thought, that thought takes form in language' (1983: 25). Form, here, is not to be conceived as a frame or container, or as opposed to content, but as 'a mode of activity that shapes and projects' (25); in the words of Humboldt, 'languages are not really means for representing already known truths but are rather instruments for discovering previously unrecognized ones' (qtd. in Adams: 25). The phrase describes Valente's own approach to language in his early essays, and shares with it a vision of language as a creative, constitutive act. Indeed, in 'Conocimiento y comunicación' Valente reproduces Humboldt's contention that languages do not reflect a given state of affairs: 'A causa de la mútua dependencia entre pensamiento y palabra, es evidente que los lenguajes no son solo medios de representar la verdad que ya ha sido determinada, sino, en medida mucho mayor, medios de descubrir una verdad no previamente conocida' (II: 43). Humboldt's vision of language is the Romantic antecedent for Valente's conception of the creative, knowledge-forming capacity of poetry.

Valente's reception of this Romantic legacy is mediated by the thought of twentieth century German philosopher, Ernst Cassirer. Cassirer advanced an elaborate theory for the constitutive powers of language in his three volume *The Philosophy of Symbolic Forms* and the shorter *An Essay on Man*. In these works, Cassirer argued that all forms of knowledge were inseparably and fundamentally derived from the language in which they were expressed. Rather than reflecting a given world, the concepts of science and the problems and solutions they provide are symbolic systems, just one of a range of ways of getting to grips with the real. The variety of symbolic systems run from scientific or mathematical systems that reduce the real to abstract categories, to the language of myth, which collapses the distinction between word and thing, appearance and reality. Artistic expression develops from myth and, like myth, combines the image and the real. These distinctions lead Cassirer to argue in *An Essay on Man* that artistic expression, unlike everyday language or scientific knowledge — 'abbreviations of reality' (1944: 143) that depend upon a process of abstraction — is a 'discovery of reality' (1944: 143). Art intensifies and purifies that which is given to the senses, and thereby restores a sense of the 'infinite possibilities which remain unrealized in ordinary sense experience' (1944: 145). There are clear links between Cassirer's theory of art and Valente's arguments in 'Conocimiento y comunicación'. Both describe an artistic image-language that, resisting the abstractions of empirical method, would constitute a privileged form of knowledge.

In a footnote to 'Conocimiento y comunicación', Valente cites the arguments of a disciple of Cassirer, the American-born philosopher Susanne K. Langer, who explored the implications for aesthetics of the philosophy of symbolic forms. In an influential work first published in 1941, *Philosophy in a New Key: A Study in the Symbolism of Reason, Rite, and Art* (1962), Langer developed the notion of 'presentational form'. Presentational form refers here to those elements of music, painting, myth, and lyric poetry which can express aspects of experience that escape the 'discursive forms', as defined by the logical positivists. In 'Conocimiento y comunicación', Valente adds his own version of the term, describing the poem as 'una forma aparicional del conocer' (II: 40–41). In each case, the terms refer to the presence within the poem of symbols that are meaningful in ways not reducible to discursive logic. Thus, many years later Valente will define the poem as the 'fulgurante aparición de la palabra' (II: 458). These symbolic 'apparitions' are not determined by conscious deliberation; they require what Valente will later describe as a process of self-emptying or kenosis in which the poet's receptivity allows for the manifestation within the poem of that which is beyond subjective intention.

Crucially, Valente is able to connect Cassirer and Langer's notion of symbolic form to politics, through his reading of the work of Ernst Bloch. Bloch's thought had, by the end of the 1960s, achieved the height of its influence in the West, as its emphasis on the utopian potential of art responded to the feeling held by the leftist radicals of the 1960s that cultural change would be a fundamental part of any revolutionary process. Bloch's theorization (1988: 141–55) of the *vor-schein*, the intuitively available 'pre-appearance' of elements of a utopian world in works of art, allows Valente to develop his thinking on the philosophy of symbolic forms in terms of radical politics. *Vor-schein*, which can be literally translated as a pre-appearance, in Bloch's writings refers to the anticipatory glimmer of that which has not yet come into existence that announces itself in the artwork. Valente describes the *vor-schein* as a concept that designates the aesthetic 'modo del ser que despierta la conciencia utópica y le indica lo que todavía no ha llegado a ser en todo el abanico de sus posibilidades' (II: 302). For Bloch, cultural artefacts that express the utopian are irreducible with regard to the intentionality of their authors. They contain a surplus or *uberschuss* that allows us to glimpse the non-actual. Bloch's *uberschuss* and *vor-schein* return in Valente's poetry and poetics in the guise of what he calls the 'sobreintencionalidad' of the poem that relates to a foundational 'palabra inicial o antepalabra, que no significa aún porque no es de su naturaleza el significar sino el manifestarse' (I: 302). As we will see, Valente, throughout his career, defines poetry in terms of its capacity to make visible this ungraspable, or unsayable, *antepalabra*, and this understanding of poetry is related in Valente's work to a semantic field that describes liminal states — the angel, dawn, the edge, the tightrope. Paradoxically, in Valente's thought this *antepalabra*, the Word at the beginning, is related both to the past and communal memory as well as to a utopian future. This paradoxical conflation of past and future in poetic language also defines a central aspect of Valente's poetics — his reading of the mystic tradition.

Memory and Mysticism

It would be misleading to give an account of Valente's thought that ignores the various mystical traditions — Christian, Jewish, Islamic, and Buddhist — that inform his understanding of the poetic. Valente dedicates two collections of essays to the mystic tradition and his library provides abundant evidence of his erudite explorations of mystics from various world religions. One of Valente's earliest, and most significant, discussions of mysticism is his 1969 essay, 'La hermeneutica y la cortedad del decir' (II: 81–90). Here, Valente develops the arguments already made in 'Comunicación y conocimiento' on the links between poetry and memory. He opens with a citation from 'The Dry Salvages' section of Eliot's *Four Quartets*: 'We had the experience but missed the meaning | And approach to the meaning restores the experience' (II: 81). As in 'Conocimiento y comunicación', Valente here describes his vision of poetry's restorative capacity, the way that, for him, it embodies the memory of an experience we underwent but could not fully assimilate. The poetry of the mystics would be, in this context, an especially clear example of how poetry relates to experiences that are otherwise unknowable. San Juan de la Cruz enters into a territory beyond all science or knowledge — 'toda ciencia transcendida'; the most effective way to register the emotional impact of this shattering experience is in the contradictory and paradoxical language of mystical poetry. In this way, what Michel de Certeau describes as the illogical 'manières de parler' (1982: 156) of the mystics[11] make visible the incapacity of discursive language to fully comprehend the experience of the divine:

> En efecto, la cortedad del decir, la sobrecarga de sentido del significante es lo que hace, por virtud de éste, que quede en él alojado lo indecible o lo no explícitamente dicho. Y es ese resto acumulado de estratos de sentido el que la palabra poética recorre o asume en un acto de creación o de memoria. (II: 88)

The strange language of the mystics shows the signifier's insufficiency with regard to that which it signifies; expressing this insufficiency allows for the presence in language of the unspeakable. That which is an 'olvido', the mystic experience impossible to comprehend in language, comes to presence in the poem: 'La experiencia de lo indecible sólo puede ser dicho como tal en el lenguaje: memoria de un olvido, voz de un silencio' (II: 85).

In a wider sense, Valente believes that the lost or forgotten experiences of entire generations can only be expressed through a demonstration of the necessary insufficiency of language. In witnessing to its own insufficiency, poetic language becomes an echo of all that has been lost:

> El más breve poema lírico encierra en potencia toda la cadena de las rememoraciones y converge hacia lo umbilical, hacia el origen. [...] Toda operación poética consiste, a sabiendas o no, en un esfuerzo por perforar el túnel infinito de las rememoraciones para arrastrarlas desde o hacia el origen, para situarlas de algún modo en el lugar de la palabra, en el principio, en *arkhé*. (II: 82–83)

Valente insists that lyric poetry is a privileged source of communal memory, even when compared with epic, which refers explicitly to the events of the past. The *llanto*, the simplest expression of grief, implies hidden levels of meaning and memory that narration elides. It is from this perspective that Valente cites Michel Foucault's arguments in *Les mots et les choses* as to the infinite interpretability of poetic language. According to Foucault, in modernity only poetry has retained a sense of the enigmatic materiality of words, and this preoccupation with the insignificant materiality of language allows for the continuance of commentary, a secular version of religious interpretative practice that Foucault opposes to a more superficial criticism. The very opacity of poetic language, those aspects of the poetic — sound, rhythm, breath — that exceed the semantic, means that it becomes an inexhaustible source of commentary and interpretation, a space for the open-ended creation of communal understanding.

It is important to note here the centrality to Valente's discussions of Jewish mysticism and theories of language. Valente maintained a profound interest in Jewish mysticism and the Kabbalah from the early 1960s on, as reflected in the wide range of literature dedicated to the theme that remains in his personal library. While in Geneva, he attended seminars on the subject given by Carlo Suarès, author of the well-known work on the Kabbalah from 1962, *La Kabale des Kabales. La Genèse d'après la tradition ontologique.*[12] But perhaps the central reference for Valente in his reading of Jewish mysticism is the work of Gershom Scholem, a mediation that is perhaps unavoidable given Scholem's dominance of the study of Kabbalah in the twentieth century. Valente's library contains fourteen titles, the earliest dating from 1960, of Scholem's authorship, and Valente cites him on numerous occasions, most notably in 'La hemeneutica y la cortedad del decir,' in which the Spanish poet describes Scholem's works as 'indispensables' for an understanding of Jewish theories of language.

In 'La hermeneutica y la cortedad del decir', Valente recounts Scholem's description of the practices of Abulafia de Zaragoza, for whom the repetition of a single verse of Genesis over a whole day, a process that empties the signifier of its apparent meaning, could reveal the hidden properties of scripture that link it to the transcendent. Paradoxically, the evacuation of sense through the rote repetition of the verse makes visible hidden depths of meanings in sacred language. Abulafia's practices bear directly on what could be called Scholem's linguistic theory. As Scholem notes in his *Major Trends in Jewish Mysticism,* for the Kabbalists, God's creation of the world is a linguistic act, a result of divine self-expression:

> All creation — and this is an important principle of most Kabbalists — is, from the point of view of God, nothing but an expression of His hidden self that begins and ends by giving itself a name, the holy name of God, the perpetual act of creation. (1995: 117)

The world is a linguistic structure, a decipherable reality that ultimately points to the ineffable Name of God, which is the ultimate foundation of both the world as language and language as spoken by humans. The Name as the fundamental but absent ground of language is analogous to the Kabbalistic conception of the hidden God, the boundless or infinite *Ein Sof,* which is the divine in itself, as opposed to the characteristics of the divine that are manifest in creation. The existence of this foundational and ungraspable Name, as Scholem writes in an essay from 1972, determines the intuition among mystics that 'language includes an inner property, an aspect which does not altogether merge or disappear in the relationships or communications between men' (1972: 60). Human reason can only deduce the existence of the Name or the *Ein Sof* through an experience of the infinite possibility of linguistic interpretation, the abyss that constitutes both tradition and the limits of language. As the practices of Abulafia had shown, there is mystery in even the simplest of words.

As we have already seen, Valente also places the mysterious origin of words at the center of his considerations. In 'La hermenéutica y la cortedad del decir', he writes:

> La imaginación poética moderna ha reflejado — aunque negativamente, en buena parte — esa impulsión hacia el origen, pues no ha dejado de girar en círculos cada vez más angostos en torno a la palabra plena de sentido y a la vez históricamente cortada del mundo de las significaciones. (II: 83)

But for Valente, this Word cannot remain completely removed from the created world, 'ha de poder hablar de su sentido, de los estratos de sentido que en ella se unifican, o posibilitar esa aproximación al sentido en que solo — poéticamente — puede ser restaurado la experiencia' (II: 83). If history implies loss and destruction, and if in modernity language has been divorced from its sacred origins, Valente believes that poetry remains as a 'reverberation' that in its very materiality retains something of that which has perished.

Interpreting Valente's Poetics

José Manuel Cuesta Abad, in his contribution to *El silencio y la escucha,* 'La enajenación de la palabra', places Valente's discussions of language in the context of modern poetics:

> Las creaciones poéticas en las que toma forma la crisis ideológicamente múltiple de la modernidad comparten con las más antiguas concepciones de la poesía una aparente fascinación común: la experiencia imaginaria de la plenitud del Ser. En términos demasiado generales, digamos que la poetización de esa experiencia tiende en sus comienzos a una plasmación afirmativa de las intuiciones ontológicas, mientras que cede, en los casos más significativos del agonismo estético moderno, a la seducción de una negatividad abismal que se recrea a menudo en un sentimiento de vacuidad metafísica. (Hernández Fernández 1995: 49)

That is to say, if the crisis of modernity has meant the death of God and the absence of metaphysical grounding for human knowledge and language, this crisis has been felt in the tension between Romantic conceptions of poetry according to which Being comes to presence in the poem through the workings of the imagination, and a post-Romantic, or counter-Romantic, poetry, in which the poem points to the abyss or absence of a fundamental metaphysical ground. For Cuesta Abad, however, this absence of a fundamental metaphysical ground coincides with a modern 'concepción *in-trascendente*' of poetic language, an ambivalence that implies that 'la negación de trascendencia metafísica convive con la sacralización formal de la inmanencia (meta)poética' (1995: 51). It is in this context that Cuesta Abad understands Valente's work as 'un modelo de tematización de la crisis ideológica que subyace a los principios constructivos de numerosas poéticas de la modernidad post-romántica' (1995: 52). The pathological desire to experience the plenitude of Being in words that are perceived as alienated from this foundation, a suffering for the *logos*, manifests in the poems in images of solitude, darkness, and emptiness, which accompany an evocation of an originary linguistic foundation, but also a thematization of the materiality of poetic language. In this way, Valente's poetry and poetics reflect a 'deseo de expresar el Lenguaje genesíaco y purificador que el mito eternamente nos promete y la historia en el tiempo nos deniega' (1995: 66).

We might refer here to another distinguished reader of Valente's work, the Italian philosopher, Giorgio Agamben. In a text written in 1984, 'The Idea of Language', Agamben argues that, in modernity, the place of the Divine as guarantor of our words is replaced by the simple recognition of the existence of language as the ultimate horizon of our knowledge. In light of this, modern philosophy becomes aware of its epistemological limitations, of the impossibility of constructing a metalanguage that could speak of the necessary presupposition of language that is implied in every instance of speech. For Agamben, this is the case with hermeneutics, in which 'every act of speech also renders present the unsaid to which it refers, as an answer and a recollection' (1999: 44), but also with the grammatology of Derrida, though in the 'negative structure of writing and the *gramma*' (Agamben 1999: 44).[13] But if it is true that language is the absolute presupposition of all enunciation, and that we cannot return to a foundational ontology or theology that would ground our truth claims, the task of philosophy, for Agamben, is to find, beyond nihilism, a way to speak the medium of our knowledge, to maintain 'a discourse that, without being a metalanguage or sinking into the unsayable, says language itself and exposes its limits' (1999: 46). In this essay, Agamben identifies this discourse in a Platonic 'idea of language' itself, which he describes as language which is neither a word (a metalanguage), nor an object outside language (God, the Name, etc.). Rather, the 'idea of language' is language perceived in its immediacy, a 'vision of language itself' that 'constitutes the sole possibility of reaching a principle freed of every presupposition' (1999: 47).

Agamben's description of the 'vision of language' is similar to what Valente describes when he writes, taking from Ernst Bloch's notion of the *vor-schein*: 'Palabra inicial o antepalabra, que no significa aún porque no es de su naturaleza el significar sino el manifestarse' (II: 302). In each case, there is an attempt to think beyond what José Olivio Jiménez describes as the dialectic of 'palabra plena, palabra hueca' (1972: 238), the claim that the poetic word relates directly to that to which it refers and the claim that language cannot grasp that of which it speaks. In a short essay, 'No amanece el cantor', included in the 1996 collection, *En torno a la obra de José Ángel Valente*, Agamben discusses Valente's poetry in terms of this struggle, framing his exploration in terms of the relationship between poetry and experience. For Agamben, the founders of the vernacular lyric tradition, the medieval troubadours, do not combine poetry and experience as conceived in terms of a Romantic poetics of expression, but neither do they absolutely separate the two. Rather, when the poems speak of love this should be understood as referring to the 'tentativa de experimentar el acontecimiento vivo del lenguaje como fundamental experiencia amorosa' (1996: 49). Love in the poems is 'la experiencia del puro acontecimiento de la palabra' (1996: 50), an experience of language as a fundamental opening or revelation.[14]

Valente's poetics are determined, then, by the intuition that poetry allows for the manifestation of a fundamental aspect of language that is beyond subjective intention, and that in so doing it relates both to the past, to experiences that have remained inarticulate, and to the future, to possibilities that are beyond our imagination. In this way, they betray a specifically modern, and, one might argue, Jewish orientation towards language, history, and memory, one that obsessively turns towards the dead and the defeated, and expresses the melancholy of those whom Flaubert, cited by Benjamin, describes as sufficiently sad so as to 'enterprendre de ressuciter Carthage' (qtd. in Benjamin 1999: 248). The desire for an alternative experience of history, one that shatters conceptions of linear progression, places Valente's thought within a twentieth century tradition of Jewish thinkers and poets — Scholem, Canetti, and Benjamin, but also Franz Rosensweig, Ernst Bloch, Emmanuel Levinas, Jean Luc Nancy, Jacques Derrida, Paul Celan, and Edmond Jabès who hold a vision of history defined by a commitment to alterity and a sympathy for those who are crushed under the weight of what the powerful perceive as teleological progress. Stepháne Mosès traces the development of the tradition of three of its most important figures: Rosenzweig, Benjamin, and Scholem. For Mosès, 'all three presented a radical critique of historical reason and its axioms: the idea of continuity, the idea of causality, the idea of progress' (2009: 10). They oppose an indefinitely extended, homogenous time in which utopia can only exist as an asymptotic ideal, to a purely internal, qualitative time, in which 'the present moment lived in all its intensity interrupts the tedious unfolding of the day and polarizes in its force field the utopian potentials put off very far into the future by historical reason' (2009: 9). This vision of the traces of utopia in the present is aligned to a perception of the contingency of history, the paradoxical capacity to see the possible defeat of Rome in the ruins of Carthage, to, like Benjamin, see the traces of different presents in the possibilities offered by the past. Valente's poetics, whether in his discussions of mystical poetry, the philosophy of symbolic forms, or what he calls the *sobreintencional* poetic language of the surrealists takes on the essential characteristics of this tradition. In each case, Valente describes a language defined by its capacity to lodge within itself an alterity that exceeds subjective intention. This excessive aspect of poetic language can be understood in two ways: as the 'memoria de un olvido', the marking of that which has been lost, but also, facing the future, the awakening of a utopian consciousness.

Notes to Chapter 1

1. For the context and significance of these debates within the contemporary discourse on poetic language in the Spanish literary sphere, and Valente's protagonism in this regard, see Ramos Abreu (2008: 23–58).
2. I refer here to the title of the opening poem of Blas de Otero's collection from 1955, *Pido la paz y la palabra*: 'A la inmensa mayoría'.
3. Bousoño's ideas were set out in his influential *Teoría de la expresión poética* (1952). Aleixandre's views were first expressed in a series of aphorisms published in 1950 in *Ínsula* under the title 'Poesía, moral, público', and later elaborated upon and published under the title *Algunas caracteres de la nueva poesía española* (1955).
4. Juan José Lanz Rivera (2009) has compiled an anthology of the critical essays written in response to the comunicación/conocimiento debate, which includes, among others, texts by Valente, Barral, Jaime Gil de Biedma, Juan Ramón Jiménez, Antonio Gamoneda, and Gabriel Celaya, in his *Conocimiento y comunicación. Textos para una polémica poética en el medio siglo (1950–1963)*.
5. Manuel Fernández Rodríguez (2012: 311–490) provides a full account of Valente's time in Oxford, and the poetic influences he cultivated there, in *Valente vital (Galicia, Madrid, Oxford)*. Ioana Ruxandra Gruia explores the influence of Eliot in the work of Valente and Jaime Gil de Biedma in her doctoral dissertation, *Escribir el tiempo: Huellas de T. S. Eliot en Jaime Gil de Biedma y José Ángel Valente* (2008).
6. Inspired by Martz's *The Poetry of Meditation* (1954), the results of Valente's research would be published in 1962 as 'Luis Cernuda y la poesía de la meditación' (II: 132–44) in *La Caña Gris*, and later included in *Las palabras de la tribu*. These ideas are reiterated in 'Una nota sobre relaciones literarias hispano-inglesas' (II: 349–64), an essay written in 1982 that forms part of the collection *La piedra y el centro*. For a critical appraisal of these essays, see Julián Jiménez Heffernan (2004b: 79–117).
7. Valente indicates the Romantic provenance of these ideas when he quotes, in the same essay, a letter Schelling writes to Hegel in 1796: 'Mientras no hayamos transformado las ideas en obras de arte, es decir, en mitos, careceran de interés para el pueblo' (II: 161). It is important to note that the Modernists were also concerned with the possibility of creating a new mythology for contemporary life. As Robert Langbaum writes in his *The Poetry of Experience*, in words that Valente underlines in his edition of this work held in his personal library at the University of Santiago de Compostela: 'Eliot and Joyce show with uncompromising completeness that the past of official tradition is dead [...]. But they also dig below the ruins of official tradition to uncover in myth an underground tradition, an inescapable because inherently psychological pattern into which to fit the chaotic present' (1957: 10).
8. These arguments are expressed in more concise form in the essay 'Tendencia y estilo', published in *Ínsula* in 1961, the title of which alludes to Lukacs's *Tendenzliteratur*, a term that describes propagandistic literature of poor aesthetic quality.
9. Claudio Rodríguez Fer and Tera Blanco de Saracho give a detailed account of Valente's political commitments during the 1960s in *Valente Vital: Ginebra, Saboya, París* (2014: 201–35). Valente also discusses these experiences in interview with Rodríguez Fer in 'Entrevista vital a José Ángel Valente: de Xenebra a Almería' (Rodríguez Fer 2000: 185–210).
10. María Lopo (2013) describes the centrality of the work of Lautréamont for Valente, and also the possible connections between Valente's 'Agone,' the name he gives to his son Antonio in the poems, and the adolescent 'Aghone' of the *Cantos*. Valente read Lautréamont in the first half of 1969, an experience he describes in his diaries: 'La lectura y anotación de *Maldoror* me ha llevado estos meses a una serie de lecturas *irradiadas*' (DA: 138).
11. Referring to the deictic status of the mystical oxymoron, De Certeau writes: 'D'autre part, l'oxymoron appartient à la catégorie des "métasémèmes" qui renvoient à un au-delà du langage, comme le fait le démonstratif. C'est un déictique: il montre ce qu'il ne dit pas. La combinaison des deux termes se substitue à l'existence d'une troisième et le pose comme absent. Elle crée un trou dans la langage. Elle y taille la place d'un indicible' (1982: 198–99). I will discuss the importance of deixis in Valente's work in a later chapter, in the context of Giorgio Agamben's writings on Auschwitz and poetic testimony.

12. Claudio Rodríguez Fer and Tera Blanco de Saracho discuss Valente's attendance at these seminars in *Valente Vital: Ginebra, Saboya, París* (2014: 272–74).
13. For a discussion of the complex relation between Agamben and Derrida that describes the commonalities and difference in their approaches see Donohue (2013) and Attell (2015).
14. It is notable that Valente, in his speech at the *Círculo de bellas artes* of 1999, paraphrases Agamben's words almost to the letter: 'Los trovadores entendían por amor el fundamento de la palabra poética. La mujer es igual en el mundo trovadoresco al acontecer de la palabra, al acontecimiento del lenguaje. La mujer es la razón del trovar y así se unifican cuerpo, palabra y mundo' (II: 1596).

CHAPTER 2

Memory and Signs

Mourning and Melancholy

With Miguel Casado and Julián Jiménez Heffernan, we have identified a fundamental emotional tonality that runs through Valente's work that is linked to feelings of loss and mourning. This sense of primordial loss relates to the historical context of the Spanish post-war, but equally to a conception of history, inflected by a tradition of twentieth-century Jewish thought, defined by both an ethical commitment to the defeated as well as a desire for an alternative or utopian future. In his early collections, Valente explores these themes in the Catholic idiom of death and redemption. The poem that opens Valente's first collection, 'Serán ceniza...' of *A modo de esperanza*, is an example of this mode:

> Cruzo un desierto y su secreta
> desolación sin nombre.
> El corazón
> tiene la sequedad de la piedra
> y los estallidos nocturnos
> de su materia o de su nada.
>
> Hay una luz remota, sin embargo,
> y sé que no estoy solo;
> aunque después de tanto y tanto no haya
> ni un solo pensamiento
> capaz contra la muerte,
> no estoy solo.
>
> Toco esta mano al fin que comparte mi vida
> y en ella me confirmo
> y tiento cuanto amo,
> lo levanto hacia el cielo
> y aunque sea ceniza lo proclamo: ceniza.
> Aunque sea ceniza cuanto tengo hasta ahora,
> cuanto se me ha tendido a modo de esperanza. (I: 69)

The poem intertextually alludes to Quevedo's 'Amor constante más allá de la muerte' (2009: 136), a sonnet that describes the survival of love despite the separation of body and soul in death. In Valente's poem, solitude in the desert, which we can understand in both theological (the absence of God) and political (the desolation of post-war Spain) terms, is mitigated by a relationship to the other that allows for the experience of hope. The 'luz remota' that traditionally refers to the alterity of the divine is here incarnate in the hand's touch. As in Bloch's *vor-schein*, the poem describes an immanent experience that surpasses the limits of human intentionality, while its reference to Quevedo's sonnet reminds us that the approach to the other is not limited to our real-life contemporaries, but also to those others that leave traces of past experience in literary artefacts, artefacts that can be recuperated to take on new meaning in the present.

The themes of death, mourning, and absence are central to *A modo de esperanza*. 'Lucila Valente' and 'Epitafio' are both elegies to maternal figures in Valente's life — his aunt and a domestic assistant. In both cases, survival of the past in the present and the capacity to commemorate the dead are related to the proper name: 'Dejó su nombre puro | solo frente a la noche: | Lucila o siempremadre' (I: 70) and 'Francisca | el nombre de la muerte tiene' (I: 73). Language, and more specifically, the inscription of the name, allows for the survival in the present of the memory of dead loved ones. José Manuel Cuesta Abad notes here the importance for Valente, as for Stephane Mallarmé, of elegy and the written name, in which the 'escritura-epitafio' of the tomb poems becomes a 'fragmento de una teoría de la ausencia' (Cuesta Abad 2010b: 204). For Cuesta Abad, Valente's poems register that which remains after absence; they are not signs of a past that would be straightforwardly available for representation, but signs that testify to all that is irrecoverably lost. Such a reading is confirmed in the tension within the poems of this collection between, on the one hand, a desire to communicate with and testify for those who have passed and, on the other, an acceptance of the ultimate absence and unapproachability of the dead. It is in this context that we can read 'Aniversario', in which the poet apostrophizes an unnamed ghost:

> Tú no comprenderás
> para qué he vuelto.
> Tal vez, ahí tendida,
> no comprendes
> nada de lo que vive.
> (Está mojada
> y limpia la colina).
> Aún te pienso
> con el rostro de siempre
> y los cabellos, en su reino
> de humo, un poco grises.
> No tengo ojos
> para más. Tal vez
> no eres así y eso es la muerte.
> He vuelto para hablarte.
> Estoy aquí. Tú no comprendes
> nada. Te he olvidado
> tanto y he podido
> olvidarte tan poco
> [...] (I: 74)

Here, the power of poetic address, the capacity of lyric to conjure an abstract or absent entity, a capacity that Jonathan Culler (2015) posits as a defining aspect of the poetic, confronts the limits of human finitude. The poem reminds us that although the imagination can lead us to picture a life after death, filled with grey smoke and aged wraiths, our separation from the dead is absolute: 'no importa; | no puedes comprenderme. | Todo ha sido cortado' (I: 75). Communication with the dead is impossible, but we cannot stop ourselves from imagining that alterity, from clothing otherness in images, as we represent the Divine in idols. The pathos of these last lines reflects both faith in the capacity of poetry to conjure that which is absolutely other and a simultaneous recognition of the limits of this power.

It is in this context, too, that we can consider the choice of title for Valente's second collection, *Poemas a Lázaro*. The figure of Lazarus come back from the dead is resonant in a post-war context. Significantly, in his correspondence with the philosopher María Zambrano, Valente links the figure of Lazarus to Spanish historical memory. In a letter to Valente in 1968, Zambrano writes: 'Lázaro ha de resucitar en cada época o momento de eso que llaman historia. Y ahora ha llegado el momento de que resucite entre estos escombros, escombros que a ti más que a mí se te han dado...' (qtd. in Blanco de Saracho 2010: 86). In his reply, Valente agrees with Zambrano, and emphasizes the entwining of memory and renewal in the figure of the dead man come back to life: 'Hablas de Lázaro. Yo te preguntaba por la memoria. Lo que me dices es, sin embargo, una respuesta. ¿Está lejos el que resucita del que recuerda?' (qtd. in Blanco de Saracho 2010: 86). Valente frames his discussion of in terms of remembrance. Lazarus is the uncanny figure of a death that refuses to seal itself from the living, marking the failure of the mourning process and the impossibility of forgetting.

We might refer here to Sigmund Freud's short essay from 1917, 'Mourning and Melancholia'. In Freud's telling, mourning is marked by a refusal of absence. As we grieve we maintain our connection with the departed, so as to resist the 'reality principle' and delay facing up to the definitive loss of the object of our libidinal desire. For Freud, the healthy process of mourning becomes a pathological melancholy if the mourner fails to discharge his or her libidinal attachment to the cause of grief. In this case, the mourner internalizes the lost object, which is now identified with the ego. The identity of the object of libidinal attachment then becomes unclear, giving way to a more generalized sense of loss marked by introspection and self-accusation. In the historical context in which Zambrano and Valente write, Lazarus would symbolize an incomplete process of mourning, a result of the societal refusal to publicly mourn the Republican dead of the Civil War. The dead who lie in unmarked graves and whose memory is traduced return in the melancholy figure of Lazarus.

Giorgio Agamben discusses Freud's theories of mourning and melancholy in his *Stanzas: Word and Phantasm in Western Culture*. Agamben notes the centrality of the imagination in Freud's discussion of melancholy, observing that, for Freud, an important part of the melancholic's experience is the contemplation of 'phantasms of desire' (1992: 23), imaginary projections that help him endure an unbearable reality. For Agamben, this melancholic creation of 'phantasms' is a fundamental part of the Western lyric tradition; the founders of this tradition, the troubadour poets, create a poetry in which the introspective contemplation of a purely imaginary beloved compensates for an essential absence. Lyric can be understood, from this perspective, as a cultural activity that creates and desires fetishistic objects which, like all fetishes, are signs of absence. The courtly poet is a melancholic who desires to possess loss, to hold nothing in his hand in 'a process in which what is real loses its reality so that the unreal becomes real' (1992: 25). Valente's employment of the figure of Lazarus in his work would be but one of many examples of the appropriation of the unreal in Western poetic tradition, in which 'covering its object with the funereal trappings of mourning, melancholy confers upon it the phantasmagorical reality of what is lost' (1992: 20).[1]

Agamben's discussion of Freud's theory of melancholy sheds light on many of Valente's poems from his first collections. 'El corazón', from *A modo de esperanza* describes a descent towards an inner emptiness that accords with Agamben's description of the melancholic poet's introspection and obsession with lack:

> Ni una voz, ni un sonido
> conviviéndose en él.
> Si hundo mi mano extraigo
> sombra;
> si mi pupila,
> noche;
> si mi palabra,
> sed.
>
> Como nada puebla el desierto,
> tal esta soledad;
> como la caída de una piedra en el sueño,
> tal esta soledad.
>
> Como la sombra
> está, la noche
> está, la sed,
> la muerte verdadera
> en su reino impasible
> reina y aguarda en pie. (I: 76)

The process of self-contemplation, the excavation of the heart, reveals absence, *sombra*, *noche*, *sed*, and, ultimately, death. The melancholic desire to grasp absence is realized in a hand that grabs shadow, an eye that sees night, and a word that speaks thirst. Similarly, 'Noche Primera', again from the first collection, describes the poet's exercise of kenosis:

> Empuja el corazón,
> quiébralo, ciégalo,
> hasta que nazca en él
> el poderoso vacío
> de lo que nunca podrás nombrar.
> Sé, al menos,
> su inminencia
> y quebrantado hueso

> de su proximidad.
> Que se haga noche. (Piedra,
> nocturna piedra sola.)
> Alza entonces la súplica:
> que la palabra sea sólo verdad. (I: 79)

Here, the poetic voice prescribes the creation of an unnameable void in a poem that takes, in the words of Agamben, 'unappropriability as its most precious possession' (1992: xvii). The excavation of the self the poem describes complements Valente's declarations as to the nature of poetry, which he repeatedly identifies in his poetics as relating to the creation of an essential 'nada'. It also relates to his constant attempts to give figurative shape to absence in the poems, the constant reiteration of tropes of absence — concavities, empty rooms, empty mirrors. Valente relates these themes to the question of memory, but it is important to remember that for Agamben, the melancholic affirmation and denial of its object, or the poet's capacity to maintain a relationship to absence as absence, is a project 'constantly orientated in the light of utopia' (1992: xix). It implies an understanding of history according to which the melancholic relation to loss is a necessary element in the shaping of new historical realities. It is this double aspect of melancholy that I will trace in my discussion of three of Valente's earliest collections: *Poemas a Lázaro*, *La memoria y los signos*, and *El inocente*.

Poemas a Lázaro

The poems of the first section of *Poemas a Lázaro* communicate loss in a Christian vocabulary informed by Valente's Catholic upbringing. They also reflect his readings of Spanish mystical writers and English Metaphysical poets, interests he was able to cultivate during his time as a lecturer in Oxford.[2] Typically, the voice in these poems addresses an absent God and begs for a revelation of the divine. 'El emplazado' is indicative of this mode:

> No me llames después
> ni quieras
> a eternidad remota
> aplazarme y juzgarme.
>
> No me llames después
> hay tantas cosas
> de llanto y luz urdidas
> — ahora, cerca
> de mí — que la vida limita.
>
> No a eternidad me llames, no me llames
> después, ni quieras
> emplazarme remoto
>
> Mira estas manos tristes
> de recordarte en tanto
> humano amor, en tanto
> barro que te reclama y no me llames

> después: júzgame ahora,
> sobre el oscuro cuerpo
> del amor, del delito. (I: 110)

Again, as in 'Serán ceniza', the speaker craves an experience of transcendence in the immanent here and now of the flesh. The impossibility of separating the spirit and the flesh is reiterated in the following poem, 'El alma', which is introduced with a citation from the sermons of John Donne, '...therefore the soul hath a resurrection'.[3] Donne's sermon argues for a 'second' resurrection of the soul, when, at the end of days, it is reunited with the resurrected body of the saved. It is in this context that we can read the final section of Valente's poem:

> No, tú no existirás
> en la espera terrible
> sin rama en que posarte,
> hasta que el barro sople sobre ti
> y en nueva luz te alce
> a tu reino completo,
> para hacerte visible a los ojos del Padre. (I: 110)

Although these poems are written in a Christian idiom, we can see the motifs that will become central in all of Valente's writing: a desire for an experience of transcendence in the here and now that would confirm the possibility of redemption. Yet, as Jiménez Heffernan (2004b: 183–92) points out, for all Valente's use of religious terminology, his poems depict a de-transcendentalized universe. The central question in these poems, and in Valente's poetry as a whole, is whether, after the death of God, it is possible to maintain a mysticism of the flesh, of the *ceniza*. The vocabulary Valente holds in common with the early modern poets and their modern interpreters — *ceniza, polvo, carne,* ash, dust, flesh — reflects a specific form of modern (ir)religious discourse that, as Lucien Goldmann (1964) demonstrates in his readings of Pascal and Racine, is an inherent part of the disenchantment of the post-Renaissance world. Reference to the soul, in this case, refers to what remains of faith in a world that no longer provides legible evidence of divine providence. It refers to a faith in the power of fallen language to describe that which is not, to create, in the words of Agamben, 'a topology of the unreal' (1992: xviii). As Jiménez Heffernan writes: 'La palabra es alma-pájaro que genera escritura en su batir de alas [...] No hay trascendencia en ese batir de alas: estamos siempre en la palabra, y la palabra es materia' (1998: 361)

The second section of *Poemas a Lázaro* begins with 'Entrada al sentido':

> La soledad.
> El miedo.
> Hay un lugar
> vacío, hay una estancia
> que no tiene salida.
> Hay una espera
> ciega entre dos latidos,
> entre dos oleadas
> de vida hay una espera

> en que todos los puentes
> pueden haber volado.
> Entre el ojo y la forma
> hay un abismo
> en el que puede hundirse la mirada.
> Entre la voluntad y el acto caben
> océanos de sueño.
> Entre mi ser y mi destino, un muro:
> la imposibilidad feroz de lo posible.
>
> Y en tanta soledad, un brazo armado
> que amaga un golpe y no lo inflige nunca.
>
> En un lugar, en una estancia — ¿dónde?
> ¿sitiados por quién?
>
> El alma pende de sí misma sólo,
> del miedo, del peligro, del presagio. (I: 113)

The opening five lines describe a vacant space common to many of Valente's poems. A solitary voice speaks from this liminal space: 'entre dos latidos', 'entre dos oleadas', 'entre el ojo y la forma', 'entre la voluntud y el acto', 'entre mi ser y mi destino'. The lines recall Eliot's 'The Hollow Men':

> Between the idea
> And the reality
> Between the motion
> And the act
> Falls the Shadow   *For Thine is the Kingdom*
> Between the conception
> And the creation
> Between the emotion
> And the response
> Falls the Shadow
> Between the desire   *Life is very long*
> And the spasm
> Between the potency
> And the existence
> Between the essence
> And the descent
> Falls the Shadow
> (1963: 85–86)

But whereas Eliot links the space between ideal and real to the creative sterility of the modern 'Hollowmen', for Valente the capacity of the melancholic poet to allow absence and negativity to come to presence in the poem constitutes its 'feroz' power. As in the orphic tradition, the poet has the gift of creating through nomination — the soul, a 'lugar vacío', exists only as a result of this capacity to name the intangible. The poetic capacity to create through naming has a relation both to danger and to the future, 'peligro' and 'presagio'. Taken in its historic context, the poem can be taken to refer to the hope that remains within the dead time of the dictatorship, the renewal that can be glimpsed even in the aftermath of catastrophe.

'Los olvidados y la noche', the longest poem of the second section of *Poemas a Lázaro,* directly addresses the question of the responsibility of the living to the dead. Here, the poetic voice explores the power of poetry to recuperate that which has been lost in the passing of time:

> Cuando aparecen ante mí, terrible,
> suavísimos rostros,
> sus contornos se mezclan
> y adelantan una sola figura.
> Bajo la transparente piel
> de aquel amor y el agua solitaria
> brillan los ojos de mi madre antes
> de haberme concebido.
> ¿Soy yo quien pasa o sois vosotros?,
> ¿quién está detenido?,
> ¿quién abandona a quién?,
> ¿quién está inmóvil o quién es arrastrado?
> Madre después de tanto
> hilarme a tu pupila,
> después de haber edificado un reino de esperanza,
> después de haber soñado
> cuanto soy, cuanto tengo,
> no habré hablado contigo.
> ¿Pero podríamos hablar?,
> ¿hay tiempo?
> Dadme un día,
> detened un día
> el implacable paso,
> el terrible descenso
> — vuestro, mío —
> para que pueda así
> escoger la palabra, el adiós, el silencio:
> para que pueda hablaros.
> Mientras escribo sobre mi cuerpo,
> el mundo habrá pasado,
> habrá cerrado el ciclo,
> completado el retorno
> de su nada a su origen,
> y yo seré antepasado pálido
> de mi futuro olvido.
> Puedo deciros que esta misma noche
> vuestro feroz recuerdo ha devorado
> mi amor,
> envejecido el rostro de mis hijos,
> mutilado los besos,
> reducido mi pecho a soledad.
> Porque nada de lo vivido
> puede daros más vida:
> sé que no soy,
> que no me pertenezco.

> Pasé por vuestros ojos
> y creí desgarrarlos, arrastrarlos conmigo,
> mas fue vuestra pupila la que hizo presa en mí.
> [...]
> (I: 118–19)

The poem is set out in terms of vision. The poetic voice imagines the faces of the dead combining to form a single terrible figure, from which shine the eyes of his mother. The mother's eyes are creative, her dreams creating the man who speaks in the poem. The poetic voice desires that his own creative powers will allow for communication with a ghostly mother, but the passing of time is implacable, and writing only confirms the impossibility of recuperating past experience: 'Mientras escribo sobre | la resistencia de mi propio cuerpo | el mundo habrá pasado | habrá cerrado el ciclo | completado su retorno | de su nada a su origen, | y yo seré antepasado pálido | de mi futuro olvido'. The voice, which exists only in writing, refers its own paradoxical temporal status — we experience the proximity of a voice but are reminded that this voice, as writing, stands apart from any authorial presence, a remnant of an 'antepasado pálido', of a living human being. The rupture in the thread of generations leads to a brutal confrontation with the necessity and solitude of death. Here, the contemplation of the gap between present and past selves reveals the impossibility of complete self-identity and provokes feelings of guilt regarding the dead:

> [...]
> Jirones de mi ser,
> banderas,
> viento como un gemido
> largo en el corazón.
> Inmóviles aún,
> como os dejó mi olvido,
> pálidos de mi sangre,
> conjurados en una sola acusación.
> ¿Soy yo el culpable?
> [...]
> (I: 120)

The poem, the space/stanza/remnant that survives the absence of the speaker, testifies to the ultimate power of death:

> [...]
> Inmensa noche. Solitaria noche.
> (Despojado de mí busco mi cuerpo en vano,
> sigo en vano mi voz.)
> Noche: mi sueño
> no la puede durar.
> (I: 120)

This conception of the poem as remnant or fragment, reflecting the futility of modern desires for the total comprehension and mastery of the self, is a fundamental aspect of Valente's poetics, and relates to a broader criticism of the modern quest for totality in the political sense. As José Olivio Jiménez writes: 'Para José Ángel Valente la poesía es *un* resto, en el que se refleja la fragmentariedad del mundo en que vivimos. Un mundo en el que la aspiración a la totalidad, característica del clasicismo, se ha hecho ya inviable' (1996: 60).[4]

'Son los ríos,' the title of which is derived from Manrique's *Coplas*, and which appears in the third section of the collection, repeats the descent to the underworld of 'Los olvidados y la noche'. The poem opens with an orphic warning: 'No te detengas, sigue: | no vuelvas la mirada' (I: 128). Here, rather than expressing a desire to recuperate the past, the poetic voice warns against memory. The past self — the cadaver of a child, a failed love — are memories from which the voice attempts to escape. Rather than face the dead, who follow the speaker with the 'opaca | tenacidad de muertos' (I: 128), it is better to 'saltar ciegamente' from river to river until time slows, and present and past dissolve into the anonymity of death. If poetry, identified by Maurice Blanchot (1955) with Orpheus's turning back to gaze upon the face of Eurydice, is defined by the melancholic desire to possess absence, this poem is almost a plea against poetry, against its tortuous rememberings, its broken images that reveal only death and darkness, the absence of that which is recalled.

The single long poem, 'La salida', which constitutes the fifth part of *Poemas a Lázaro* concludes this poetic cycle and initiates the more explicit social engagement characteristic of the collections of the 1960s.[5] It describes a train journey, an allegory for the passing of time, but also a device that allows us to contemplate the barren landscape of Francoist Spain. The journey starts with a description of the desolate shanty towns that had sprouted up around Madrid in the years after the Civil War:[6]

>Después el paso largo
>y a través de arrabales perezosos,
>los primeros yerbajos, los desmontes
>donde se amontonaban las basuras,
>el cinturón de lo olvidado, hombres
>que alzaban su silueta indiferente
>y seguían despacio. (I: 153)

The train passes this depressing terrain and enters a dark tunnel, symbolic of both the darkness of the present as well as the possibility of future political change: 'Parecía la sombra demasiado larga, | demasiado hondo y invencible. | Pero al cabo saltaba, siempre otra vez, la vida | del lado de la luz' (I: 153). Symbols of darkness and light return in the speaker's self-reflective struggle against sleep, which in the poem is linked to complacency and deceit:

>*Luchando a solas contra el sueño.*
>*Siempre.*
>*En la alta vigilia*
>*conjurando mi vida*
>*contra su maleficio.*
>*Como un atleta oscuro*
>*ha avanzado,*
>*invadiéndolo todo. Apenas*

> *resiste el pensamiento,*
> *allá en lo hondo,*
> *a su dominio.*
> *Un gallo canta lejos,*
> *remota, en la frontera*
> *difícil de la sombra.*
> *Siempre, siempre.*
> *Y a la luz me encomiendo....* (I: 154)

The speaker describes a lonely vigil, a resistance against the powers of sleep, this latter an invasive 'atleta oscuro' that only the extreme edges of thought can resist. Yet, this short meditation ends on a note of hope, signaled by the coming of dawn and the distant crowing of the cockerel. In the political context of the poem's writing, the terms sleep/darkness and vigil/light can be read to refer to the inauthenticity of a life lived under dictatorship and the necessity of maintaining hope in such circumstances. The Biblical resonances of the cock crowing suggest the struggle to summon the courage to resist what appears to be insurmountable adversity.

Although the allegory of the train journey implies hope in the future, memory is an overwhelming force in the poem, conjuring a cruel child who taunts the speaker: 'y un niño me persigue | dando voces crueles | arrojándome piedras | de inocencia y blancura'.[7] Similarly, memories of loved ones and, more broadly, the dead, bring feelings of guilt:

> Henos al cabo sitiados,
> rodeados de figuras lejanas
> que mastican
> una ceniza humedecida y triste
> y nos hablan de tú,
> de: 'tú regresas,
> tú recuerdas
> tú sabes...', más y más y no podemos
> reconocer a nadie en tantos rostros. (I: 155)

In italics, the speaker meditates on the nature of memory:

> *De cuantos reinos tiene el hombre*
> *el más oscuro es el recuerdo.*
> *Oh qué feroz acometida*
> *contra una vida de tantas muertes.*
> *La sombra cierra a las espaldas*
> *con un bramido lento y sordo.*
> *Sobre las huellas del que huye*
> *su ciego reino se proclama.* (I: 156)

The speaker's responsibility towards the dead becomes an overwhelming burden that inspires terror and the desire to forget. But it is impossible to consign the past to oblivion; even the landscape seen from the train window reveals the marks of temporal and historical destruction: 'Un río queda atrás, después | una pequeña casa arruinada | por la guerra tal vez o por el tiempo | o solo porque se desmoronaran los suspiros' (I: 158). And yet, the images outside the carriage pass rapidly, and few of them can be retained: '[...] más y más | imágenes veloces nos envuelven. | Van devorándose | unas y otras sin cesar y tantas | presencias hacen | solamente un olvido' (I: 158). Like the rapidly passing landscape seen from the train window, our lives are marked by inevitable processes of forgetting and loss: 'Cien veces más veloz | que nuestro pensamiento, | pasa del amor a olvido | ciegamente la vida' (I: 158). At this irreparable loss, the poetic voice cries out to a higher power:

> *Por eso ahora,*
> *a medio caminar,*
> *en medio del camino*
> *— porque éste es el tiempo*
> *y no lo ignoro — digo*
> *otra vez la plegaria:*
> *'Que despertemos en tu nombre,*
> *que despertemos en tu reino,*
> *que despertemos en tu duración,*
> *así en la tierra*
> *como en el cielo,*
> *Padre'....* (I: 159)

There is a sense that this cry is made more in desperation that in any real expectation of fulfillment. It is simply the capacity for address, the invocation of the divine as distinct from its presence, that constitutes the religious pathos of this moment. After this invocation, the tone moves towards calmness and acceptance:

> Ahora sumo imágenes,
> rostros, acciones, nombres,
> peso el amor.
> Ésta es la cuenta al cabo:
> estamos solos.
> Alrededores son, postrimerías,
> ecos remotos cuanto llega ahora
> de más allá de la distancia. (I: 160)

Images are remote echoes of that which is beyond reach. They fail to embody experience, and perhaps even delude, but this delusion may point to a greater truth, the ultimate nature of loss and the concomitant necessity of remembering the past, clothing it in the figures, the *peso* and *cuenta*, of the poem. In the context of the post-war, this melancholic task constitutes a fundamental ethical responsibility. It is in this sense that the voice declares that 'Todo | se hace destino', and at the same time implies that we will never finish our task, but that rather 'con paso lento | y el corazón entero en la firmeza, | ingresemos despacio en la enorme salida' (I: 160).

Left Melancholy: *La memoria y los signos*

By the time of the writing of *La memoria y los signos*, the years 1960 to 1964, Valente had left his position in Oxford for a post as translator in the headquarters of the World Health Organization in Geneva. Although he had harboured ambitions to continue in academia, as a young man with the responsibility of providing for a family, the salary and stability of the post in Geneva were difficult to refuse.[8] Nevertheless, Valente maintained contact with his British colleagues and paid regular visits to England, to take advantage of British libraries or to give talks and seminars. A record remains of the poems he chose to present in some of these readings. The following list, from a talk given in Southampton in 1964, is indicative of a more general tendency: 'Patria cuyo nombre no sé', 'Sobre el lugar del canto', 'A Don Francisco de Quevedo, en piedra', 'Cementerio de Morette-Gliéres', 'Tiempo de guerra', 'Si supieras', and 'John Cornford'.[9] These poems, which all deal in one way or another with the Spanish Civil War, reflect Valente's desire during this period to emphasize in his poetry political and communitarian themes, themes that are central to *La memoria y los signos*.

In reading the poems of *La memoria y los signos*, we might again turn to the concept of melancholy, but in this case, melancholy in political as opposed to religious terms. Here, the faith lost, or at least questioned, is a dogmatic Marxism that maintained a belief in the capacity of Communist regimes to create an egalitarian world. As already mentioned, Valente belongs to a generation of poets who came to question the totalitarian tendencies of the Communist Parties, a critical attitude that, in Valente's case, would be reinforced by his experiences in Cuba, and which colours his attitude to the social poetry of the 1950s and 1960s. It is notable in this respect that in his diary Valente reserves some of his most acerbic comments for the communist poet Gabriel Celaya and the Russian poet Yevgeny Yevtushenko, and also that he writes poems that on first glance seem gratuitously cruel in their dismissal of Spanish Republican exiles.[10] It is important to remember that Valente's rejection of the Communist Party was common among leftists in the 1960s: the driving forces in the student revolts of Paris in 1968 would hold the Party in almost as much disdain as the De Gaulle's government — Daniel Cohn Bendit's *Obsolete Communism: The Left Wing Alternative* typifies this scepticism. This distrust of the Party does not, however, preclude a utopian desire for fundamental social and political change. In fact, it is the tension between utopian desire and the more sordid realities of actually existing socialism that provides the pathological force of Valente's collection as a whole.

In this sense, the poems in *La memoria y los signos* reflect an attitude to the past that the Italian theorist Enzo Traverso terms 'left-wing melancholy', an outlook that he contrasts with a contemporary, depoliticized understanding of the events of the twentieth century that has become prevalent since the disintegration of the Soviet Union and the so-called 'end of history'. For Traverso, contemporary memory cultures are the result of the late twentieth century 'eclipse of utopias' (2016: 9). Here, the responsibility we feel towards the victims of totalitarian violence can cause us to forget the fundamental political stakes at play in twentieth-century conflicts.

The sanctification of the figure of the victim leads to an erasure of libertarian struggles, so that 'the memory of the Gulag erased that of revolution, the memory of the Holocaust erased that of anti-fascism, and the memory of slavery eclipsed that of anti-colonialism' (2016: 10). The consequences of such a vision of history become clear in the contemporary understanding of the Spanish Civil War, in which 'the conflict between democracy and fascism [...] becomes a sequence of crimes against humanity' (2016: 16). In contrast, Traverso describes the 1960s as a time in which the principle of hope had not yet been replaced by the principle of responsibility and argues that today's 'presentist' understanding of the past is lacking compared to a 'left melancholy' in which memory of the past is orientated towards the future. The pathological development of Stalinism and the totalitarian aspects of Communist regimes or the experience of crushing defeat in the Spanish Civil War would not, in this context, eclipse the desire for utopia that motivated socialist endeavours. Rather, left melancholy resists the passing of socialism and holds to 'memory and awareness of the potentialities of the past: a fidelity to the emancipatory promises of the revolution, not to its consequences' (2016: 52). Benjamin's exhortation that we remember the vanquished and see in their experiences of defeat the seeds of an egalitarian future, would exemplify this attitude.

La memoria y los signos is marked by the melancholic dialectic that Traverso identifies as typical of the 1960s, commemorating past defeats but also gleaning from them possibilities for the future. The opening poem, 'La señal', describes this process:

> Porque hermoso es al fin
> dejar latir el corazón con ritmo entero
> hasta quebrar la máscara del odio.
>
> Hermoso, sí, de pronto, sin saberlo,
> dejarse ir, caer, ser arrastrado.
>
> Tal vez la soledad, la larga espera,
> no han sido más que fe en un solo acto
> de libertad, de vida.
>
> Porque hermoso es caer, tocar el fondo oscuro,
> donde aún se debaten las imágenes
> y combate el deseo con el torso desnudo
> la sordidez de lo vivido.
>
> Hermoso, sí.
> Arriba rompe el día.
> Aguardo sólo la señal del canto.
> Ahora no sé, ahora sólo espero
> saber más tarde lo que he sido. (I: 163)

Beauty, here, is linked to the capacity for enthusiasm, the capacity to allow the heart full rein or to allow the body to move freely with the current. This openness to experience is linked to the motif of descent, a journey both towards the past and towards an interiority in which elements of the subconscious would become manifest in images. The exploration of the subconscious allows for new ways of thinking that can inform utopian ideals, in which 'deseo' can overcome the depressing 'sordidez de lo vivido.' The willingness to act without knowledge of consequences, to commit oneself entirely to a 'solo acto' of liberty, is necessary for the achievement of a future that is symbolically marked by the coming of day. The historical significance of a given course of action can only be known in time, when the speaker can come to a retrospective understanding of his own place in the world, when he will 'saber más tarde lo que he sido'. Similarly, 'El testigo', describes the relation between the burdens of the past and a longed-for future:

> Amanece sobre la nieve.
> La noche ha sido larga.
> Hay una hiriente claridad o amenazadora inocencia.
>
> No podría decir que velo aunque esté en pie,
> sino que alguien que tal vez contemplara mi sueño
> me impidiese cerrar los ojos
> con su muda presencia.
>
> Los que duermen están
> lejos en su recinto,
> y aunque gritara ahora
> no podría alcanzarlos.
>
> Me pregunto qué ha pasado esta noche,
> por qué acudo a mi mesa,
> con quién es el convite.
>
> Amanece sobre la nieve.
> ¡Y a qué altura sobre mi frente
> inmóvil
> nace la claridad!
> Aguardo.
> Alguien puede llegar, venir de pronto,
> no sé quién, conociendo
> más que yo de mi vida. (I: 164)

Again, the poem links hope in the future to a sense of responsibility to the past, to those who sleep 'lejos en su recinto' and whose 'muda presencia' forestalls any sense of complacency. Again, the unknowability of the future is emphasized — 'no podría decir', 'no podría alcanzarlos', 'alguien puede llegar, venir de pronto, no sé quién'. The poem describes an immobile point, symbolized by the dawn, between a past that weighs heavy on the present and a more just future that has yet to arrive.

Dawn in 'La señal' and 'El testigo' symbolizes hope and new beginnings, but it is also the uncanny moment between light and darkness, when the coming day comingles with the night. These liminal moments are recurrent in Valente's poetry, reflecting his belief that an anticipatory foreshadowing of utopia can become manifest in the here and now of the poem. Hope in new beginnings and the instauration of an alternative social structure is tempered, however, by an understanding of the ways in which, to use Valentean terminology, political ideals become 'crystallized', turned unto empty slogans, in the bureaucracies of state socialism. Two poems in the first section of *La memoria y los signos*, both dialogues with an unnamed interlocutor, describe the regret felt after the loss of the Spanish Republic and the promise it entailed, but also the struggle to retain a sense of hope in the wake of political defeat. The first is titled 'Hablábamos de cosas muertas':

> Hablábamos de cosas muertas
> o de todo
> lo que nunca ha existido.
>
> La sombra amenazaba
> con su olor triste el pálido
> recinto.
> Dije: hemos dejado
> la oración por el grito.
> La pasión solitaria
> por el miedo de muchos.
>
> Hablábamos de nuestra fe,
> aunque era inútil.
> Pero no importa.
> Había
> tiempo, toda una vida,
> un largo espacio de interrogaciones
> y ojos desiertos.
> Sí,
> hablábamos, previamente enlutados,
> de nuestra mutua muerte.
>
> Hablábamos a la caída de la tarde,
> sin nadie por testigo,
> de cuanto contempláramos un día
> partir de nuestros manos,
> de la fe que tuvimos,
> del vacío que en ella
> acaso nos unía. (I: 165–66)

Here, a religious vocabulary — *oración*, *fe* — allows us to read the poem in two ways. Firstly, as a description of a loss of Christian belief, and secondly, as a struggle to sustain belief in the possibility of radical political change. Traverso, in his discussions of left melancholy, links the two, describing how in the early modern period, Christian uncertainty in the wake of the rationalistic and empirical desacralization of the cosmos resulted in the increased doctrinal centrality of faith. The failures of twentieth-century revolutions provokes, for the believer in socialism, a similar melancholy to that felt by the religious believer in the early modern period, but now there can be no return to faith and 'the culture of defeat takes the form of a melancholic retreat into meditation and introspection' (Traverso 2016: 42). For Traverso, this melancholic culture of defeat is expressed in representations of emptiness, in the deserted landscapes of De Chirico's paintings. Valente's poems from this period also inhabit this melancholic space — 'el pálido | recinto', 'un largo espacio de interrogaciones | y ojos desiertos'. Paradoxically, however, it is precisely the melancholic experience of absence, loss, and solitude that can allow for future solidarities with those who are willing to speak of 'cosas muertas' and '… la fe que tuvimos | del vacío que en ella | acaso nos unía'.

'Extramuros', again from the first section of *La memoria y los signos*, is a companion piece to 'Hablábamos de cosas muertas'. Here, the speaker inhabits a desolate suburban landscape reminiscent of the films of Michelangelo Antonioni or the novels of Luis Martín-Santos: '[…] en los desmontes macilentos | donde la vegetación raquítica no puede | dar más señal del hambre' (I: 167). Again, we are presented with the description of a dialogue between the speaker and an unknown interlocutor. But here, dialogue is impossible, as the language and shared beliefs that had previously constituted their relationship have atrophied:

> Ocupamos después
> el centro, mudos,
> igual que dos actores
> que a mitad de la obra se mirasen
> en un suspenso tácito, sabiendo
> que el hilo estaba roto,
> el argumento falseado,
> el público difunto
> y la palabra que correspondía
> estúpida, grotesca, caída entre los dos. (I: 167)

All that remains of the past are half-destroyed scraps of material that provoke confused feelings of memory and regret:

> El viento alzó de pronto un negro andrajo
> cuya ceniza nos hirió la boca
> con un sabor amargo o un recuerdo
> quizá impreciso ya para los dos. (I: 167)

It is significant that Valente describes the workings of memory with the image of the rag blown by the wind. Walter Benjamin uses precisely this image when he describes the melancholic writer Siegfried Kracauer, the epitome of the outsider:

> Thus, in the end this writer stands alone. A malcontent, not a leader. No pioneer, but a spoilsport. And if we wish to gain a clear picture of him in the isolation of his trade, what we will see is a ragpicker, at daybreak, picking up rags of speech and verbal scraps with his stick and tossing them, grumbling and growling, a little drunk, into his cart, not without letting one or another of those faded cotton remnants — 'humanity,' 'inwardness' or 'absorption' — flutter derisively in the wind. A ragpicker, early on, at the dawn of the day of the revolution. (Benjamin 2005: 310)

The writer takes decayed words and ideals and stores them in the hope that they may someday return and take on revolutionary force. It is in this sense that we can understand Valente's stance as 'Extramuros', or 'un poco en las afueras de la vida'. Like Benjamin's writer, Valente places himself at the dawn of revolution, sifting through language to reactualize for the present words and images that can once more become operable in political struggle. It is in this sense, too, that we can understand the final lines of the poem, in which the speaker refuses to remain indifferent to past ideals:

> Sin odio o sin amor nos contemplamos,
> aunque no indiferentes
> a cuanto al fin y al cabo compartiéramos,
> y con un leve gesto de cabeza, en silencio,
> abandonamos el final brillante
> en que una muerte falsa sustituye el adiós. (I: 168)

But while Valente maintains in this collection hope in egalitarian ideals, he does not underestimate the forces that frustrate them. Throughout, the question arises as to what can remain of socialism in a world of ascendant Anglo-American capitalism. This is precisely the question put in 'Ramblas de Julio, 1964':

> Me pregunto qué queda de esta tierra,
> de ayer, de hoy mismo,
> de hace un momento apenas,
> de nuestra propia juventud a punto de no serlo
> ya nunca más y para siempre.
> [...]
> Y me pregunto qué queda de esta tierra
> y de su lento espacio poderoso,
> del pertinaz recuerdo de lo nunca vivido,
> pero sobrevivido a golpes
> de violenta luz
> contra el aire vacío. (I: 203)

The question arises in the context of Spain's opening to Western capitalism and development:

> La ciudad industrial tiene gratos ruidos
> de economía en pleno desarrollo,
> de bien compuesta burocracia,
> alegres avenidas,
> barriadas escuálidas en vías de mejora,
> pulso muy europeo.
> Aquí la burguesía
> ha dulcemente florido. (I: 203)

In this bustling scene, the 'liberales acentos de la Europa vecina' and the 'seminal y heroico tantán de los turistas' drown out the poetic word that can only be spoken 'a media voz'. The poem ends with the question: 'Me pregunto qué queda, pues, de todo | o de tan poco como fuimos, | bajo el tendido cielo del estío | enorme y duro, solo y sin nostalgia' (I: 204). The use of the word 'nostalgia' is significant. The melancholic relationship to the past is not nostalgic, it does not seek to recuperate what has been lost, nor does it mystify the past in order to console. Rather, the melancholic's dialectical relationship with the past recognizes loss but from it takes hope for future change.

It is in this context that we can understand the controversial poem Valente dedicates to the Republican exiles, 'Melancolía del destierro':

> Lo peor es creer
> que se tiene razón por haberla tenido

> o esperar que la historia devane los relojes
> y nos devuelva intactos al tiempo en que quisiéramos
> que todo comenzase.
> Pues no antes ni después existe ese comienzo
> y el presente es su negación y tú su fruto,
> hermano consumido en habitar tu sombra.
>
> Lo peor es no ver que la nostalgia
> es señal del engaño o que este otoño
> la misma sangre que tuvimos canta
> más cierta en otros labios.
>
> Y peor es aún ascender como un globo,
> quedarse a medio cielo,
> deshincharse despacio,
> caer en los tejados de espaldas a la plaza,
> no volver al gran día.
>
> La gloria de aquel acto
> era toda futura.
> Pero tú olvidas cuanto
> pusiste en él, mientras los muertos
> brotando están a flor de tierra ahora
> para hacer con sus manos
> la casa, el pan y la mañana nuestra. (I: 196)

Here, the word melancholy is used in a negative sense, to describe the nostalgic desire to dwell on a glorious past without facing present difficulties. Staying in the past removes the exile from current concerns while his vainglorious words inflate his sense of self-importance and diminish his capacity for social intervention. He becomes like a bloated balloon, floating away from the 'plaza' or place of public discourse. The exile forgets that the glory of any act is its orientation towards the future, and that the sacrifices of the dead were made so as to create 'la casa, el pan, y la mañana nuestra' (I: 196).[11] Similarly, in 'El visitante', Valente decries the clichéd language of the Republican exiles. The visitor, in this case Marcos Ana, who had been imprisoned for more than twenty years in Francoist jails and who attended Geneva in a Communist party-organized conference in the 1960s, speaks in 'palabras usadas | que de otro recibiera' (I: 198). For Valente, this means that the capacity to create among younger generations a genuine understanding of past suffering is lost. A reified language leads to an exhibition of pain as if it were an object to be bought or sold: 'como peines, navajas u otro objeto de venta | en inerte muestrario' in which experience is 'dispuesto, mas no dicho, todo | extrañamente desvivido' (I: 198).

But if the Republican exiles have lapsed into nostalgia and cliché, Valente finds in the language and example of past writers inspiration for future struggles. This is especially visible in the three elegies of section VI of *La memoria y los signos*: 'John Cornford, 1936', 'César Vallejo', and 'Si supieras' (dedicated to Antonio Machado). In his commemorative poem for John Cornford, Valente eulogizes the young poet and Communist who was killed in battle at the age of twenty-one near to Cordoba.

In the poem, Valente uses elements of Cornford's own writings — an epigraph, 'Only in constant action was his constant certainty found. He will throw a longer shadow as time recedes', from Cornford's 'Sergei Mironovitch Kirov', as well as references taken from Cornford's essays on the failures of artists to engage directly in political struggle. The poem ends with a eulogy to Cornford's capacity to merge life and literature in the fight against fascism:

> Un solo acto vida y muerte,
> la fe y el verso un solo acto.
> Ametrallados, no vencidos,
> veintiún años, en diciembre,
> Córdoba sola, un solo acto
> tu juventud y la esperanza. (I: 195)[12]

Similarly, the short poem dedicated to César Vallejo ends with three lines that emphasize the revolutionary potential that survives in the Peruvian poet's work, despite his miserable end: 'El roto, el quebrantado, | pero nunca vencido. | El pueblo, la promesa, la palabra' (I: 199). The poem to Antonio Machado also stresses the need to take up the example and revitalize the language of an earlier generation. Addressing Machado, the poetic voice declares:

> Si supieras cómo acudimos
> a tu verdad, cómo a tu duda
> nos acercamos para hallarnos,
> para saber si entre los ecos
> hay una voz y hablar con ella. (I: 205)

The present generation exists in the shadow of the vision of the future held by the dead and defeated, its artists measuring themselves on this scale:

> Dinos si en ella nos tuviste,
> si en tu sueño nos reconoces,
> si en el descenso de los ríos
> que combaten por el mañana
> nuestra verdad te continúa,
> te somos fieles en la lucha. (I: 205)

The final section of the collection considers the ways in which poetic language can embody and communicate experience. In 'El signo' the poetic word is compared to a clay pot: 'un cuenco de barro cocido al sol, | donde la duración de la materia anónima | se hace señal o signo, | la sucesión compacta frágil forma, | tiempo o supervivencia' (I: 211). The poem allows for the embodiment of otherwise ungraspable experience in the same way that the shaping of a clay pot transforms formless earth into an element of human culture. The choice of metaphor is telling. Benjamin, in 'On Some Motifs in Baudelaire' (1999: 152–96), also used the image of a clay pot to describe the difference between the purveying of information and the transmission of experience. In the essay, Benjamin draws from the philosophy of Bergson to argue that the capacity for experience does not depend on the individual alone, but on their relationship to a collective memory that is passed on through generations. In traditional societies, experience is passed on through oral tradition; in modern societies, the traditional communication of knowledge is lost, and is compensated for by a flood of information in newspapers and mass media. This explains the distinction in Proust's work between the *memoire volontaire* and the *memoire involontaire*: the first, like the newspapers, recalls information; the second, exemplified in the memories and sensations provoked by Marcel's tasting a Madeleine pastry, recalls experience. For Benjamin, Proust's novel is an attempt to produce synthetically for the modern world what was once a given of pre-modern existence, in which traditional stories did not give information about an event but rather 'embed[ed] it in the life of the storyteller in order to pass it on as experience to those listening' (Benjamin 2007: 159). The story, in this context 'bears the mark of the storyteller much as the earthen vessel bears the marks of the potter's hand' (Benjamin 2007: 159).[13]

This desire that the poem should somehow embody elements of experience, and that this experience be made available to the reader, is the fundamental motif in the final section of the *La memoria y los signos*. Thus, 'El signo' ends with a description of the way experience is embodied in the poem and the impact of this latter on the life of the reader:

> Aquí, en este objeto
> en el que la pupila se demora y vuelve
> y busca el eje de la proporción, reside
> por un instante nuestro ser,
> y desde allí otra vida dilata su verdad
> y otra pupila y otro sueño encuentran
> su más simple respuesta. (I: 211)

But poetry that alters another's consciousness cannot base itself on tired ideas and vocabularies, what in 'Un canto' is described as '...la palabra como ídolo obeso, | alimentado | de ideas que lo fueron y carcome la lluvia' (I: 213). Poetry, for Valente, needs to name that which has until now been unnameable, to become 'la explosión de un silencio' (I: 213).

Like Benjamin's ragpicker, the speaker in 'Como una invitación o una súplica' sees his task as sorting language, looking within our tired words for linguistic rhythms and combinations that would reveal 'una brizna del mundo' (I: 214). But it is important to note that the glimpse of a more just world is only possible in dialogue with the past, however difficult this dialogue may be to sustain:

> En la casa desierta o desertada,
> en la casa nocturna o sola
> en vano busco una respuesta.
> Hay un hilo perdido,
> una señal, la réplica que acaso
> permitiría proseguir el diálogo roto
> hasta después del alba. (I: 214)

Paradoxically, it is in this relationship to the defeated, to those whose vision of justice led to their suffering and death, that justifies continuing socialist struggle, and which compels the poet to renew the language of egalitarianism:

> En vano vuelven las palabras
> pues ellas mismas todavía esperan
> la mano que las quiebre y las vacíe
> hasta hacerlas ininteligibles y puras
> para que de ellas nazca un sentido distinto,
> incomprensible y claro
> como el amanecer o el despertar. (I: 215)

The final poem of the collection, 'No inútilmente', brings together the concerns of this final section. In the opening lines, the speaker considers the basic tension between existing conditions and a utopian future that underlies the collection as a whole:

> Contemplo yo a mi vez la diferencia
> entre el hombre y su sueño de más vida,
> la solidez gremial de la injusticia
> la candidez azul de las palabras. (I: 218)

While poetry may seem a weak tool in the fight against fascism, the speaker affirms a belief in the capacity of literature to form new vocabularies, or reactivate old ones, that might inspire political struggle. The moments in the past when poetry embodied a lived experience of utopian egalitarianism are cause enough for faith in its capacities: 'Haber llevado el fuego un solo instante | razón nos da de la esperanza' (I: 219). These 'solo instantes' or 'solo actos' are what Bloch calls *vor-scheinen*, or what Benjamin calls 'dialectical images': sudden illuminations that give a foretaste of a different world, and which, beyond the pamphleteering of clichéd social realism, can create subjectivities willing to imagine alternative social, political, and cultural conditions:

> Pues más allá de nuestro sueño
> las palabras, que no nos pertenecen
> se asocian como nubes
> que un día el viento precipita
> sobre la tierra
> para cambiar, no inútilmente, el mundo. (I: 219)

Melancholy and Resistance: *El inocente*

Valente reiterates the themes of *La memoria y los signos* in his other major collection from this period, *El inocente*. Many of the poems from *El inocente* were written in the aftermath of Valente's trip to Cuba, where, as he relates in his diary, he could witness for himself the creeping authoritarianism of the Castro regime, especially evident in its treatment of dissenting writers. During this period he also became friends with the homosexual Cuban writer Calvert Casey, who, despite having returned to Cuba from the United States in order to support the revolution, was marginalized because of his sexual orientation. Casey, who spent time in Geneva and developed a close friendship with Valente, with whom he shared an interest in the work of the seventeenth-century mystic and theologian Miguel de Molinos, would ultimately commit suicide, an event that Valente attributed in part to the Castro regime's treatment of gay men and women.

El inocente is dedicated to the memory of Casey, but also bears an epigraph from Flaubert's *La tentation de Saint Antoine*: 'Le vent que passait emportait les prophetes'. The phrase in Flaubert's short novel is spoken by a disempowered Old Testament God, who laments the destruction of the temple, the dispersal of his chosen people, and the ultimate triumph of atheistic science. The wind here refers to the power of the God, who was able to carry his word with the all-reaching swiftness of that element, but also alludes to historical change and destruction, which in the novel is reflected in the God's lament that 'les parfums de l'holocauste se sont perdus à tous les vents' (Flaubert 1954: 228). In the context of the writing of the poems, the wind symbolizes the power of revolutionary change and the prophets that announce it, but also the destruction of a belief system along with its sustaining communal celebrations.

The second poem of the collection, 'El viento trae sobre todas las cosas' explores aspects of these complex allusions:

> El viento trae sobre todas las cosas,
> lejanas, leves, polvorientas, dispersas,
> desde el cielo cubierto y bajo,
> vertiginosamente bajo, una amenaza.
> [...]
> El viento viene doblegando el cielo,
> sobajando la luz,
> organizando un gran concierto en medio del otoño
> de puertas herrumbrosas y trémulos maullidos.
> [...]
> El viento hace sonar gruesas fanfarrias
> con predominio de una larga tuba
> y triunfantes, más de qué, marchamos
> entre oscuros pañuelos y latas golpeadas.
>
> El viento loco del otoño brama
> como hembra marchita.
> Adiós, adiós.
> Ya nunca dejaremos
> que entre negros crespones el sueño nos confunde. (I: 281–82)

Here, the wind signifies the destruction of historical events as well as the creation of rituals that consolidate a new social and political order. The speaker refuses to participate in ritual, the ceremonial marking of time which confirms membership of a community and celebration of inaugural historical events. The refusal of communal celebration recurs in the following poem, 'Lugar vacío en la celebración', in which the speaker looks back with great bitterness at his childhood experiences in wartime Galicia and claims that his growth took place in opposition to the rituals of his city:

> Y yo empecé a crecer entonces
> como toda la historia ritual de mi pueblo,
> hacia adentro o debajo de la tierra,
> en ciénagas secretas, en tibios vertederos,
> en las afueras sumergidas

> de la grandiosa, heroica, orquestación municipal.
>
> Nací en la infancia, en otro tiempo, lejos
> o muy lejos y fui
> inútilmente aderezado para una ceremonia
> a la que nunca habría de acudir. (I: 283)

The speaker's refusal of the public ceremonies of his country registers a profound resistance to the hegemonic cultural memory that such rituals presuppose and reinforce. In the context of Francoist Spain, these rituals are the National Catholic celebrations of Church and Patria, events that could only alienate defeated Republicans. Given the ethical impossibility of participating in the public life of Francoist Spain, the speaker's predicament is like that of Baudelaire's alienated city dwellers, who could no longer enjoy the holidays that once marked communal memory and experience. As Benjamin puts it, 'the man who loses his capacity for experiencing feels as though he has dropped from the calendar' (2017: 184). Valente, too, drops from the calendar, refusing to collude with the rites of the Francoist parody of tradition. In order to do so, he constructs alternative visions of history and temporality.

The time and space from which Valente's voice speaks in these poems precludes any triumphant, or conciliatory, vision of Spain's history. Rather, the voice in Valente's poems speaks from a temporal position defined by disaster, ruin, and death, from the position of the hanged man in François Villon's 'Ballade des pendus', a citation from which serves as epigraph to the centrepiece of the collection, the long poem 'Sobre el tiempo presente':

> Escribo desde un naufragio
> desde un signo o una sombra,
> discontinuo vacío
> que de pronto se llena de amenazante luz.
> [...]
> Con lenguaje secreto escribo,
> pues quién podría darnos ya la clave
> de cuanto hemos de decir.
> Escribo sobre el hálito de un dios que aún no ha tomado
>   forma,
> sobre una revelación no hecha,
> sobre el ciego legado
> que de generación en generación llevará nuestro nombre.
> Escribo sobre el mar,
> Sobre la retirada del mar que abandona en la orilla
> formas petrificadas
> o restos palpitantes de otras vidas.
> Escribo sobre la latitud del dolor,
> sobre lo que hemos destruido,
> ante todo en nosotros,
> para que nadie pueda edificar de nuevo
> tales muros de odio.
> [...]
> Escribo desde nuestros huesos

> que ha de lavar la lluvia,
> desde nuestra memoria
> que será pasto alegre de las aves del cielo.
> Escribo desde el patíbulo,
> ahora y en la hora de nuestra muerte,
> pues de algún modo hemos de ser ejecutados.
>
> Escribo, hermano mío de un tiempo venidero,
> sobre cuanto estamos a punto de no ser,
> sobre la fe sombría que nos lleva.
>
> Escribo sobre el tiempo presente. (I: 298–300)

Writing after the disaster, the speaker takes on the responsibility of testifying for the defeated in a prophetic language whose recourse to anaphora is reminiscent of Biblical declamation, in this way reaffirming a belief in the ideals that inspired socialist movements. 'Escribo sobre las humeantes ruinas de lo que creímos | con palabras secretas | sobre una visión ciega, pero cierta' (I: 299). The faith that was lost in *La memoria y los signos* here returns, informed by the struggles of 'la muchedumbre que padece | hambre y persecución' (I: 300). Writing from a now that is marked by irreparable loss, the speaker awaits the revelation of a new language or vision that would inspire the struggles of those who long for 'un tiempo venidero' (I: 300).

But while the speaker in *El inocente*, as in *La memoria y los signos*, longs for the revitalization of a language that would be worthy of utopian ideals, the poems also express a commitment to those who become victims of crude teleological visions of history. Whereas previously, Valente had chosen the 'solo acto' of John Cornford as an emblematic gesture from the past that might inspire revolution in the present, in one of the final poems of *El inocente*, 'Una oscura noticia', he chooses as his Benjaminian 'dialectical image' the baroque mystic Miguel de Molinos's public humiliation at the hands of the Inquisition in the Rome of 1687. Valente had worked with Calvert Casey on a new edition of Molinos's *Guía espiritual* and reference to his persecution could not but recall Casey's persecution at the hands of the Cuban authorities. In a wider sense, the poem alludes to the humiliating public retractions forced on Cuban writers by the regime, events which had shaken the faith of European intellectuals, including Valente, in the moral authority of Castro's government. In the third section of the poem, the speaker describes the solitude of the 'extranjero' Miguel de Molinos:

> Estabas, extranjero, Aragonese, en medio
> de los que acaso más te habían amado,
> extranjero, engendrado por tu tierra
> extranjero, como todos nosotros,
> extranjero y de hinojos, Michele,
> Aragonese, con un cirio en las manos
> y las manos atadas,
> cargado con el peso estrafalario
> de tantas conclusiones, setenta y ocho creo,
> adversus quietisarum errores,
> mientras en tu tierra, extranjero,
> ninguno acaso nunca volvería a leerte

> por estar defendido desde antiguo
> contra herejes e idos
> por el arsenal invicto de las refutaciones,
> por el lenguaje heroico de todas las censuras
> y la represión sexual con que ya se escribían
> Triumphos de la Castidad contra tu diabólica lujuria. (I: 316–17)

In a motif that will become more central in Valente's work, Molinos is portrayed as a foreigner, as unwelcome in his own country, where his writings will be censored and forgotten, as in Rome, where he feels the full weight of ecclesiastical repression. It is not difficult to see the parallels between the existential solitude described here and the experiences of Casey and other Cuban poets. Molinos responds to the Church's persecution by deepening his journey of inner contemplation:

> Y tú en medio,
> tú solitario bajo las insignes galas
> del otoño romano, vestido de amarillo,
> taciturno y secreto,
> aragonés o español de la extrapatria, ibas,
> aniquilada el alma, a la estancia invisible,
> al centro enjuto, Michele,
> de tu nada. (I: 317)

Molinos's exercise of contemplation could also represent the development of Valente's poetry, which from this moment on becomes less directly referential and more attentive to the figure of the outsider. I will attempt to show, however, that this development does not imply a lessening of political commitment, nor a turning away from utopian ideals. Rather, the melancholic desire to relate to absence as absence, to grasp hold of nothingness, implies in Valente's work a profound commitment to political change that is informed by a heightened sense of the historical and the communal, but which is tempered by an ethical sense of responsibility to marginalized others. In my next chapter, I will discuss these issues in the context of contemporary theories of community.

Notes to Chapter 2

1. Significantly, one of the first poems in the *Lazarus* cycle, written in 1955 but not included in the published collection, refers to a Lazarus who 'Yacía entre los melancólicos | desperdicios del día' (I: 801).
2. The majority of the poems that make up *Poemas a Lázaro* were written in the period from 1954 to 1958, comprising Valente's final year in Madrid and his years in Oxford. For a detailed discussion of this period and a contextualization of the writing of the collection see Marta Aguda and Manuel Fernández Rodríguez's contributions to *Valente Vital* (Rodríguez Fer, Agudo Ramírez, and Fernández Rodríguez 2012: 264–70, 405–09). Jordi Doce (2005: 27–28) provides the background to the arrival of Eliot's work in the Spanish literary sphere in the attempts of the poets gathered around the *Cruz y raya* literary magazine to 'rehumanize' Spanish literature in a neo-Catholic vein after the exhaustion of the avant-gardes, an influence that is especially noticeable in *Poemas a Lázaro*. Valente describes *Poemas a Lázaro*, perhaps due to its overtly Catholic tone, as 'el libro que menos me gusta' but also recognizes that 'ese libro ha sido muy importante para mí' (DA: 150).

3. The quotation is taken from Donne's sermon 'Blessed and Holy is He that hath Part in the First Resurrection' (1953: 62), preached on at St. Paul's Cathedral on Easter Day, 1624.
 4. Stefano Pradel explores Valente's fragmentary aesthetic in his *Vértigo de las cenizas: estética del fragmento en José Ángel Valente* (2018).
 5. In the entry for 3 November 1959 of the *Diario Anónimo* Valente writes: 'Cuando escribí 'La salida' (varias semanas de la primavera del 56) es posible que tuviera más inmediatamente presente la estructura de los *Cuartetos* de Eliot, por ejemplo. Creo ahora, sin embargo, que el poema se relaciona por vínculos más estrechos con Baudelaire. En realidad podía haberse desprendido enteramente de este verso: 'Amer savoir, celui qu'on tire du voyage!' (DA: 39).
 6. Michael Richards (2013) describes the expansion of precarious dwellings in Spanish suburban spaces of the 1940s and 50s due to the migration of the rural poor, many of whom were escaping the consequences of their war-time allegiances, to Spain's major cities.
 7. Miguel Casado notes Valente's ambivalent relation to personal memory in this and other poems: 'Queda ahí, en todos los casos, la amenaza de un peligro grave, surcado de hechos y términos violentos, que parece poseer una fuerza incontrolable y ante lo cual solo cabe la huida. La mención de la infancia siempre conlleva esta turbiedad oscura y viscosa, que no deja de fluir en vida. La memoria no es una facultad intelectual abstracta e implica por fuerza la constitución del inconsciente y, entreverados con sus oscuridades, los conflictos en que se delucida y conforma la identidad. La negación de la memoria conlleva el velado, la negación de estos ámbitos; de ellos se huye, se quiere huir' (2012: 164–65).
 8. In interview with Claudio Rodríguez Fer, Valente describes his motivations for taking up the Geneva post: 'Porque eu tiña xa unha familia, tinha xa dous fillos e non tiña un salario moi bon en Oxford. Entón propuxeronme o de Xenebra e pagaron moi ben' (Rodríguez Fer 2000: 185).
 9. Manuel Fernández Rodríguez (2012: 346–47) gives an account of the reading, based on the testimony of the Hispanist Nigel Glendinning, in *Valente Vital (Galicia, Madrid, Oxford)*. For Fernández Rodríguez: 'Aquella lectura constituyó [...] una revisión de la memoria colectiva española y europea, así como una interpretación del papel de la poesía como un instrumento de búsqueda de la verdad, en perfecta sintonía y coherencia con las preocupaciones dominantes en el Valente de los años 60' (2012: 349).
10. Valente's difficult interaction with Gabriel Celaya and his wife during their trip to Cuba in 1967 is recorded in his *Diario Anónimo* (DA: 121). Valente was later to write a fiercely satirical poem on the couple — 'Fábula de payaso en la ancianidad y su pareja', which was published in the *Índice* literary magazine in 1969. Of Yevtushenko's reading of poems at the PEN congress of 1965 in Bled, Valente remarks: '[...] decía versos, huecos y llenos de erres, con gestos de actor barato' (DA: 91). 'Melancolía del destierro' (I: 196–97) and 'El visitante' (I: 198), included in *La memoria y los signos*, both criticize what seemed to Valente the empty rhetoric of Republican exiles.
11. The poem refers to José Herrera Petere, an older poet and common friend of Rafael Alberti and María Zambrano who also lived in Geneva. Claudio Rodríguez Fer and Tera Blanco de Saracho discuss the context of its writing in *Valente Vital* (Lopo, Blanco de Saracho, and Rodríguez Fer 2014: 123–41).
12. For a history of the failed attempt to censor this poem see José Antonio Llera, 'Poesía y censura previa. A propósito de José Ángel Valente', *Cuadernos Hispanoamericanos*, April (2019).
13. Valente refers to Benjamin's essay and these specific issues in a diary entry for February 1966: 'Bergson: *Materia y memoria*. La duración es la esencia de la experiencia. Es la actitud contemplativa la que permite actualizar el curso vital: la *memoria*. Para Proust, que se sumerge en la duración, la operación de restaurar la experiencia no depende de la libre elección, sino de la *memoria involuntaria*.' (DA: 100).

CHAPTER 3

Poetry and Community

Antigone: Speaking for the Other

Valente's defence of outsider figures like Calvert Casey becomes, from the late 1960s onwards, an essential aspect of his work. This concern for alterity is linked to Valente's exploration of the relationship of the poet to the community and its language. Like Paul Celan, whose importance for the Spanish poet we will discuss in a later chapter, Valente believes that a given political circumstance — National Socialism in Germany or National Catholicism in Spain — can lead to the corruption of public language. In a world of corrupt public discourse, the task of the poet is to forge a language that, to adapt the title of his first collection of essays, purifies 'las palabras de la tribu'. This ambition is related, in Valente's thought, to his conception of poetry as remembrance, a fulfillment of our ethical duty to the victims of violence. In the late 1960s, Valente articulates these concerns in his reading of a classical figure of alterity, Sophocles's Antigone.

Valente writes two essays on Antigone: 1968's 'Ideología y lenguaje' and 1969's 'La respuesta de Antígona'. Both readings are closely related. In the later text, Antigone's loyalty to her brother, who has been refused the rites of burial by the victors in a civil war, is framed in terms of the achievement of a new horizon of possibility for historical experience. Antigone's resistance to the law of the city, according to which those deemed traitors are refused the dignity of ritual burial, is, for Valente, an attempt to reconceive the political. If, in the Periclean model of the state, the civic law (justice) coincides with the law of the revealed Gods (truth), in Sophocles's tragedy, Antigone's task is to 'negar esa verdad' (II: 73), to fight against the Gods of the city so as to reveal hidden Gods and new forms of political life. In this sense, 'parece naturaleza del héroe trágico romper con su sacrificio los condicionamientos históricos que le han dado existencia para abrir una nueva posibilidad temporal, una nueva expectativa humana' (II: 69).

In an interesting twist on traditional interpretations of the tragedy, Valente does not consign Antigone to the realm of the pre-political; rather, for the Galician poet, she is the only character in the play capable of effecting political change:

> Antígona es la aberración peligrosa del espíritu, una nueva manifestación de la conciencia libre del hombre en la materia de la historia que la imposición de lo estatuido reifica. Por eso, de la pareja Antígona-Creonte sólo Antígona es creadora de historia, de devenir. (II: 75)

Valente's reading of Antigone coincides to some degree with Judith Butler's arguments in her *Antigone's Claim*, in which the American thinker critiques influential Hegelian and Lacanian interpretations of the play. In the Hegelian scheme, Antigone stands for the kinship relationships that must be partially overcome so that the male citizen can come into being; the mother must give up her son so that he may fight for the polis, a process that she resists, thus becoming both the foundation and the enemy of the state, the 'everlasting irony of the community' (Butler 2000: 4).[1] Similarly, for Lacan, the realm of the Symbolic (a quasi-transcendental category that is not natural but at the same time not contingent or social), is derived from an understanding of the incest taboo as the universal norm that transforms biological relations into cultural ones. The Lacanian Symbolic is, in Butler's reading, 'what sets limits to any and all utopian efforts to reconfigure and relive kinship relations' (2000: 20). In Lacan's theory, the transcendental kinship positions determine the linguistic structures of the Symbolic, which are the basis of social life. Antigone, in this context, is understood as speaking from an impossible subject position with regard to the transcendental symbolic structures of kinship, and her destruction is the consequence of the sheer incoherence of her enunciative position in relation to these constitutive norms.

Butler argues that both Hegel and Lacan's approaches to Antigone ignore the fact that we can 'critically assess the status of these rules that govern cultural intelligibility but are not reducible to a given culture' (2000: 17). In the context of kinship relationships, the contemporary legalization of gay marriage and, perhaps more subversively, the recognition of familial relations that do not coincide with the strictures of marriage, demonstrate the possibility of reconfiguring what are perceived in modern thought as necessary structures for cultural intelligibility and reproduction. Antigone, from this perspective, is 'precisely the one with no place who nevertheless seeks to claim one within speech, the unintelligible as it emerges within the intelligible, a position within kinship that is no position' (2000: 78). In her enunciation of subject positions and relations that are beyond cultural intelligibility, Antigone performs the ultimately political act, which is to question the boundaries between the political and the private, to question the naturalized and depoliticized categories upon which the polis is founded. As Butler remarks:

> If kinship is the precondition of the human, then Antigone is the occasion for a new field of the human, achieved through political catechresis, the one that happens when the less than human speaks as human, when gender is displaced, when kinship founders on its own founding laws. (2000: 82)

Butler's reading of *Antigone* is similar to Valente's reading of the play in 'Ideología y lenguaje'. Here, the 'inflación del estado' (II:76) limits a given language's revelatory capacity: '[T]odo orden institucionalizado lleva siempre consigo una institucionalización del lenguaje, pues éste ha de eludir las formas pugnaces de una realidad que, por su propia naturaleza, tiende a irrumpir del subsuelo histórico' (II: 76). For Valente, Creon's language is like that of any totalizing social order; it is what Henri Lefebvre (1966) terms *discours,* a reified public language that Antigone's words, which are 'de raíz poética' (II: 76), denounce.[2] It is in this sense that Valente argues for the political efficacy of poetic language, which does not have to conform to the tenets of social realism to be politically significant:

> La corrupción del lenguaje público, del discurso institucional, falsifica todo el lenguaje. Sólo la palabra poética, que por el hecho de ser creadora lleva en su raíz la denuncia, restituye al lenguaje su verdad. He ahí uno de los ejes centrales de la función social (tan debatida y tan poco entendida entre nosotros) del arte: la restauración de un lenguaje comunitario deteriorado o corrupto, es decir la posibilidad histórica de 'dar un sentido más puro a las palabras de la tribu'. (II: 78)

In these lines we have a succinct exposition of Valente's argument for the social value of poetic language, one that he will repeat on many occasions throughout his career. For Valente, a corrupt language is one that reinforces and naturalizes a social order that is hostile to change, that is without *fissura*, and the poet's task in this context is to reveal new linguistic possibilities that would imply the possibility of a new social order, new divisions between the political and the non-political. In the context of our reading of *Antigone*, this possibility is related to the emergence within the political of those who, according to the divisions upon which the political sphere is defined, have no voice within it, someone who, as in Butler's understanding of Antigone, 'is dead in some sense and yet speaks' (77).

Thus Valente can argue that the political import of his work, in the context of the post-war Spain in which he writes, lies in the attempt to create a poetic language that would resist a Francoist public language which he later describes as constituting a linguistic 'estado de ocupación' (II: 1216).[3] The figure of Antigone is especially resonant in post-war Spain, as her ethical stance is based on a desire to declare publicly a grief that can find no legitimate expression within the polis. It is impossible not to link this desire to the contemporary silencing of the suffering of the losing side in the Civil War, and the fact that, even today, the bodies of the victims of violence lie in unmarked graves throughout the country. Perhaps no figure exemplifies the injustice of a society in which the victims of violence cannot receive proper burial than that of Lorca, to whom Valente dedicates the following memorial in *Fragmentos de un libro futuro*:

> Desde Granada subimos hasta Víznar. Vagamos por el borde sombrío del barranco — ¿Dónde?, decíamos. Era el otoño. Los hermanos, las viudas, los hijos de los muertos venían con grandes ramos. Entraban en el bosque y los depositaban en algún lugar, inciertos, tanteantes. ¿En dónde había sucedido? — Lo mataron a él, decía la mujer, pero también mataron a otros muchos, a tantos, a ésos que ahora nadie ya recuerda. — Él ya no es él, le dije. Es el nombre que toma la memoria, no extinguible, de todos. (Víznar, 1988) (I: 558)

The body of Lorca, like the unburied body of Polyneices, becomes the figure through which a grief that could not find legitimate expression within the Francoist state begins to speak, and reflects the way in which, for Valente, the subversion of language and the exploration of the enunciative complexity of testifying for the victims of violence constitutes the political task of the poet within his community.

Language and Community in the Early Poems

The problems evoked in Valente's reading of Antigone — the relation between the poet, his language, and the cultural memory of the wider community — are taken up in many of the poems of his first five major collections of poetry — *A modo de esperanza* (I: 69–101), *Poemas a Lázaro* (I: 105–60), *La memoria y los signos* (I: 161–219), *Breve son* (I: 235–64), and *El inocente* (I: 277–318). Many of the poems in these collections are defined by the language that Valente describes as existing in an 'estado de ocupación', the overdetermined jargon of Stalinism, National Catholicism, and American militarism that he presents in a collage work from 1970, *Presentación y memorial para un monumento*. Valente's critical attitude towards public discourse brings with it, however, complexity and contradiction, aspects of which are reflected in the figurative resources he employs when referring to language in his poems. Valente depicts the language of a corrupt public sphere in organicist images of putrefaction and decay, but he also denounces empty words, meaningless signifiers that float in a vacuum, in a vocabulary relating to the semantic field of air and lightness. The language of truth is also figured in organic terms, with a healthy growth opposed to the rotten fruit of the language of lies. In these early collections, the desire to break with existing linguistic conventions and create new political and social relations exists alongside a desire to restore the memory of generations to a society that experiences the traumas of war as a profound rupture. The poet longs for a poetic language that could establish or celebrate a sense of community, but at the same time recognizes the dangers inherent in the jingoism that can cause a false sense of solidarity based on the exclusion of others. I will argue that these rhetorical contradictions, which are present in Valente's poetry up to *Interior con figuras*, allow us to read the political import of the stylistic and thematic transformation visible in the poet's work from this collection on, and also allow us to explore the difficulties involved in writing poetry that is attentive to historical and political context, while at the same time negotiating a literary and philosophical tradition in which the desire to cast poetry as a 'new mythology' that would found a community in which each member identifies themselves with a communitarian essence entails the dangers of a totalitarian exclusion of otherness. I will begin with a reading of poems from the first five collections that explore the themes of language and community.

In 'La rosa necesaria,' from *A modo de esperanza*, the poetic voice appeals for a language that would allow for the creation of a polis bound by shared experience:

> La rosa no;
> la rosa sólo
> para ser entregada.
>
> La rosa que se aísla
> en una mano, no;
> la rosa connatural al aire
> que es de todos.
>
> La rosa no,
> ni la palabra sola.

> La rosa que se da
> de mano a mano,
> que es necesario dar,
> la rosa necesaria.
> La compartida así,
> la convivida,
> la que no debe ser
> salvada de la muerte,
> la que debe morir
> para ser nuestra,
> para ser cierta.
> Plaza,
> estancia, casa
> del hombre,
> palabra natural,
> habitada y usada
> como el aire del mundo. (I: 85)

Despite the Heideggerian overtones of a language that would be 'estancia, casa | del hombre', this early poem accords with the social realist vision of poetry of the 1940s and 50s, in which poetic language must be 'normalized' so that it can freely circulate between members of a community metonymized as a 'plaza'. The social realist desire to give voice to the everyman is repeated in the penultimate poem of the collection, 'Acuérdate del hombre que suspira...' (I: 98), which, in existentialist tones, opposes the singular experience of the Unamunian subject — 'tan singular, tan oscuro, tan diario | que me toco, río, y muero a la vez' (I: 100) — to the language of the political representatives who claim to speak for all: 'Ellos, los poderosos | los que suelen hablar | en representación de todo el mundo' (I: 100).[4]

Poemas a Lázaro shows a more ambiguous attitude towards the capacity of poetic language to effect political change. In the 'Primer poema' that opens the collection, the 'odiosamente inútil' poetic voice questions its own powers: 'cuento los caedizos latidos | de mi corazón y ¿qué importa?, | ¿qué sed o qué agobiante | vacío llenaré de un vacío más fiero' (I: 107). Beyond lyrical self-examination, the political relevance of poetry arises through a process of self-abnegation:

> Para vivir así,
> para ser así anónimamente
> reavivida y cambiada,
> para que el canto, al fin,
> libre de la aquejada
> mano, sea sólo poder,
> poder que brote puro
> como un gallo en la noche,
> como en la noche, súbito,
> un gallo rompe a ciegas
> el escuadrón compacto de las sombras. (I: 108)

Here, the political efficacy of poetry lies in the destruction of the poetic prerogative to speak and express subjective interiority. The anonymity of the poetic voice allows for the expression of heretofore unvoiced communitarian desires.

'Objeto de poema', from the same collection, seems to flatly contradict the linguistic optimism of 'La rosa necesaria'. Here, the 'object' of the poem is hidden by an excess of words. The capacity to deceive is related precisely to the airy lightness of words that in the previous poem was a virtue: 'Te pongo aquí cercado| de palabras y nubes: me confundo' (I: 133). There is a distrust of common language, and a Cavafy-influenced disdain for the public sphere: '...hablo | de lugares communes, pongo | mi vida en las esquinas | no guardo mi secreto' (I: 133). This distrust of public language is not, however, a retreat into solipsism, but should be viewed more as a reaction to a corrupt society. 'La plaza' expresses this suspicion of contemporary discourse in a nostalgic description of pre-war political speech:

> Aquí alguien habló
> tal vez a hombres unidos
> en la misma esperanza.
> Tal vez entonces
> tuvo en verdad la vida
> cauce común y fue la patria
> un nombre más extenso
> de la amistad o del amor.
> Aquí
> latía un solo corazón unánime. (I: 146)

This pre-war language is described as articulating the voice of a community that moves in unison with the rhythm of the heart. In 'La mentira', the possibility of a language that would unite a community and express the truth is described in organic terms, a language that would 'enarbolar la verdad' (I: 149) opposed to the 'palabras de globos hinchados' (I: 149) of the 'mercaderes de mentira' (I: 149). In the following poem, 'Sobre el lugar del canto,' language is again described with organic metaphors of generation:

> La cólera terrible de la tierra
> que no alimenta la raíz del aire
> y se acuesta en la tierra boca abajo.
> La palabra que nace sin destino.
> [...]
> Un fruto triste se desgarra y cede
> más débil que su propia podredumbre. (I: 150)

Already in these first two collections we can see a tension between, on the one hand, a poetics of generation in which poetic language figured as organic growth would unite a community as a totality, and, on the other, a vision of language as unbounded, a transparent substance 'connatural al aire' (I: 85), the very lightness of which allows for linguistic exchange and thereby communitarian relation. Language conceived in this, second, sense can be understood either positively or negatively, as that which can freely circulate among citizens or as that which deceives, a sterile word, 'ebrio de nada', which empties the plaza, once the place for the celebration of community, but, in the context of the post-war, the site that reveals the destruction of solidarity: '[...] piadosamente, | en el aire extinguido, | mi mano toca ahora | la soledad' (I: 146).

La memoria y los signos again takes up the thematics of a new poetic language that would work against the corrosive language of the Spanish public sphere. 'Con palabras distintas' imagines a poetry that 'hirió de muerte al necio | al fugaz señorito de ala triste' and that would provide a new vocabulary to replace the tired language of cliché: 'vino a nuestro encuentro | con palabras distintas, que no reconocimos, | contra nuestras palabras' (I: 201). The final section of the collection, section VII, deals almost entirely with the question of the relation between poetic language and community. In 'Un canto' we can read again the aspiration that poetry might allow for the public expression of marginalized voices:

> La explosión de un silencio.
> Un canto nuevo, mío, de mí prójimo,
> del adolescente sin palabras que espera ser nombrado,
> de la mujer cuyo deseo sube
> en borbotón sangriento a la pálida frente,
> de éste que me acusa silencioso,
> que silenciosamente me combate,
> porque acaso no ignora
> que una sola palabra bastaría
> para arrasar el mundo,
> para extinguir el odio
> y arrastrarnos. (I: 213)

As with Antigone, the emergence of these voices — the adolescent, the desirous woman — into the public sphere has world-transforming potential. 'Como una invitación o una súplica' recounts the difficulty of discovering a 'brizna del mundo' (I: 214) behind the shroud of a cliché-ridden language whose 'ritmos componían | el son inútil de la letra muerta | y de la vieja moralidad' (I: 214). The revolution that would allow for political change must be accompanied by a radical subversion of the language of totalitarianism. Words, in this moment, would be emptied of their old meanings, and the utopian impulse would become visible in the blinding light of revolutionary speech: 'pues ellas mismas todavía esperan | la mano que las quiebre y las vacíe | hasta hacerlas inintelligibles y puras | para que de ellas nazca un sentido distinto, | incomprensible y claro | como el amanecer o el despertar' (I: 215).

The following poem, 'No puede a veces', is more pessimistic as to poetry's powers. There is, perhaps, a time for poetry within a community that celebrates and sacralizes itself through song, but equally, as the first line of the poem reads, 'No puede a veces alzarse al canto lo que vive' (I: 216). In a recurrent trope in these poems, the failure of language is linked to the failure of generation. What in 'Como una invitación o una súplica' is described as a 'hilo perdido', in 'No puede a veces' finds its equivalent in 'la solidificación del tibio | fluido seminal en los lechos vacíos' (I: 216). Moreover, the 'plaza' or place of communitarian celebration is replaced by 'vastos salones preparados | para un ceremonial que no veremos' (I: 216). The restorative function of poetry, dear to Wordsworth (spots of time) and Eliot (the objective correlative) is lost: 'Y la memoria | irreparable, hunde su raíz en lo amargo' (I: 216).

The penultimate poem of this section, 'Para oprobio del tiempo', is a devastating dissection of this time that makes the celebration of community in poetry an impossible task, and of all Valente's poems, the one that makes most obvious reference to *Antigone*. Like the stench that exposes the corruption of Thebes, the broken world of the poem contains 'algo que había quedado sin sepultar | y hedía' (I: 217). The resonances of this reference to the unburied in the context of twentieth century Spain and its Civil War needs no elaboration. In this world, the public sphere is falsified; rather than a plaza where the community can convene, it has become '[...] un ensayo general | con trajes, música, el director de escena | y un telón espantoso cayendo de improviso | antes de terminar el tercer acto' (I: 217). Behind the spectacle of monarchal power, the '[...] sucesión | de los monarcas godos', there is something 'roto o insepulto' (I: 218), something that remains to be said, but unsaid, diminishes language itself: 'Unas palabras eran | por su sonido falsas, se veía. | Otras por su inocencia, peligrosas y aleves' (I: 218). But if this time is not propitious to poetry that might inspire an effective revolution in the present, there is the possibility that the 'candidez azul de las palabras' (I: 218), might in the future reach actors with the capacity to change the given order: 'las palabras, que no nos pertenecen, se asocian como nubes | que un día el viento precipita | sobre la tierra | para cambiar, no inútilmente, el mundo' (I: 219).

The tension between generation and discontinuity, empty or decaying words against the organic language of truth, returns in the final work of Valente's most explicitly political writings, *El inocente*. The first two sections of the long poem 'Sobre el tiempo presente' crystallize these tensions:

> Escribo desde un naufragio,
> desde un signo o una sombra,
> discontinuo vacío
> que de pronto se llena de amenazante luz.
> Escribo desde el tiempo presente,
> sobre la necesidad de dar un orden testamentario a nuestros
> gestos,
> de transmitir en el nombre del padre,
> de los hijos del padre,
> de los hijos oscuros de los hijos del padre,
> de su rastro en la tierra,
> al menos una huella del amor que tuvimos. (I: 298)

Emerging from the historical rupture of war, the poetic voice assumes the task of restoring the memory and the experience of generations in an anaphoric language reminiscent of Biblical declamation. But, paradoxically, this task can only be carried out through the creation of a new language and under the aegis of a new mythology:

> Con lenguaje secreto escribe,
> pues quién podría darnos ya la clave
> de cuanto hemos de decir.
> Escribo sobre el hálito de un dios que aún no ha tomado forma,
> sobre una revelación no hecha,

>   sobre el ciego legado
>   que de generación en generación llevará nuestro nombre. (I: 299)

The poet's task is not only to write about the past, but to write in a new language that redefines that which can be said, creating, like Antigone, 'una nueva manifestación de lo divino' that would allow for 'una nueva órbita de humana libertad' (II: 76), and, paradoxically, through rupture create a new generational thread.

'El poema', from the same collection, describes this language:

>   Si no creamos un objeto metálico
>   de dura luz,
>   de púas aceradas,
>   de crueles aristas,
>   donde el que va a vendernos, a entregarnos, de pronto
>   reconozco o presencie metódica su muerte,
>   cúando podremos poseer la tierra. (I: 303–04)[5]

This 'objeto incruento', paradoxically, allows for the communal possession of the earth; that which refuses exchange, 'resistente a la vista | odioso al tacto' (I: 304), is precisely that which founds a community that shares a common world. This hard, metallic language is opposed to the decaying language of 'Crónica, 1968':

>   Las palabras se pudren.
>
>   El que da una palabra da un don.
>   El que da un don deja vacío el aire.
>   El que vacía el aire coloniza la tierra.
>
>   Pero bajo la tierra las palabras se pudren.
>   Las palabras se llenan de un hipo triste de animal ahíto
>   de un hipo de hipopótamo tardío,
>   y que mucho que brille su arco iris no traen la paz,
>   sino el sebáceo son del salivar chasquido
>   y el hilo deglutido de la muerte.
>
>   Las palabras se pudren, son devueltas,
>   como pétreo excremento,
>   sobre la noche de los humillados. (I: 308)

Here, the twin aspects of language are invoked. Language can freely circulate in exchange, in this way allowing for the construction of a common world. But this can also be a language that creates a 'vacío,' which, in this context, has the negative connotations of 'empty words'. Putrefaction, on the other hand, suggests the semantic field of rot and decay that Valente uses to describe both Spanish society, which like Thebes suffers the stench of unsanctified corpses, and a corrupt or outdated public language. In this context, literature that conforms to traditional norms or to the fixed vocabulary of social realism is inadequate to the memory of the victims of Francoist violence.

The major collections from the first part of Valente's career — *A modo de esperanza, Poemas a Lázaro, La memoria y los signos, Presentación y memorial para un monument, Breve son*, and *El inocente* — are characterized by a sustained critique of the public language of Francoist Spain, and the expression of the need to create a new poetic language that would lay bare the shortcomings of that social and political world, and at the same time serve in the foundation of a new communitarian self-understanding. The language of the regime is figured rhetorically as both a 'vacío' and as a rotting corpse, the language of the empty plaza or the ceremonial room from which the public is excluded. Opposed to this is a poetic language, which is the organic language of generations, that which connects the present and the past, but also that which allows for the rupture of existing conditions, the inclusion of enunciative positions that are excluded from the public sphere, and the opening of horizons towards a future of liberty. It is clear, however, that there are profound tensions within Valente's approach to the political potential of poetic language and its relation to the wider community. Whereas 'La rosa compartida' describes a transparent language that would be easily shared among members of a community, 'El poema' describes an 'objeto incruento' that would resist any facile reading, while 'La mentira' imagines an organic language that would 'enarbolar la verdad'. The desire to break with existing linguistic convention and to include the excluded within the public sphere coexists with a more conservative ambition that poetry restore the memory of generations, framed in terms that are themselves exclusive — 'del hijo al padre'. We might also ask ourselves whether there are dangers in the belief that poetry should found a community. The organic metaphors that Valente uses to describe the language of truth have disturbing echoes of the blood and soil rhetoric of National Socialism. Similarly, the description of the empty, floating words of lies is disturbingly reminiscent of the nationalist distrust of the *luftsmensch*, the overly intellectual cosmopolitan Jew. Valente himself seems to point to these possible dangers in the 'Canción de cuna' included in *Breve son*, in which a motley group of Francoist dignitaries chant in unison:

> — *¡Somos las fuerzas vivas,*
> *somos las fuerzas vivas,*
> *somos las fuerzas vivas*
> *de toda la nación!* (I: 262)

The nationalist rhetoric invoked, and implicitly criticized, reminds us of the dangers inherent in the belief that poetry can become a new foundational mythology for a community, a danger that was central to intellectual exploration of the notion of community that began in the late 1970s and early 1980s in the work of a series of philosophers — Michel Blanchot, Jean Luc Nancy, Giorgio Agamben — responding to the development of the European Union. In the next section, I bring the insights of Jean Luc Nancy's influential text, *La communauté désoeuvrée*, to bear on Valente's later poetry, and argue that it can allow us to read it in terms of a paradoxical notion of community based on difference and singularity.

The Inoperative Community

Nancy's major work on community was published in 1986 under the title *La communauté désoeuvrée*, and later published in English in 1991, with the addition of two further chapters, as *The Inoperative Community*.[6] In the preface to his work, Nancy defines the question of community in terms of a politics of the left. Politics of the right would be, from this perspective, concerned with administration and order. Politics of the left, on the other hand, implies 'at the very least, that the political, as such, is receptive to what is at stake in the community' (1991: xxxvi). This means that the very possibility of the political, which in contemporary democracies seems to give way to economic models of efficiency, is based on life in community. And life in community is, for Nancy, necessarily bound up with relation to an alterity. In fact, in order to *be* at all, we must first *be in relation* to that which is other, and Nancy here adopts a Levinasian discourse of the 'face of the other' in order to describe this 'being-in-common' within community, an existence whose 'exemplary reality is that of "my" face always exposed towards others, always turned toward an other and faced by him or her, never facing myself' (1991: xxxvii–xxxviii).

Nancy argues that thinking of the political and the community as the expropriation of the self in its being-in-common with another has been replaced, in modern conceptions of community stemming from Rousseau, by an idea of the immanent community, conceived as 'the sharing, diffusion, or impregnation of an identity by a plurality wherein each member identifies himself only through the supplementary mediation of his identification with the living body of the community' (1991: 9). These conceptions are precisely the 'closure' of community, whereas being-in-common is a relation that never allows itself to be absorbed into a common substance outside of relation. As opposed to communion, being in common means '*no longer having, in any form, in any empirical or ideal place, such a substantial identity, and sharing this* (narcissistic) "lack of identity". This is what philosophy calls "finitude"' (1991: xxxviii). That is, community is the ecstatic experience of the singular (as opposed to the atomic individual) being, the *clinamen* it undergoes in its relation to the other that is excessive, that does not allow itself to be appropriated in a process of self-identification.

It is from this understanding of community that Nancy constructs a critique of modern conceptions of 'lost' community. Nancy identifies a tendency in modern thought, developing from Rousseau but also present in Hegel, to describe a prior state of social development in which a pristine state of community prevailed. Though this vision of community can be framed in the historical context of Rome, the first Christian communities, or medieval brotherhoods, for Nancy, the most important model for community as conceived by the moderns is the Christian Eucharist. The modern conception of community would, from this perspective, be a way of conceiving the irruption of the divine into the immanence of human existence. Modern ideas of community would be a reaction to the withdrawal of the divine in modernity, the replacement of the *Deus Absconditus* with the *Deus Communis*. For Nancy, this modern desire for absolute immanence in community is destructive of the very spacing, the relation with alterity, which constitutes true community. In fact, the desire for immanence in community constitutes its very suppression. Absolute immanence can only be achieved in death, and for Nancy this explains the self-destructive tendencies of nationalist societies. Nazi Germany, which moved from the extermination of those considered other to the brink of absolute self-destruction, would be the prime example of this tendency, and it is possible to argue that in this case societal self-destruction actually took place, at least, as Nancy notes, 'with regard to certain aspects of the spiritual reality of the nation' (1991: 12).

A similar process can be seen in the mythico-literary figure of the self-destructive suicide of lovers, or in the self-sacrifice of the subject for the state, which for Hegel was a profound expression of the achievement of objective spirit. Thus Nancy argues:

> The fully realized person of individualistic or communistic humanism is the dead person. In other words, death, in such a community, is not the unmasterable excess of finitude, but the infinite fulfilment of an immanent life: it is death itself consigned to immanence; it is in the end that resorption of death that the Christian civilization as though devouring its own transcendence, has come to minister to itself in the guise of a supreme work. (1991: 13)

If, for Hegel, death can be sublated in the dialectical movement of history towards the absolute community yet to come, for Nancy, death is never comprehended in the pseudo-communitarian terms of homeland, soil, blood, or nation; on the contrary, death reveals the true nature of community as the impossibility of immanence. That is, when we witness the death of the other we are presented with what we cannot ourselves experience but that which is at the same time our innermost truth, our finitude. The most profound experience of ourselves as finite beings (since we cannot experience our own birth or death) is this witnessing which simultaneously tells us a profound truth of community — the impossibility of immanence or fusion within it. As Nancy writes: 'In a certain sense community acknowledges and inscribes — this is its particular gesture — the impossibility of community' (15). It is in this sense that Nancy argues that the community is that which is 'unworked', as it is constituted by the sharing or co-appearance of a finitude that cannot be made into a work — there can be no transcendent embodiment of community outside of the communication-without-communion of singular beings.

But what is the relevance to literature of Nancy's discussion of community? A hint is given at the end of the first essay of *The Inoperative Community*, in which Nancy describes the place of lovers in the work of Georges Bataille, for whom, as Nancy notes, 'community was first and finally the community of lovers' (1991: 36). For Nancy, if lovers reveal something about community it is not that they form a special bond above society, but because they 'expose that fact that communication is not communion' (1991: 37). Lovers are at the extreme limit of communication, touching each other in the joy of intimacy, but nevertheless retaining their singularity. As such, lovers, are exemplars of true community, which is defined by proximity and address. Literature, for Nancy, would be the writing of this speechless co-appearance of beings in the singularity of loving relation:

> There is community, there is sharing, and there is the exposition of this limit. Community does not lie beyond the lovers, it does not form a larger circle within which they are contained: it traverses them, in a tremor of 'writing' wherein the literary work mingles with the most simple public exchange of speech. Without such a trait traversing the kiss, sharing it, the kiss itself is as despairing as community is abolished. (1991: 40)

Because being-in-common is constituted by the mutual 'compearance' (*comparution*) or exposure of singular beings to one another in relation, there is always resistance to mythological conceptions of community that would in effect drown being-in-common in an absolute structure of social immanence. Whereas myth would imagine itself as a language that enacts absolute communion, what Nancy terms 'literature' or 'writing' would be a language that bears witness to its own incapacity, to the 'limit upon which communication takes place' (1991: 67), it would be 'the indefinitely repeated and indefinitely suspended gesture of touching the limit, of indicating it and inscribing it, but without crossing it, without abolishing it in the fiction of a common body' (1991: 67).

Language and Community in the Later Poems

It is here that we can return to the tensions that we identified in Valente's exploration of language and community in the first half of his career. Ultimately these tensions can be reduced to the division between a mythic language that unites word and world and binds a community, and a corrupt language which ruptures a community that has lost its connection with past generations. The call for a new language and for the inclusion of the voices of the excluded within public discourse is framed in terms of a restoration of the public sphere in which the celebration of community would be the expression of an genealogical history in which each member identifies with an original and total Word which absorbs him or her, 'para ser así anónimamente | reavivada y cambiada' (I: 108).

That this division leads to tensions within Valente's poetry is inevitable. Working from the presupposition of an opposition between community and nihilism puts the poet in a difficult position — either he accepts a loss of linguistic value and meaning, or he defends the existence of a mythic poetic language that unites word and world, thereby falling into the trap of the totalizing discourse of community that Nancy identifies. The Italian philosopher Roberto Esposito (2009), writing in a similar vein to Nancy, allows for a reformulation of this opposition that might help us to create an alternative to the path that Valente takes in his earlier works. For Esposito, modern thought on the relation between community and nihilism pits the presence of the *thing* of community against the destructive *nothing* of nihilism. What is necessary, for Esposito, is to recognize that nihilism and community are bound up with each other. Like Nancy, Esposito identifies community with the *munus*, the sharing that constitutes community, the fact that to enter into community the subject must encounter the other, and that being in common is precisely this — the 'sequence of alterations that never coalesce into a new identity' (2009: 26). Subjects in community do not possess any quality that constitutes their essential identification with a communitarian totality; rather, their very dispossession, their alteration in the face of the other, constitutes their place within a commonality. Thus, 'community is structurally inhabited by an absence — of subjectivity, identity, and property' (2009: 26–27). In fact, the very being of community is this absence, the gap that relates subjects in a common giving of themselves without recompense; as Esposito notes, the term *munus* refers to a gift given, that which is always excessive with regard to an economy of exchange.

For Esposito, modern thought on community since Hobbes has erred in attempting to fill in this lack, creating the totalizing category of the sovereign in an attempt to guarantee the coherence of a community, but in effect annihilating the essence of community, the gap of relation between subjects, replacing it with a direct relation between the individual and the sovereign, or the absolute identity of subjects united under the general will. But these schemes, based as they are on a false conception of inter-relation, the anomic fight of all against all, creates a more radical nihilism, as that which they are supposed to recreate, a non-historic golden age of pristine community, is non-existent. The communitarian attempt to retrieve the lost origin that would inaugurate community inevitably leads to violence, as this origin that would allow for an absolutely saturated community is always unavailable; the search for the origin leads to violence against those perceived as outside the community, and ultimately also to the self-destruction of the community itself. For Esposito, the contemporary world, in which the lack of stable meanings is exacerbated by globalization, allows for the opportunity to escape modern concepts of community. The sheer lack of sense would allow us to ultimately let go of the illusion of transcendent categories that would ground our understanding of the world and would reveal a 'world reduced to itself, able to be simply what it is' (2009: 35). Our communities would be the passage 'between this immense devastation of sense and the necessity that each singularity, each event, each fragment of existence must be in itself meaningful' (2009: 35). I take Esposito here to mean that, in the absence of illusions of transcendent grounding of our communities, we can reappraise their constitutive lack as something other than privation. If there were communal celebration in this society it would be based not on the Word made flesh of the Christian Eucharist, but on the ephemeral garlands of incense that Mallarmé describes in his *Divagations*.[7]

It is in this context that we can read the relation between community and poetry in the second half of Valente's career, which stretches from *Interior con figuras* to his final *Fragmentos de un libro futuro*, and in which the references to political and communitarian themes diminish, and his poetic language becomes more abstract and self-referential. This movement from a more obvious engagement with political themes, whether through direct reference to political events and cultural decay, or through the collage poems in which the clichés that lent support to the totalitarian regimes of the twentieth century are laid bare, does not mean that Valente completely discontinues his exploration of the relation between poetic language and community. Paradoxically, it might be best to explore the notion of community in Valente's later work by approaching that which is generally taken to be its opposite, the emptiness of the 'vacío'.[8]

From this perspective, the second half of Valente's career is not a solipsistic turning from communitarian issues towards a hermetic discourse that refuses communication. Rather, the development of Valente's poetry reflects the radicalization of his communitarian impulse, but one in which the immanent transcendence of relation becomes the centre of the poems. This tendency is nowhere more evident than in the erotic poetry of the later collections.[9] 'El deseo era un punto inmóvil' from *Interior con figuras* is an outstanding example:

> Los cuerpos se quedaban del lado solitario del amor
> como si uno a otro se negasen sin negar el deseo
> y en esa negación un nudo más fuerte que ellos mismos
> indefinidamente los uniera.
>
> ¿Qué sabían los ojos y las manos,
> qué sabía la piel, qué retenía un cuerpo
> de la respiración del otro, quién hacía nacer
> aquella lenta luz inmóvil
> como única forma del deseo? (I: 356)

The lovers in the poem negate themselves so that the ecstatic relation they share becomes the expression of their love. The 'lenta luz inmóvil' that inhabits the space of relation is the form of their desire, that which binds them in the separation of unknowing eyes, hands, body, and breath. Similarly, 'La noche', from the same collection, describes a relation in which each lover enjoys the never satisfied desire of the other:

> Déjame ahora
> que igual que tú con la palabra tú
> que así prolongas
> para que sea el nombre que has querido darme,
> acaricie tu largo cuerpo duro,
> el brillo de tu piel que un vaho
> mortal humedecía.
>
> Y déjame aún beber
> la sed inagotable de la noche.
>
> Cuánta sed engendramos
> para que nunca nadie de aquella sed dijera:
> fue extinguida.
>
> Y ahora te digo déjame aún beber
> en la manida misma de tu sed
> tu sed.
> Retenme, cierva,
> poder lunar,
> en la raíz del agua. (I: 353)

'La noche' and the 'cierva' are allusions to the poetry of San Juan de la Cruz, a poetry that, like the lyrics of courtly love, describes a desire that never achieves fulfilment. The poem is an apostrophe, an address to the lover, who, like the speaker, is depersonalized in deixis, each one becoming a "tú" that exists for another in ecstatic relation. Love, here, is a becoming other in relation, in the 'infinita perpetuación del deseo' (II: 396) that can never come to rest in the union of lovers.[10]

The collection *Mandorla*, from 1982, is dedicated entirely to this space of relation. The *mandorla*, as Valente explains in an essay from 1999, 'La experiencia abisal', is the space formed in the intersection of two circles, a space that in the Christian tradition was often used to signify the incarnation of the divine, but which for Valente is 'la mandorla — espacio vacío y fecundante, donde se acoplan lo visible y lo invisible — es símbolo del sexo femenino' (II: 747). It is in this context that we can understand the motif of 'concavidad' which reappears throughout the collection. The *mandorla* is the space within which creation can occur, symbol of the female sex, but it also represents the nothing of community, the space that is produced in the intimate and joyful separation of lovers, as described in 'Borde':

> Tu cuerpo baja
> lento hacia mi deseo.
> Ven.
> No llegues.
> Borde
> donde dos movimientos
> engendran la veloz quietud del centro. (I: 411)

It is difficult not to recall here Nancy's invocation of the lovers as the exemplars of community to which literature testifies. In describing the erotic relation, Valente makes visible the extreme limits at which singularities are mutually exposed in the sharing that constitutes community. Whereas in Christian tradition, the *mandorla* surrounds representations of Christ and signifies the presence of divine power in the flesh, here it is the empty space of a communion that is never realized. It is in this sense that we can understand the desacralization of communion that opens the collection *Al dios del lugar*, in which an unknown God inhabits the dark sediments at the 'fondo' of the chalice. There is transcendence, but this transcendence should be understood as an alterity of the flesh, in the 'oscuro, sombra, cuerpo | mojado en las arenas' (I: 463). Relation is the limit, the unassimilable remainder, that resists the absolute immanence of communion.

In his *The Coming Community*, Giorgio Agamben describes the contemporary world of spectacle and linguistic alienation in terms of the Kaballistic 'isolation of the Shekinah' (Agamben 1993: 80.1), the isolation of the manifestations of the divine from the divine itself. (1993: 80.1).[11] Valente at times responds to this isolation of language from its ground in the relation to an *arche-palabra*, the Word before the word, that occurs in various guises throughout his work, and which remains present in many of his declarations on poetry right up to his death. The difficulty of such a stance in terms of community, and in terms of Valente's commitment to those who are excluded from nationalistic communities, is clear — the Word before the word is a hierarchical and inevitably totalizing grounding of the communal. Valente's poetry, however, along with the various essays in his career dedicated to figures of ungrounding — *silencio, nada, vacío* — make clear the complex tensions that underlie his, and modern poetry's, relation to politics and community. For Agamben, the attempt to reground language is futile. Rather, it is better to attempt to derive from achieved nihilism the separation of language from being that would allow language itself, the opening to another that language implies, to be revealed as the immanent grounding of community:

> Only those who succeed in carrying it to completion without allowing what reveals to remain veiled in the nothingness that reveals, but bringing language itself to language will be the first citizens of a community with neither presuppositions nor a State, where the nullifying and determining power of what is common will be pacified and where the Shekinah will have stopped sucking the evil milk of its own separation. Like Rabbi Akiba, they will enter into the paradise of language and leave unharmed. (1993: 82.3)

It is perhaps this experience of language without metaphysical ground that Valente describes in the third fragment of *El fulgor*, which bears the epigraph 'Materia': FORMÓ | de tierra y de saliva un hueco, el único | que pudo al cabo contener la luz (I: 463). The poem reveals both the negative power of the linguistic, which forms a 'hueco', the gap between words and the things to which they refer, but also its somatic production in the commerce of saliva and earth. The relation between this 'hueco' and the 'saliva' and 'tierra' of embodied enunciation, the very *materia* or matter of language itself, is for Agamben, and, I believe, for Valente, the axis around which turns the community to come.

Notes to Chapter 3

1. The phrase refers to Luce Irigary's reading of Hegel's interpretation of the play in *Speculum of the Other Woman* (1995). For a concise summary and criticism of Hegel's reading of Antigone see Mills (1986: 131–52). George Steiner's *Antigones* (1984) remains a standard introduction to the enormous literature on, and adaptations of, Sophocles's text.
2. Valente takes from Lefebvre's Marxist theory of the reification of language discussed in *Le langage et la société* (1966). There are two editions of this work in Valente's library, one, the French edition from 1966, the other, the Spanish edition from 1967.
3. As Valente notes in his interventions to the congress '40 anni di poesia in spagna: tra realism e avanguardia,' which took place on 7–8 October 1976 in Venice: 'En regímenes fascistas, cuya naturaleza totalitaria es manifiesta, el poder opera sobre el lenguaje brutal y directamente, mediante sistemas de censura o incluso de eliminación física. En otros sistemas se actúa sobre el lenguaje por manipulación indirecta, ocupando el lenguaje — gracias, en gran parte, a los llamados *mass media* — con contenidos prefabricados, con paquetes de información (packaged information)' (II: 1219–20). We might turn here to a contemporary, neoliberal version of this institutionalized language, the 'bankspeak' described by Franco Moretti and Dominique Pestre (2015).
4. The poem recalls Unamuno's distrust of the abstract 'humanity' to which he counterposes, in *Del sentimiento trágico de la vida*, 'El hombre de carne y hueso, el que nace, sufre y muere' (1986: 20).
5. These lines are reminiscent of Blanchot's description of Lautreamont's *Chants de Maldoror*, which Valente underlines in his copy of the volume *Lautréamont et Sade* from 1967: '[...] cette coupure âpre, froide, des mots, exactement semblable à celle du rasoir dans un visage, cette décision acérée qui déjà s'affirme et, si elle ne renverse pas la langage, fait de lui une lame si tranchante que, par quelque côté qu'on la saisise, elle coupe, elle déchire' (155–56).
6. For purposes of convenience I will quote from the English version of the text (1991), which includes essays excluded from the earlier French edition.
7. Betrand Marchal (1988: 316) reads the section of Mallarmé's *Divagations* entitled 'Catholicisme' as a response to the modern death of God, in which the ultimate foundation of religiosity

— a fear of human finitude that was covered over with the figure of the Divine — is finally confronted, and absence becomes the foundation for the celebration of community.

8. In this regard, I argue against Miguel Posada's criticism, which is indicative of a tendency within Spanish letters of the time, which sees Valente's later poetry as the work of: 'un poeta hermético, intransitivo, fragmentario, que alumbraba de tan incandescente como misterioso belleza, abismado en su propio ensimismamiento, que hacía de la palabra poética un absoluto' (qtd. in Mayhew 2009: 7).
9. Christine Arkinstall draws a distinction in Valente's work, similar to the one I note here, between his description the destruction of difference in communal relation under fascism and the maintenance of difference in erotic relation: 'Esta fusión amorosa de dos cuerpos en uno es la antítesis de la asimilación del cuerpo colectivo de España a la ideología franquista. Mientras que en la primera instancia los cuerpos de los amantes, aunque unidos, siguen conservando su individualidad, en la segunda las diferencias individuales se hallan completamente borradas por la homologación forzada del pensamiento' (1993: 102).
10. For Valente, writing in the context of the mystics, it is precisely unsatisfied desire that constitutes the human, as it is what exceeds necessity. Writing on San Juan de la Cruz, Valente comments: 'El deseo sería la faz verdaderamente humana de la necesidad. No hace el hombre que desaparezca, sino que la hace sobreaparece, la hace sobrevivir a su satisfacción. Sería así el deseo la necesidad sobrevivida. En cierto modo, la reducción de la necesidad, de las necesidades — fin de toda ascética — es inversamente proporcional al crecimiento del deseo — fin de toda mística' (II: 396)
11. Valente heavily underlines this section of in the French edition of Agamben's work which is in the personal library that he donated to the University of Santiago de Compostela.

CHAPTER 4

Valente and Jabès

The 'Figural Jew' in Post-war Thought

As we have seen, from the 1960s on, Valente's commitment to profound social change is tempered by his distrust of what he sees as totalizing political and philosophical schemes that are destructive of difference. This distrust is the fruit of his having grown up in the repressive atmosphere of Francoism, but it is also due to his personal disappointment with the Spanish Communist Party, as well as his experiences in Cuba and his friendships with homosexual writers who were marginalized by Castro's regime. Valente's concern for the marginalized informs his understanding of the development of Spanish history, which is inflected by the writings of contemporaries Américo Castro and Juan Goytisolo, for whom Franco's national-catholicism is but one more episode in a long history of Castilian supremacism and its destruction of religious and cultural alterities within the Iberian peninsula.[1] It is in this context that Valente develops a sensitivity to the experiences of cultural and ethnic minorities within Spain, taking a special interest in the complex history of the Jews in Spain, as well as in contemporary Jewish writers in Europe. A political exile, having lost the right to a Spanish passport, Valente saw himself as part of the wider tradition of Republican writers, intellectuals, and leftists who fled Spain in the aftermath of the Civil War, and in this way subject, with the Jews, to the experience of enforced exile, part of a 'prolongado y tenaz proceso de aplastamiento de la diferencia en un país que había nacido y se había conformado en la diversidad' (II: 681).[2]

We can also, however, situate Valente's interest in Jewish experience and culture in the context of wider European understandings of Judaism in the nineteenth and twentieth century. The discourse of Jewish exile has, of course, a long history, stemming from Biblical texts and from the historical experiences of the Jews. In the nineteenth and twentieth centuries, however, figurations of the exiled or rootless Jew take on a specific valence in the context of developing nationalisms. Sarah Hammerschlag (2010) explores this discourse on Judaism in the context of French nineteenth- and twentieth-century culture, paying special attention to its development in the wake of the Second World War. She shows how in the nineteenth century, the figure of the Jew was taken to represent both a stubborn particularism resistant to enlightened progress, and, at the same time, a rootless cosmopolitanism, a danger to the nationalist ideals of community. The figure of the 'wandering Jew' becomes the emblem of the Jew as cursed outsider, whose suffering is a direct result of the supposed complicity of Jews in the killing of Christ. In the twentieth century, however, discourses develop that reappropriate these stereotypes in a positive manner. In the immediate post-war, Jean Paul Sartre took the supposed Jewish 'restlessness' as an authentic recognition of the groundlessness of any subject position. It is those who in 'bad faith' imagine themselves tied to a specific 'ground' or national territory that are bound to lives of unfreedom. Furthermore, Sartre, in interviews with Benny Lévy recorded in 1980, describes the importance for him of thought inflected by Jewish messianism. This tradition, exemplified in the twentieth century by thinkers such as Rosensweig, Benjamin, and Bloch, offers for Sartre a vision of futurity that does not rely on a conception of a progressive and planned realization of steps towards an ultimate goal. The title given to the interviews, *Hope Now*, reflects Sartre's adoption of elements of Jewish messianism as part of an attempt to rejuvenate left wing politics in the face of the emerging neoliberalism.

Sartre's pairing of the trope of Jewish uprootedness and the tradition of utopian Jewish messianism is mirrored in the work of the philosopher Emmanuel Levinas. Levinas, too, criticizes what he sees as totalizing philosophical systems under which all singularity would be subsumed. For Levinas, as he comments in interview with Philippe Nemo, 'Toute la marche de la philosophie occidentale aboutissant à la philosophie de Hegel, laquelle, a très juste titre, peut apparaitre comme l'aboutissement de la philosophie même' (Levinas 1982: 80). And it is precisely this tradition, of which Hegel is the ultimate representative, and which is founded on the notion of the primacy of ontological Being, that Levinas's philosophy resists.[3] On the other hand, Levinas is also careful to avoid the temptation to confine his thought to a narrow particularism. This, as Hammerschlag shows, is how Levinas understands the work of Heidegger. The German philosopher's emphasis on particularity and rootedness, the authenticity of the world of the peasant, is potentially exclusionary, a return to a philosophy without transcendence that Levinas sees as a type of 'paganism'.[4] Against Heidegger, Levinas formulates a first philosophy based on a fundamental ethical responsibility to the other, a primacy of relation that Hammerschlag sees as derived from a specifically Jewish concern with the ethical duty to the neighbour. Furthermore, it is precisely the traditional trope of Jewish rootlessness that becomes the condition for responsibility towards the other. As opposed to the autonomous subject of modern philosophy who is secure in his identity, Levinas poses the figure who is called by another, removed from his dwelling place. The Jewish Abraham who sets out to answer the call of God replaces the adventurer who is always homeward bound, the Greek Odysseus. The Levinasian subject is thus 'literally without situation, without a dwelling place, expelled from everywhere and from itself' (qtd. in Hammerschlag 2010: 143). If for the Hegel of *The Spirit of Christianity and its Fate*, the Jews were alienated from nature because of their enslavement to God, here, estrangement, the exile of the self in its responsibility to the other, becomes the basis of ethical subjectivity.

Hammerschlag places Levinas's description of the exilic self as part of what she describes as the 'postmodern trope of the Jew', a discourse and understanding of

Jewishness that develops in the work of a series of post-war French thinkers — Sartre, Levinas, Derrida, Blanchot — who rearticulate powerful and sometimes anti-Semitic discourses around Jewishness in order to thread a philosophical path between the exclusive nostalgia of nationalism and the vacuity of universalizing humanism. Responding to what they see as the 'totalizing' systems of modernity, these writers devise a model of subjectivity that is symbolized by what Hammerschlag terms the 'figural Jew', 'an archetype for a new kind of difference in particularity whose function is to suggest that there is a positive moral valence to resisting the discourse of belonging that dominates both the universalist and the particularist versions of political identity' (Hammerschlag 2010: 18). But it would be a mistake to read the work of these thinkers in terms of a depoliticized individualism that would provide ideological support to a developing neoliberalism. As we have seen in the previous chapter, a commitment to singularity does not mean a refusal of communitarian ideals. Rather, the notion of community in these thinkers' work resists the atomistic conception of the individual of liberal tradition. The commitment to singularity runs parallel to a utopian hopefulness, a belief in the possibility of a break in temporal continuity and the irruption of radically new forms of social relation and organization that could be described as secularized versions of Jewish messianism. In this chapter, I will describe the development of Valente's understanding of Jewish culture, experience, and thought from the 1960s on, tracing the ways in which he engages with the 'postmodern trope of the Jew' in the context of his estrangement from the Communist Party and the wider development of what we now term 'identity politics'. I will specifically look at Valente's relationship to a poet whose exploration of Jewish identity can be compared to the work of Levinas, Blanchot, and Derrida: Edmond Jabès.

Edmond Jabès and the Poetics of Exile

Valente's interest in Jewish culture was profound. Many of his fundamental ethical and intellectual reference points are Jewish authors — Kafka, Canetti, Benjamin, Bloch, Levinas, Jabès, Celan — whose response to the conditions and traumas of modernity retain, in the broadest sense, religious elements. He was also fascinated by the Jewish tradition in Spain, and especially the medieval Jewish esotericism of the Kabbalah, attending seminars in Geneva delivered by a noted specialist in the field, Carlo Suarès. Motifs from Jewish mysticism would become an important part of Valente's poetry and poetics from the 1960s onwards, culminating in a collection from 1980 based on letters from the Hebrew alphabet — related to the Sefirot, emanations of the divine in Kabbalistic cosmology — *Tres lecciones de tinieblas*. Although Valente drew from a range of sources in his understanding of medieval Jewish writings, his central reference is the work of Gershom Scholem, the most important twentieth-century interpreter of Jewish mysticism. Central elements of Valente's poetics are informed by Scholem's discussions of Jewish mysticism, specifically his description of the writings of sixteenth-century mystic Isaac Luria, whose cosmogony has at its heart the experience of exile.

In his *Major Trends of Jewish Mysticism* (1995), Scholem describes the doctrines of Luria, who taught among a community of exiled Sephardic Jews in Sefad, in what is today Israel. Luria's doctrines diverge from previous Kabbalistic formulations, especially in his description of the cosmological process. Scholem relates how earlier Kabbalistic descriptions of creation imagined an emanative neo-platonic process, in which God projects from within himself an external world from which he is separate. Luria explored the fundamental paradoxes inherent in this conception of divine creation. If God is in all things, how could He create a world that is separate from Himself? If God is eternal and omnipresent, how can a world come into being? Luria's solution was the doctrine of the *Tsimtsum*, according to which 'God was compelled to make room for the world by, as it were, abandoning a region within Himself, a kind of mystical primordial space from which He withdrew in order to return to it in the act of creation and revelation' (Scholem 1995: 261). The first act of creation is the creation of an empty space — the divine retreats in order to allow for the creation of a universe that is not himself. Scholem interprets the doctrine of the *Tsimtsum* with regard to the historical experience of Jewish exile. For the German scholar, the effective retreat or self-banishment of God in the *Tsimtsum* would be a type of Divine exile, a mystical version of the historical exile of the Jews from Spain, in effect 'the deepest symbol of exile that could be thought of' (Scholem 1995: 261).[5]

Valente draws on Scholem's interpretation of Luria's thought in the construction of his own poetics, which describe a similar intertwining of creation and nothingness. In one of the 'Cinco fragmentos' dedicated to his friend, the Catalan artist Antoni Tapiès, included in the collection *Material memoria*, from 1979, Valente describes the artistic process in terms that are recognizably 'Lurianic':

> Quizá el supremo, el solo ejercicio radical del arte sea un ejercicio de retracción. Crear no es un acto de poder (poder y creación se niegan); es un acto de aceptación o reconocimiento. Crear lleva el signo de la feminidad. No es un acto de penetración en la materia, sino pasión de ser penetrado por ella. Crear es generar un estado de disponibilidad, en el que la primera cosa creada es el vacío, un espacio vacío. Pues lo único que el artista acaso crea es el espacio de la creación. Y en el espacio de la creación no hay nada (para que algo pueda ser en él recreado). La creación de la nada es el principio absoluto de toda creación:
>
> > Dijo Dios –Brote la nada.
> > Y alzó la mano derecha
> > hasta ocultar la mirada.
> > Y quedó la Nada hecha. (I: 387)

For Valente, poetic creation requires a primary self-negation, analogous to Scholem's description of the withdrawal of the divine in Lurianic cosmogony, in which the first thing to be created is an inner space from which the poem would emerge. If the poetry of Valente's generation is founded on an absence, an absence of the dead, the victims of violence, and the poets and writers forced to leave Spain, poetry as a process of self-exile is the singing of this loss:

> Perdimos las palabras
> a la orilla del mar,
> perdimos las palabras
> de empezar a cantar.
> Volvimos tierra adentro,
> perdimos la verdad,
> perdimos las palabras
> y el cantor y el cantar. (I: 237–38)[6]

For Valente, then, as he writes in an essay dedicated to one of the major post-war exiles, Luis Cernuda, and which is titled 'Poesía y exilio', the historical experience of exile in the post-war inflected his, and his contemporaries', understanding of poetic creation: 'El exilio del treinta y nueve nos hizo reflexionar sobre el exilio mismo como forma de la historia *y de la creación*' (II: 682, italics mine). Here, however, Valente pays more attention to the ways in which exile is bound up with the desire for redemption. As Valente notes, the messianism of Sabbatai Zevi develops within the world of Sephardi Jews of Spanish heritage, among whom 'rebrota con particular intensidad [...] la idea de redención, y ésta tiene su correspondencia en la visión mesiánica del fin de los tiempos' (II: 684). Valente sees in the exile's nostalgia for a lost home the possibility for thought of a utopian future. It is in this sense that he understands Cernuda's assumption of exile as 'una misión o un destino', quoting Cernuda's 'Peregrino':

> ¿Volver? Vuelva el que tenga,
> Tras largos años, tras un largo viaje,
> Cansancio del camino y la codicia
> De su tierra, su casa, sus amigos,
> Del amor que al regreso fiel le espere.
>
> Mas, ¿tú? ¿Volver? Regresar no piensas,
> Sino seguir libre adelante,
> Disponible por siempre, mozo o viejo,
> Sin hijo que te busque, como a Ulises,
> Sin Ítaca que aguarde y sin Penélope.
>
> Sigue, sigue adelante y no regreses,
> Fiel hasta el fin del camino y tu vida,
> No eches de menos un destino más fácil,
> Tus pies sobre la tierra antes no hollada,
> Tus ojos frente a lo antes nunca visto. (Qtd. in I: 688)

The poet poses as a new Odysseus, but now bound to travel without hope of return. Here, nostalgia looks to the future, towards the possibility of a world redeemed, not as it was, but as it might have been.

If Jewish thinkers are central to Valente's understanding of the links between exile and the creative process, so too are Jewish poets, none more so than the French language poet who would have a profound influence on Valente's thought and work, Edmond Jabès, with whom he developed a close personal relationship from the 1970s onwards.[7] Jabès, along with many Jewish and other non-Muslim citizens, was expelled from Egypt in 1957, victim of the rise of Egyptian nationalism that climaxed in the years of the Suez Crisis. Jabès remarks how political circumstances forced him to take on one of the traditional elements of Jewish experience, exile:

> Cette rupture m'a, en effet, cruellement marqué. Je crois l'avoir donnée à voir, presque physiquement, dans chacun de mes livres. J'ai quitté l'Égypte parce que j'étais juif. J'ai donc été amené, malgré moi, à vivre une certaine condition juive, celle de l'exilé (1980: 53–54).[8]

The experience of exile is reflected in a poetry that is dedicated to the marginalized and displaced, to Sarah and Yukel, the survivors of the Shoah who are the protagonists of the multivolume *Livre des questions*. As Valente notes in a newspaper article written in 1990, 'La imagen que más nos aproxima a la poesía de Edmond Jabès sea la del exilio o la extranjería, la figura del extranjero en la que se perfila el rostro del otro, apenas visible, a punto de desaparecer en la soledad natural del camino' (II: 637). Valente, as a political exile himself, and as a poet with a firm commitment to marginalized others, clearly sympathizes with Jabès's personal experiences and his explorations of the themes of solitude and displacement. In fact, on reading the French language poet's work for the first time in the 1970s, Valente claims that he came to a renewed understanding of his own life and poetry: 'Hace el encuentro con Jabès que yo me reconozca a mi mismo, me dota de una identidad, de una estirpe, de una ascendencia' (II: 663)

When Valente comes across Jabès's poetry, then, he recognises in the Jewish writer the articulation of concerns that are central to his own project. Valente shares with Jabès a desire to explore limit experiences, an ascetic tendency that is symbolized for both poets by the emptiness and solitude of the desert. Jabès claims in his dialogues with Marcel Cohen that his experiences as a young man in the desert outside Cairo were fundamental to his later understanding of poetic creation. For him, the absolute solitude and silence of the desert were necessary conditions for the discovery of his poetic voice. As Gabriel Bounoure notes, as opposed to the Heideggerian rootedness of the peasant dwelling, Jabès makes the desert the centre of his imaginative universe. If the world of the peasant implies a rootedness in the land, the desert excludes '[...] la demeure, [et] ouvre l'infini de l'ailleurs à l'errance fondamentale de l'homme' (Bounoure 1984: 32). For Valente, too, the desert is a fundamental landscape, a topos that recurs as throughout his work. On reading Jabès's descriptions of the desert, Valente could not fail to recall the first lines of his first collection, in which he describes the sense of spiritual and existential solitude the desert evokes:

> Cruzo un desierto y su secreta
> desolación sin nombre.
> El corazón
> tiene la sequedad de la piedra
> y los estallidos nocturnos
> de su materia o de su nada.
>
> Hay una luz remota, sin embargo,
> y sé que no estoy solo;
> aunque después de tanto y tanto no haya
> ni un solo pensamiento

> capaz contra la muerte,
> no estoy solo.
>
> Toco esta mano al fin que comparte mi vida
> y en ella me confirmo
> y tiento cuanto amo,
> lo levanto hacia el cielo
> y aunque sea ceniza lo proclamo: ceniza.
>
> Aunque sea ceniza cuanto tengo hasta ahora,
> cuanto se me ha tendido a modo de esperanza. (I: 69)

As Vicente Luis Mora (2010) notes, the desert in Valente's work represents fundamental alienation: 'Desgarramiento, fractura. He ahí la clave. Desajuste *orgánico* entre el interior del hombre y el mundo, sensación de herida, soledad interior, apartamiento' (426) But while Biblical tradition had always depicted the desert as the space of Jewish exile, and if in Valente and in Jabès's work it relates to a fundamental sense of alienation, it is also the place of revelation, where the Word of God becomes manifest. Thus, in an essay from 1987,[9] Valente discusses Jabès's experiences of solitude in the desert outside of Cairo in terms that describe his own creative process:

> Estado, pues, de disponibilidad y de receptividad máximas caracterizado por la tensión entre ausencia e inminencia que tan profundamente marca la entera tradición judía. Ausencia e inminencia del Nombre en el no lugar donde se inicia la revelación, en el desierto, en el exilio — o marcha infinitamente prolongada en el interior de esa ausencia — único espacio real en que esa palabra encuentra manifestación. (II: 432)

Exile in this sense is both an historical experience but also an exercise of self-negation through which fallen human language can approach the divine language from which it derives. Only with words that are divorced from subjective intention, that 'se pronuncian a si mismas' (II: 433) can we approach the unspeakable divine Name from which, according to the tradition of the Kabbalah, our human languages have fallen.

Cantigas de alén and the Impossibility of Return

The valorization of exile and solitude that Valente and Jabès share can be related to what Hammerschlag calls the 'postmodern trope of the Jew' (2010: 10) that develops in the work of a series of thinkers working in the continental tradition — Scholem, Levinas, Blanchot, Derrida — from the 1960s on. As opposed to the what they see as the closure of identity and historical temporality in the modern philosophical tradition that stems from Kant and Hegel, these authors emphasize the contingency of history and the instability of identity, the gaps that emerge in our relation to ourselves and to others. Questions of language, often influenced by Jewish conceptions of revelation and interpretation, are at the heart of their writings. Scholem's discussions of the divine Name, Levinas's conception of the 'saying' as opposed to the 'said', Blanchot's theorization of the Book, and Derrida's discussions of *différance* are theoretical constructions that have much to do with Jewish hermeneutic tradition; as in Scholem's description of Jewish esotericism, in each case they posit a paradoxical experience of transcendence or alterity immanent to a language infinitely open to interpretation. Valente, whose intellectual life was focused as much on French as on Spanish writers, and who had always had a sympathy for minorities as well as an understanding of the historical experience of exile, was well placed to take up this style of discourse, and the themes of essential exile and the desire to mark the non-closure of the text became central to his thought and poetry. But Valente's reception of this tradition is not seamless, as it provokes tension with another element of his thought, his nostalgic poetics of origins, his desire for a return to an originary *logos*. The tension is especially relevant to Valente's reading of his own existential and linguistic origins, the collection of poems written in his native Galician language, *Cántigas de alén*.[10]

The *Cántigas de alén*, which were first published in 1981, and in expanded editions in 1987, 1989, and 1996, are marked by the theme of departure and return. In them, the origin is always 'desplazada' and leave-taking becomes a form of homecoming: 'Alongarme somente foi o xeito | de ficar para sempre' (II: 509), 'Terra allea e máis nosa, alén, no lonxe' (II: 511). The question of origins is directly addressed in the short autobiographical prose piece that Valente dedicates to the Galician poet, Luis Pimentel:

> Eu nacín en ningures. Ou non nacín. Ou nacín — de ter nacido, se ben cadra — nun lugar que xa non existe. Por iso lle chamo Augasquentes. Non lle atopo outro nome na miña memoria, por mais que nela furgo. E por iso ninguén podería probar que non se chama asín. Ou pode que Augasquentes fose o nome da face non visible dun lugar que cecáis se designase no mapa doutro xeito. Entón, vai saber ti ónde eu nacín, de ter nacido, digo. (I: 529)

The poetic voice, a no-one who speaks, was born no-where, in a place that no longer exists. The absence of both geographical place and enunciative reference allows, however, for the poetic freedom to name this *no-lugar*: 'Augasquentes' as opposed to the official name, 'Ourense'. The piece reveals the instability of language, the fact that our words do not derive from the things they designate. It might seem that 'Augasquentes' is a more 'authentic' name, relating to the natural world and escaping state-imposed Castilian, but the capacity of a place to have two names reflects the ultimate freedom of language with regard to the things that it designates. In this regard, Valente follows closely the example of Jabès, for whom the book is the space that denies the nativist rhetoric of place. As Jabès writes in his collection from 1978, *Le soupçon le désert*: 'Le livre est, peut-être, la perte de tout lieu; le non-lieu du lieu perdu. Un non-lieu comme une non-origine, un non-présent, un non-savoir, une vide, une blanc' (1978: 171). The book is the site that demonstrates the irrecuperable gap between meaning and being that constitutes human freedom. In it, an 'I' can speak that is free from the elements — nation, race, place — that would otherwise seem necessary to sustain an identity.

It is significant, too, that Valente writes in an idiomatic Galician that the Galician scholar María do Cebreiro Rábade Villar describes as 'muy complejo y alejado de toda uniformidad, en donde resuenan neologismos, arcaísmos, localismos, y términos remisibles a estratos de la tradición literaria tan distantes como la lírica medieval gallego-portuguesa, el neo-popularismo, el romanticismo, el simbolismo o la vanguardia (2010: 476).[11] Valente's complex linguistic choices provoke reflection on what it means to 'have' a language, and, moreover, to have a language that resists linguistic standardization. If through his use of *localismos* and *vulgarismos* Valente seems to posit a Galician mother tongue, a language of the hearth, home, and community that is authentically 'his', the complex allusions to the literary history of the language reveal the way in which our words are always mediated, never fully 'ours'. A short prose text, written in 1997, 'Figura de home en dous espellos', explores this theme. The piece describes the difficulty of autobiography, a genre which for Valente cannot be divorced from fiction:

> Da propia vida [...], só se pode falar *ex persona*, quero decir, desde ou a través da máscara ou persoa, da máscara do actor, que é o que quere decir persoa. [...] Pero nin de tal xeito ey falaría de min mesmo, se ese presunto min e o eu falante fosen una cousa só. Entón, ¿quen é ese *eu* lonxano de *min* que me mira disposto, sexa con frialdade ou con recóndita ledicia, a disecarme? [...] Óllame a min que, en definitiva, non teño existir e non son máis que o seu reflexo nun espello. ¿Cál? Non ten o escritor máis espello que a linguaxe. É ésta o espacio reflectante onde o sí mesmo se ve como un outro. (II: 1613)

Language is the mirror that reveals an essential gap between the 'I' (eu) that speaks and the subject (min) that it speaks for; language, which precedes and exceeds the subject, is never the property of a self. Valente, who could be said to have two mother tongues, Castilian and Galician, a *figura entre dous espellos,* possesses neither of them.

We might pause here and consider this statement in the context of European conceptions of our relation to what we often term our 'native' language. As Yasemin Yildiz (2012: 7–10) points out, at the end of the eighteenth century, languages, which had previously been considered in themselves insignificant with regard to a semantic content, came to be seen as inflecting content, limiting the efficacy of translation, or the possibility of true creativity in a language that is not one's own. The mother tongue becomes the repository of national spirit, and fluency in a language is conflated with genealogical belonging conceived in terms of a unique biological origin that situates the individual automatically in a kinship network and, by extension, in the nation. To have a language is to bear a property that defines one's identity as a member of a community, demarcating the boundaries between one community and another.

Thus, notions of the purity of the mother tongue are bound up with the drive for communitarian homogeneity. The violence involved in imposing standardized national languages is well known, and it is worth recalling that the first grammar of a modern European language, the Castilian, was designed both so that accounts of the royal achievements would not be forgotten, but also so that the new subjects of the Catholic Kings would be able to understand the laws to which they were now subject.[12] In modernity, however, language becomes part of a generalized biopolitics, the genealogical desire to trace the origins of a pure language, which runs alongside a desire to protect languages from outside contagion (we might recall here the efforts of the *Académie française* to resist Americanization) are analogous to the efforts of the nation state to define its communitarian origins and exclude those who are seen as threatening the health of the communitarian body. In Freudian terms, and in light of Valente's discussion of his fundamental non-possession of his languages, linguistic purity is the fetishistic compensation for a gap or absence implied in our linguistic self-constitution; it is the attempt to preserve the wholeness of the mother, or the mother tongue, in order to disavow castration and lack. Thus, to say, as Valente does, that he speaks but does not have a language is to question one of the most fundamental constructs of modern nationalist identity.

In his *Le monolinguisme de l'autre*, Jacques Derrida explores this paradoxical simultaneity of speaking and not having a language in ways that are pertinent to Valente's description of his relation to Galician. In this text Derrida makes a series of seemingly contradictory claims: I have only one language, it is not mine; it is possible to be monolingual and speak a language that is not your own; we only ever speak one language / we never speak one language. For Derrida, these paradoxical claims reveal a basic aspect of language: that every linguistic utterance carries with it a presupposition, which is nothing more than the existence of language itself, and that it is impossible for us to speak of this presupposition. This metalanguage is 'une langue [qui] est promise, qui à la fois précède toute langue, appelle toute parole et appartient déjà à chaque langue comme à toute parole' (1996: 126–27). Similar to the imagined community, the divine Name, or the *antepalabra*, the promised language does not exist and yet remains the ever-absent ground towards which our soteriological impulses tend. As much as we want to find a fundamental ground for words, the attempt to do so can only give rise to what Derrida terms 'la rage appropriatrice, à de la jalousie sans appropriation' (1996: 46) which cannot accept 'cette langue qui n'arrive pas à demeure' (1996: 129).

Derrida's discussion of the essential alterity of language allows us to understand the tension in Valente's writing of his linguistic and existential home. His writing in a non-standard Galician is an attempt to enact a 'mother tongue', a language of the home and of the fireside, which would escape the necessarily homogenizing structures of state language normalization, even if in this case it would be a matter of a minority language and a regional government. This is a jealous reappropriation of language, an attempt to return to a language that would resist exchange, an effaced coin that becomes the founder of value, a golden sun: 'o sol, será como unha velha | moeda esverdeada do ferruxe' (I: 517). As Julián Jiménez Heffernan notes, Valente's poetry aims to be original, pure donation, but cannot escape the essential repeatability of language. In the Bloomian terms that Jiménez Heffernan employs, Valente's melancholy derives from his inability to 'poner un huevo lírico y aniquilar la descendencia, acuñar una moneda y borrar su efigie, redactar un poema y cancelar su ascendencia y transmisión' (2004b: 252). His agony is a result of the impossibility of creating a language that would break absolutely with the conventions of poetic tradition and social interaction, the recognition '[...] en sus monedas, [de] trozos de habladuría heredada, fragmentos de jerga' (Jiménez Heffernan 2004b: 252). There is no original language which would be ours, that would completely express an imagined inner self. Our desire, however, is to reconstitute a 'first language' not subject to the gaps, absences, and ambiguities that historical languages necessarily imply. This is the desire for the Word that Valente expresses throughout his career, and which in the second poem of the collection is figured, as in Jabès work, as a wound of language:

> Anceio
>
> O verbo crea o movimento
> da luz no fondo
> das marguradas augas.
>
> Mañan,
> non pouses inda
> os teus paxaros louros
> no meu peito ferido. (I: 507)

The desire here is to escape a fallen language and the temporality that it implies. But this is impossible. The poems of *Cántigas de alén* are a lament for the impossibility of return and a recognition that the words we speak are never ours, that language is, in the words of Derrida, 'la langue est à l'autre, venue de l'autre, *la* venue de l'autre' (1996: 127). It is in this context of a French post-war literary and philosophical discourse of rootlessness that we can understand the refusal of return of the final and definitive poem of *Cántigas de alén,* the 'Cántiga do eterno irretorno':

> QUERO ficar asín, solo, no lonxe,
> sen ninguén, sen naide,
> paxaro que no ar infindo voa,
> no baleiro do ar
> cara ó hourizonte onde xamais se chega,
> e nunca xa poder — ficar asín —
> voltar á orixe para sempre borrada. (I: 537)

As in Cernuda's poem, the impossibility of return allows for a vision of a utopian future, the adverbs *xamais, nunca,* and *sempre* marking, if only negatively, the strange persistence in language of that which has never been.

Silence and the Question

The impossibility of return is analogous, in Valente's work, to a critical resistance to dogma. In Valente's poetics of origin, the positing of a founding *antepalabra* does not limit linguistic freedom and autonomy. Rather, the Word before the word refers to the potentiality of language, what Valente terms the 'infinita disponibilidad' of language that poetry explores. In an essay dedicated to Jabès published in 1991, 'La memoria del fuego', Valente refers to the eighteenth century Hassidic Rabbi Nahman of Braslaw, who famously burnt one of his holy texts in order to bring it to its ultimate and 'más intensa forma de existencia' (II: 433). For Valente, the story is strikingly indicative of a tradition in which the authority of the text does not imply a closure of meaning, a 'discurso impositivo o totalitario' (II: 433). Rather, the burnt book alludes to the Jewish tradition of Biblical commentary that allows, precisely because of its positing of a Divine language, tremendous creative freedom.

Gershom Scholem, who, as already mentioned, is the major interpreter of Kabbalah in the twentieth century, explored this interpretative tradition in a text that would have a major influence on both Valente and Jabès, *On the Kabbalah and its Symbolism*.[13] Here, Scholem describes the interpretative freedom of the esoteric reading of scripture:

> What happens when a mystic encounters the holy scriptures of his tradition is briefly this: the sacred text is smelted down and a new dimension is discovered in it.[...] The mystic transforms the holy text, the crux of this metamorphosis being that the hard, clear, unmistakable word of revelation is filled with *infinite* meaning.[...] The word of God must be infinite, or, to put it in another way, the absolute word is as such meaningless, but it is *pregnant* with meaning. Under human eyes it enters into significant finite embodiments which mark enumerable layers of meaning. (1969: 12)

This passage reveals a strange paradox of the Kabbalistic approach to sacred writings. The printed words of the text are veils, indirectly referring to the divine language that inhabits the white space surrounding words and that can only be approached through an infinite process of interpretation.[14] Because the divine language is posited as absolutely incomprehensible to human reason, the mystic can give free rein to his interpretation of the revealed words of the Torah. Paradoxically, and as Scholem notes: 'Precisely because they preserve these foundations of the traditional authority for all time, [the mystics] are able to treat Scripture with [an] almost unlimited freedom that never ceases to amaze' (1969: 13).

Jabès, as Rosmarie Waldrop notes, was an assiduous reader of Scholem's texts, and it could be argued that he accentuates the nihilistic elements in the German scholar's work, becoming what could be termed a Kabbalist without God.[15] For the Kabbalists, the original Torah is unavailable to us; the words we read in the sacred texts are already mediations and need human commentary to move towards the original but illegible divine writing that inhabits the spaces of the Book. This scheme retains a sense of divine authority, but it also grants great power to the human interpreters of the revealed word — to come into existence the Book requires interpretation. If God, for Jabès, is simply a 'métaphore du vide', with Judaism a concomitant 'tourment de Dieu, du vide' (qtd. in Waldrop 2002: 87), commentary is necessarily infinite, fragmented by the gaps and white spaces which surround each question of his texts. The process of commentary that is enacted in *Le livre des questions* is, then, ungrounded by divine authority. Like Kafka's parabolic texts, they retain the rumour of things sacred, the form of Talmudic commentary, but without the transcendent reference of this latter.

In an essay written in 1989, to mark the end of the decade and the fall of the Berlin Wall, Valente refers to Scholem's discussion of the Torah: 'reasumimos una muy remota tradición, según la cual la Tora está escrita en los espacios blancos que separan una letra de otra. Escritura invisible o intersticial. Lo blanco. Cerámica con figuras sobre fondo blanco' (II: 1459). Valente links the paradox of Biblical revelation and concealment to a poem that describes the contrast of coloured figures on a white vase, his 'Cerámica con figuras sobre fondo blanco', from *Interior con figuras*:

> Cómo no hallar
> Alrededor de la figura sola
> lo blanco.
>
> Dragón, rama de almendro, fénix.
>
> Cómo no hallar
> alrededor del loto
> lo blanco.
>
> Del murciélago al pez o a la rama o al hombre,
> el vacío, lo blanco.
>
> Cómo no hallar
> alrededor de la palabra única
> lo blanco.
>
> Fénix, rama, raíz, dragón, figura.
>
> El fondo es blanco. (I: 341)

The poem is indicative of Valente's obsession with the white spaces around the text, the blank canvas on which the painted figure appears, or the silence before the word. The white space stands for the nothingness, the void left after the Lurianic withdrawal of God, which allows for the emergence of language and history. The movement of figures in the poem — 'Del murciélago al pez o a la rama o al hombre' — do not imply a hierarchical structure in which the movement of signifiers would come to rest in an ultimate signified. Rather, the chain continues — 'Fénix, rama, raíz, dragón, figura'. The white space that surrounds the figures, the 'fondo,' is not a metaphysical ground that guarantees the ultimate significance of words, but rather the empty space in which they propagate in infinite dispersion.[16]

This claim for the constitutive incompleteness of the poem, the presence within it of absence, is a central aspect of Valente's exploration of the relationship between music and silence, form and material, in poems from the mid-seventies onwards. For Valente, silence is the 'materia natural' (I: 388) of both music and the poem; a 'poema no existe si no se oye, antes que su palabra, su silencio' (I: 388). It is important here to consider the Aristotelian acceptation of the word 'materia' in order to understand Valente's enigmatic statements. Matter, for Aristotle, is pure potentiality. It is unknowable, destroyed in its actualization in form. In Valente's meditation on the relationship between silence and music from this period, the effacement of the material in the passage from potential to act is resisted. Valente's fragmentary aesthetic, the use of typography to emphasize the spaces between his words and lines, reflects a desire to retain the material as such within the poetic form. We might draw a comparison here with the innovations of the avant-garde music of Valente's time, the explorations of John Cage's experimental work in which 'nothing is accomplished' (1961: xii).[17] A poem from *Interior con figuras*, 'Arietta, opus III', explores these concerns in its description of a musical piece:

1
Forma
(en lo infinitamente abierto hacia lo informe).

2
El silencio se quiebra
en trino por tres veces
y la materia de la música
ya no es sonido sino transparencia.

3
El tema se disuelve en la cadena
interminable de las formas.
El movimiento iguala a la quietud
y la piedra solar
a lo perpetuamente alzado y destruido.

4
Delgado,
tenue,
agudo,
el timbre hila
la melodía al corazón del aire.
Entra en la sombra,
busca a tientas
lo inferior disparado hacia lo alto.
¿Dónde
está tu voz que ya no encuentra
respuesta?
Ahora
se funda en la materia
feraz del mundo, en las cosas que son,
que han sido o que serán,
el solitario.
Cantible,
hacia adentro.

5
Para que el hilo tan infinitamente se prolongue,
para que sólo quede por decir
la total extensión de lo indecible,
para que la libertad se manifieste,
para que andar al otro lado de la muerte sea
semplice e cantible
y aquí y allí la música nos lleve
al centro, al fuego, al aire,
al agua antenatal que envuelve
la forma indescifrable
de lo que nunca nadie aún ha hecho
nacer en la mañana del mundo. (I: 363–64)

It is important to note that the Beethoven sonata that Valente here describes, the Piano Sonata No. 32 in C Minor, Op 111, is among the later works of the composer, which are defined by elements of dissonance and incompleteness. Theodor Adorno, in his writings on Beethoven, which would be ventriloquized in Thomas Mann's Doctor Faustus, describes the *Arietta* as part of this 'late style', in which the 'the hand of the master sets free the masses of material that he used to form; its tears and fissures, witnesses to the finite powerlessness of the I confronted with Being, are its final work' (Adorno 2002: 566). The *Arietta* refuses the ideal of the completed work. Its imperfections allow for the presence within the musical piece of the material, the 'forma indescifrable | de lo que nunca nadie aún ha hecho | nacer en la mañana del mundo'.

It is in this context, too, that we can understand the poem that follows 'Arietta, opus III' in the collection, which is titled simply 'Materia':

>   Convertir la palabra en la materia
>   donde lo que quisiéramos decir no pueda
>   penetrar más allá
>   de lo que la materia nos diría
>   si a ella, como a un vientre,
>   delicado aplicásemos,
>   desnudo, blanco vientre,
>   delicado el oído para oír
>   el mar, el indistinto
>   rumor del mar, que más allá de ti,
>   el no nombrado amor, te engendra siempre. (I: 364–65)

The poem refers meta-poetically to its own creation. It is only through a passive experience of listening, as if to a 'vientre', that the poem can arise. The material, an unnamed love, is heard as an indistinct rumour of the sea, a white noise that exceeds the intentionality of the human subject, and which remains within a poem that combines the delicacy of form with the nudity of the matter, the rhythm and assonance of 'delicado aplicásemos | desnudo, blanco vientre, | delicado el oído para oír' recalling waves breaking on a seashore.

The collection which followed *Interior con figuras*, *Material memoria*, which was published in 1979, furthers the exploration of the presence of the 'material' in the poem. It is marked by a proliferation of figures of liminality: 'aurora', 'amanecer', 'ocaso', 'funámbulo', and 'umbral'. All of these figures refer to the liminal status of a poetry that, in Scholem's terms, is 'pregnant with meaning', that holds within itself elements that cannot be reduced to the subjective intentions of an author. The figuration of dawn is paired in the collection with another liminal figure central to Valente's work, the angel:[18]

>   Al amanecer,
>   cuando la dureza del día es aún extraña,
>   vuelvo a encontrarte en la precisa línea
>   desde la que la noche retrocede.
>
>   Reconozco tu oscura transparencia,
>   tu rostro no visible,
>   el ala o filo con el que he luchado.

> Estás o vuelves o reapareces
> en el extremo límite, señor
> de lo indistinto.
> No separes
> la sombra de la luz que ella ha engendrado. (I: 379)

The mystical language of paradox — 'oscura transparencia', 'rostro no visible' — is employed here in an allegory of the creative process — the confrontation with an angel at the limit between light and darkness describing the poet's struggle to retain within words an immediacy that words efface, what in the first poem of the collection is described as the 'don de lo imposible' (I: 377). The desire of the poet, like the angel, is to combine form and material, the 'luz' and the 'sombra' from which is has arisen. This nostalgia for the *materia* is sometimes expressed in Valente's work by the symbol of the fish, as in the following fragment from the same collection:

> COMO el oscuro pez del fondo
> gira en el limo húmedo y sin forma,
> desciende tú
> a lo que nunca duerme sumergido
> como el oscuro pez del fondo.
> Ven
> al hálito. (I: 384)

For Valente, the fish is a symbol of primordial beginnings, related to an originary Word or music. To descend towards this animal is to listen to the material of poetic language, to return to its silence, its breath or 'hálito'.[19]

Tres lecciones de tinieblas, which was published in 1980, furthers this meditation on silence and creation, in this case elaborated in the context of a Jewish theology of the letter.[20] In the 'autolectura' attached to *Tres lecciones de tinieblas*, Valente describes their relation to the sacral music of the baroque composer François Couperin, but also the music of other composers in the same tradition — Victoria, Tallis, Charpentier, Delalande. For Valente 'del lento depósito de esas composiciones fue desprendiéndose o formándose un solo principio iniciador o movimiento que subyace en toda progresión armónica y que ha sido llamado justamente *Ursatz*' (I: 403).[21] The *ursatz* is pure potential, a 'potencial expresivo universal' and musical variation, from this perspective, a 'meditación creadora sobre el movimiento primario, sobre una forma universal' (I: 403). The fourteen Hebrew letters that head each of the fourteen texts that make up the collection would correspond to this *ursatz*. They are what Valente terms the 'eje vertical' (I: 403) that constitutes the axis of potentiality, the 'infinita posibilidad de la materia del mundo' (I: 403). The 'eje horizontal' (I: 403), that of the texts themselves, would be the 'eje de la historia, el eje de la destrucción, de la soledad, del exilio, del dolor, del llanto del profeta' (I: 403). The proximity of these two levels reflects their constant intertwining, the 'perpetua resurrección' (I: 404) of potentiality in actuality in a collection that Valente describes as a 'canto de la germinación y del origen o de la vida como inminencia y proximidad' (I: 404).

Tres lecciones de tinieblas begins with the *Alef*, the letter that in the Kabbalistic book of creation, the *Sefer Yetsirah*, is unvoiced. This is the letter from which the other letters arise, and which accompanies them as their negative foundation, the silence that inhabits music or the white space that surrounds the word. The first fragment of the first *lección* describes this originary position: 'En el punto donde comienza la respiración, donde el alef oblicuo entra como intacto relámpago en la sangre: Adán, Adán: oh Jerusalem' (I: 397). The fragment 'He', which I reproduce here, returns to the motif of an originary breath and the symbolism of the fish:

> El latido de un pez en el limo antecede a la vida: branquia, pulmón, burbuja, brote: lo que palpita tiene un ritmo y por el ritmo adviene: recibe y da la vida: el hálito: en lo oscuro el centro es húmedo y de fuego: madre, matriz, materia, stabat matrix: el latido de un pez antecede a la vida: yo descendí contigo a la semilla del respirar: al fondo: bebí tu aliento con mi boca: no bebí lo visible.
> (I: 398)

The poem describes a primordial respiration of what for him is the animal symbolic of origins. The rhythm of the breath is mirrored in the iambic stress patterns that repeat throughout the piece: 'branquia, pulmón, burbuja, brote'. The animating breath thus unfolds with language, on what Valente terms the 'eje de la historia', the words that make up each fragment. This intertwining of rhythm and meaning is emblematic of poetry, which can be defined by the necessary relation of sound and sense.[22] It is in this context that we might speak of an enigmatic, non-discursive element intrinsic to the poem, a claim that is confirmed by the connecting of each sentence in the text with a colon. If the colon is the sign that marks both separation and linkage, the poem describes a relation to an origin that is both separate from us but at the same time fundamentally our own. Analogous to the Divine language that fills the white spaces of the Torah, the breath that inhabits the poem is both absolutely present and absolutely other.[23]

The resistance to closure implied by Scholem's description of Jewish traditions of commentary and enacted in Valente's meditation on the relationship between music and silence in his poetry has a profound philosophical and political significance. It refers to an essential refusal of dogma that, in an essay he dedicates to Jabès in 1993, Valente ascribes to the heretical early modern figures of Spinoza and Uriel da Costa, whose non-orthodox, or paradoxically atheistic, Judaism, placed them on the margins of both Christian and Jewish communities. For Valente, it is the commitment to an infinite questioning, a specifically Jewish form of 'incertidumbre', that defines Jabès's work, and which relates it to the utopian *preaparecer* that Bloch described. It is in this context that we can understand Valente's scepticism regarding the so-called 'end of history' pronounced by the American sociologist Francis Fukuyama on the fall of the Berlin Wall. Rather than the end of history, for Valente the fall of the Wall signifies the end of a specific type of totalitarian discourse, that of the Soviet Union. Paradoxically, the fall of the Wall means that 'el comunismo [...] se acercaría no a su conclusión, sino a su nacimiento' (I: 1458). The question, like the 'unworked' work, would, in this regard, refer to an openness to that which has yet to arrive, relating to the unforeseen more than to the given. As Marc Alain

Ouaknin notes, it is the paradox of a God who is both present and absent in the words of the Torah that leads Rabbi Nahman to see his role as that of the 'holder of the question' (1986: 276). Similarly, Valente's later poems, which, in their desire to retain within their form a constitutive material — silence, the blank page — refuse to conform to a 'normal' realism that accepts the given.[24] Rather than a nostalgia for lost origins that would translate to a political quietism, the poems express a fundamental critical resistance in which 'lo inexistente o lo imposible preaparece, pero aún no pueden ser vividos' (I: 672).

Notes to Chapter 4

1. Michael Ugarte describes Goytisolo as Castro's 'unruly disciple' (1979: 353) in an article that explores the paradoxes of their shared project of undermining the myths of Castilian imperialism.
2. Valente's short prose text, 'El uniforme del general', which tells the story of the execution of an anarchist for profaning the uniform of a general, was deemed sufficiently seditious to warrant Valente's conviction, in 1971 and in-absentia, for an *ofensa a clase determinada del ejército*. Valente, living in Geneva at the time, was unable to renew his passport and his travel was limited until the passing of the dictatorship in 1975. Details of the affair can be found in *Valente Vital: Ginebra, Saboya, París* (Lopo, Blanco de Saracho, and Rodríguez Fer 2014: 236–55).
3. For a thorough discussion of the ways in which Levinas's philosophy can be read as a resistance to Hegel see Ari Simhon (2006).
4. For a discussion of Levinas's understanding of both Hitlerism and Heidegger's philosophy as contemporary types of paganism, see Samuel Moyn (2005: 190–94).
5. Scholem's projection of Lurianic cosmology onto history, as well as many other aspects of his understanding of Kabbalah, have been criticized by his successor, Moshe Idel (1988: 264–67).
6. Commenting on this poem in the context of a discussion of the post-war exile of Spanish intellectuals, Valente writes: 'Nacimos, pues, de la palabra perdida y de su vacío en nosotros. Yo mismo, en un libro temprano, sentí la intensidad de esa pérdida, y ese sentimiento se hizo canción' (II: 687).
7. For a detailed description of the relationship and correspondence between Valente and Jabès, see María Lopo, 'José Ángel Valente y Edmond Jabès. Reconocerse en la palabra' in *Referentes europeos en la obra de Valente* (Fernández Rodríguez 2007), and also the section she dedicates to Jabès, 'Edmond Jabès y la resonancia' in *Valente Vital: Ginebra, Saboya, París* (Lopo, Blanco de Saracho, and Rodríguez Fer 2014: 463–71).
8. For a history of the Jews in Egypt in the first part of the twentieth century, a history in which Jabès's family played a significant part, see Krämer (1989).
9. This essay is a version of a talk Valente gave at the colloquy *Ecrire le livre (autour d'Edmond Jabès)* held at the *Centre Culturel International de Cerisy-la-Salle* from 13–20 August 1987, the proceedings of which were published as *Ecrire le livre (autour d'Edmond Jabès)* (Stamelman and Caws 1989).
10. Valente's only collection of poetry written in Galician has been the object of insightful commentary from María do Cebreiro Rábade Villar (2010) and Margarita García Candeira (2013). Claudio Rodríguez Fer (1992, 1995, and 2010) has written the most in-depth commentary on Valente's relationship to Galician language and letters. Rodríguez Fer also carried out two 'Entrevistas vitales' (1998, 2000) with Valente in the late 1990s, in the first of which the poet speaks at length of his Galician upbringing.
11. Margarita García Candeira writes with regard to this linguistic choice: 'O emprego dunha linguaxe precaria e impura é solidario cunha refutación da ética da orixe e, nese senso, as Cántigas formulan unha proposta desterritorializada sobre a identidade galega mediante unha nostalxia violenta que matiza outras propostas máis tópicas sobre a saudade' (2013: 111). García Candeira's theoretical approach to *Cántigas de alén* in this essay, in which she combines the Freudian theorization of melancholy with the Deleuze and Guatarri's concepts of deterritorialization and minor literatures differs from the emphases of my own approach, but

arrives at similar conclusions — Valente's approach to Galician language complicates what might on the surface seem like a simple song of nostalgia for lost linguistic and existential origins.
12. Ignacio Navarette (1994) shows how Nebrija's grammar was devised with a view to arrest the perceived cultural lag of a country that was becoming an empire but had not created the cultural and linguistic hegemony that empire requires.
13. Valente takes from this text in his argument for the infinite layers of meaning in the sign in his 'La hermeneútica y la cortedad del decir'. Moshe Idel (2002: 76–79) has shown that for Jacques Derrida, too, this section of Scholem's work is important, and even traces Derrida's famous 'il n'y a pas de hors texte' (1967: 227) to Scholem's discussion of the conflation of the divine and the text in medieval Kabbalism.
14. Elliot R. Wolfson (1999: 113–54) discusses the importance of secrecy in the Kabbalah, which he defines as an esoteric, rather than a mystic, tradition, and one in which there is a simultaneity of concealment and revelation — as the name of God is written YHWH but pronounced Adonai, so 'all the matters of the supernal world are hidden and revealed' (115).
15. Waldrop, a friend and translator of Jabès, discusses his reading of Scholem in *Lavish Absence* (2002): 'When Gershom Scholem comes up in conversation Edmond always comments on his love of words. "That's what he has in common with the Kabbalists, only he calls it philology"' (2002: 87).
16. Fernández Castillo discusses the significance of the color 'blanco' in the context of the Taoist tradition that informs the poem: 'De esta forma, en el poema de Valente, el blanco propicia el cambio, la transformación, que algunos de los elementos representados como el dragón o el fénix aluden simbólicamente, unificándolo en la latencia plena de formas potenciales que rebasa en lo no presente a las presencias reveladas' (2008: 439). Castillo discusses at length throughout his study the importance of 'blanco' como un símbolo de potencialidad lingüística que informa la obra de Valente, Octavio Paz, Mallarmé, and Juan Ramón Jiménez.
17. The words are from Cage's 'Manifesto', written in 1952. Also relevant to our discussion here are Cage's remarks on the 'White Paintings' series of Robert Rauschenberg, which he describes as a 'poetry of *infinite possibilities*' (1961: 103).
18. The figure of the angel in Valente's poetry has been discussed in Julian Palley (1992) and María de los Ángeles Lacalle Ciordia (2001). Jennifer Anna Gosetti Ferencei (2010) notes a paradoxical 'immanent transcendence', similar to that which I have identified in Valente's poetry, at work in the symbolization of the angel in the poetry of Rainer Maria Rilke and Wallace Stevens. For a discussion of the figure of the angel in the work of modern Jewish writers, see Alter (1991).
19. In the entry for 21 May 1977 of his *Diario Anónimo*, Valente writes: 'El pez, la concha, y la síliba OM (Guénon, *Símbolos*)' (DA: 175). Valente is referring to the chapter entitled 'Quelques aspects du symbolisme du poisson' originally written in 1936, and contained in Guénon's *Symboles fondamentaux de la science sacrée*, a copy of which is in Valente's library. Here Guénon observes that in Hinduism the first manifestation of Vishnu is as a fish, and it is in this form that the deity passes on the wisdom of the Veda after the cataclysm and the beginning of the present cycle. According to Guénon, in Hinduism sacred wisdom is originally communicated by a non-significant sound, the equivalent to which in Christian tradition is the Johannine Word.
20. *Tres lecciones de tinieblas* has been the focus of various articles written on Valente, most of which concentrate on the mystical Jewish or Christian elements of the poem, and in this regard we can cite Frank Savelsberg (2001), Carlos Peinado Elliot (2010) and (2011), and Esther Ramon (2014). The various religious elements that are combined in the text have also been traced in detail in Benlabbah (2008: 371–411).
21. Valente takes this term from the work of musicologist Heinrick Schenker, for whom it denoted the fundamental structure of every musical composition. For a discussion of the organicism that underlies Schenker's work, and also his use of the horizontal/vertical trope, in this case a gendered, creative 'female' nature and 'masculine' human artifice, see Snarrenberg (1994: 29–56). In a wider sense, Valente's description of an originary music or mood that poetry would express can be traced to the Romantic tradition and thinkers like Coleridge and Schelling. For an insightful discussion of the relevance of *stimmung* for the theorization of modern poetry see Cuesta Abad (2010a). *José Ángel Valente. Memoria sonora* (Lopo 2003) is a collection of valuable essays exploring Valente's interest in music.

22. For Agamben, enjambment, or the opposition of a rhythmic or metrical limit to a syntactical limit, defines the exceptionality of poetic language: 'the possibility of enjambment constitutes the only criterion for distinguishing poetry from prose' (1999: 109).
23. Agamben (1999) describes the use of the semi-colon in Gilles Deleuze's 'Immanence: A Life' as referring to the paradoxical alterity within immanence that characterizes Spinoza's thought. The semi-colon, linking and separating, is the diacritical emblem of Deleuze's 'transcendental empiricism'.
24. Jonathan Mayhew (2009) has described the rhetoric of 'normality' in the *poesía de la experiencia*. For Mayhew, the aspiration of poets like Luis García Montero to describe 'normal' experiences should be seen in the context of a Spanish post-transition desire to become a 'normal' European social democracy.

CHAPTER 5

Valente and Celan

Valente reading Celan

The work and life of German language poet Paul Celan play a significant part in Valente's understanding of the poetry of post-war Europe. Writing in 1999, the Galician writer claims that Celan's poems constitute 'la obra del poeta europeo que más definitivamente ha marcado su siglo' (II: 759). Celan's importance for Valente is reflected in the references to the Romanian poet in his essays from the 1970s onwards; his translations of Celan's poetry, published first in 1978 and then, as *Lectura de Celan: Fragmentos*, in 1993; and in his incorporation of motifs from Celan's writings into his own poetic work.[1] The title of Valente's 1982 collection, *Mandorla*, refers to a poem of that name included in Celan's *Die Niemandsrose*. A direct quote from Celan's poem — 'In der Mandel — was steht in der Mandel? Das Nichts' — prefaces the text: (qtd. in Valente, I: 407). The prose fragment 'Berlin' from 1992's *No amanece el cantor* references Celan's 'Todesfuge' and two poems from the posthumous *Fragmentos de un libro futuro*, published in 2001, 'Tubinga, otoño tardío', and 'Memoria de Paul Celan, en la muerte de Gisèle Celan-Lestrange, fines de 1991', also directly reference Celan's life and work. The first recalls Celan's 'Tübingen, Jänner', a poem that Valente translated, and which references Hölderlin's descent into madness and aphasia as well as Celan's troubled relationship with Martin Heidegger. The second is a more intimate poem, addressed to the deceased Celan on the death of his wife, Gisèle Celan-Lestrange. The fragment 'SOS', from the same collection, echoes Celan's 'In den Flüssen', a poem that is also included in the *Lectura de Celan: Fragmentos*.

Valente's reading of Celan should be understood in the context of his wider interest in German letters. Valente immersed himself in German literature and philosophy from an early age. His adolescent readings of Hölderlin and Rilke were to inform his later understanding of the significance of lyric poetry. Valente was also fascinated with that aspect of German Romantic thought that sought to mediate the gap between poetry and philosophy, and was an avid reader of figures of the *fruhromantik*, such as Novalis and the Schlegel brothers, as well as the lynchpins of German Idealism: Kant, Hegel, and Schelling. As José Luis Gómez Toré (2017) has shown, however, Valente's reading of contemporary German literature develops in the specific context of discussions of the fate of poetry in the aftermath of fascism. In a diary entry in September, 1964, Valente takes note of Hans Magnus

Enzensberger's short article, 'In Search of the Lost Language', in which the German poet discussed the search in the post-war years for a new poetic language, a language that would serve to repudiate the use to which words had been put during the Nazi regime (DA: 79). For Enzensberger, even the simplest German words — soil, blood, home, land — were, after their use under Hitler, damaged. Poetry, in this context, must be written in an entirely new kind of language. Valente sees a parallel between the cultures of post-war Germany and Spain. Where the German poets of the 1940s and 1950s felt they had to rebel against the conventions of an evasive *Naturlyrik*, so the Spanish poets felt it necessary to rebel against the evasions of a saccharine *garcilicismo*. Poetry, in this context, is written from a 'nullpunkt', the phrase German poets used to refer to a language and poetic tradition that must start from zero in order to escape its association with fascism, and which Valente would adapt for the title of the first anthology of his work, published in 1972, *Punto cero*. For Valente, Celan's poetry, with its radical subversion of the German language, comes closest to achieving the linguistic break of which Enzensberger spoke, and mirrors his own rebellion against the tainted language of Francoism. Thus, in the prologue to his translations of Celan, Valente recognizes a shared attitude towards an inherited language and culture:

> Las presentes versiones son resultado breve — fecundamente frustrado — de un largo período de frecuentación de un lenguaje nuevo, de una paralela frecuentación de lenguajes gastados o vacíos, de un demorado diálogo, de un movimiento de irremediable aproximación o filia. (I: 644)

While there are obvious differences in the work of both poets — as Gómez Toré (2017) points out, Valente's purified lexicon and sinuous syntax has little in common with the radical rupturas and awkward neologisms of Celan's poetry — Valente can see in Celan a common desire to construct a new poetic language that would coincide with a public sphere that has fully broken with the ideology of fascism.

We can also understand Valente's interest in Celan's work in terms of a worldview that develops in response to the absolute violence and destruction of alterity of the twentieth century. In an interview given to the *Vanguardia* newspaper in the last year of his life, Valente responds to the question '¿Qué ha marcado tu biografía?' with the single phrase: 'Que los americanos lanzaron la bomba atómica y que los alemanes asesinaron judíos' (Valente and Sanchís: 100). As I have argued, this concern with the victims of violence develops as a reaction to the humanitarian disasters of the twentieth century. It is an attitude that we could, to use a now unfashionable word, describe as 'postmodern'. By this, I mean that Valente's intellectual and ethical itinerary is defined by a developing scepticism with regard to the teleological narratives of modernity and a concern for the victims of what he sees as 'totalizing' ideologies of progress, whether Marxist or Liberal. We can turn here to an essay from 1987, 'Modernidad y postmodernidad: el ángel de la historia' (II:1355–61), in which Valente discusses Walter Benjamin's well-known description of the angel of history that sees the modernity as a catastrophic process of exploitation, destruction, and ruin. The angel longs to rescue the dead and defeated, but a wind catches his wings, preventing his return — the wind is called progress. Benjamin imagines the proletarian revolution as the interruption of this linear, progressive time by 'messianic' time, in which the aspirations of the defeated for a life lived without domination of humans or nature are actualized. Revolution is, then, married to redemption. As Valente writes:

> El futuro del ángel está sumergido en el pasado, es decir, en cuanto ha sido, pero sin llegar a ser realmente en la historia, pues ha quedado excluido, reducido al olvido, privado de palabra por la lógica de dominación. Y así aparece, en cierto modo, como preñado de muertos que aún están por nacer. (II: 1360)

Revolution implies 'resurrección del pasado; redención de los muertos' (II: 1360). The work of Celan, in this context, becomes emblematic of the capacity of poetry to constitute a counter language to the language of power, but also for the capacity of poetry to remember and to speak for the forgotten victims of history.

Jonathan Mayhew, in his essay, 'Valente's Lectura de Paul Celan': Translation and the Heideggerian Tradition in Spain', prefers to read Valente's relationship to Celan in the context of the literary rivalries and position-takings within the Spanish literary field of the 1970s and 1980s. For Mayhew:

> Valente's main purpose in translating Celan is to affiliate himself with a European modernist tradition, or, more precisely, to situate himself within the Spanish literary tradition as the most exemplary representative of modernist poetics.[...] Celan served Valente well, since the latter was able to identify himself with one of the most prestigious poets of post-war Europe while also using Celan's theory of communicability to denounce the 'realist' poetics of his own time (2004: 87).

This is certainly the case: connection to the cultural and ethical prestige of a writer like Celan could not but bolster both Valente's standing as an author and the high modernist tradition that he defended. However, while Mayhew's comments are insightful in their appraisal of the dynamics of the Spanish literary field, this approach overlooks the wider significance of Valente's affiliation to Celan. It fails to situate Valente's reading of Celan in the wider context of his understanding of Jewish culture, which, as we have seen, is motivated by a complex set of intellectual and ethical commitments that include a reading of Spanish history attentive to difference, an interest in a critical but still utopian Marxism embodied in the work of Jewish thinkers such as Bloch and Benjamin, and a growing awareness of a post-war philosophical and literary discourse of alterity, in which the figure of the Jew is central, and which includes thinkers and poets such as Blanchot, Levinas, Derrida, and Jabès.

The influence of Levinas's thought is evident in Valente's preface to his translations of Celan's work. Here, Valente configures his understanding of Celan's poetry in terminology that refers to Antonio Machado's 'heterogeneidad del ser' but also to Levinas's ethics of alterity:

> Dar por cierto el conocimiento del otro es ignorar que este presunto conocimiento es una mera proyección de nuestro yo. Suprimida esa proyección ocultante, el otro sólo puede ser percibido como esencialmente desconocido: la faz misteriosa del otro. Y, también, sólo en la medida en que es percibido

> como un misterio, puede el otro ofrecérsenos como fuente posible del conocer y del amar. Con el que yo así percibo como otro y con el que así como a otro a mí mismo me percibe puedo construir un mundo, una relación o un espacio de fluido intercambio de la diferencia con la diferencia. El misterio está en la diferencia misma; y en ella, la raíz del conocimiento y del amor. Pensamiento, este, que no traiciona su estirpe: la del pensar, la de la radical heterogeneidad del ser. Su naturaleza esencialmente dialógica. (I: 645–46)

Valente expresses here the fundamental problem of Levinas's thought: the difficulty of creating a relation to alterity that would not bind this alterity within the horizon of the self. Instead of a relationship in which the 'I' would find in alterity its own reflection, Valente proposes a Levinasian relationship to the other, in which difference is maintained in a relation that is 'dialogic' rather than 'dialectic'.

From this perspective, the difficulty of Celan's poetry has to do with a respect for the other, a refusal to assume a facile capacity to witness extreme suffering that is registered in a language that would exceed the subjective intention of the author, a language which would be, in Valente's terms, 'sobreintencional'. This conception of Celan's poetry is similar to that expressed by Levinas in his essay, written in 1972, 'Paul Celan: From Being to the Other'.[2] For Levinas, when Celan in his Bremen address describes poetry as a handshake, reducing the poem to a gesture, he is referring to the poem as that which 'precedes all thematization; it is in that act that qualities gather themselves into things. But the poem thus leaves the real its alterity, which pure imagination tears away from it' (Lévinas 1996: 44). The reduction of the poem to a gesture is significant for Levinas as it accords with his own theory of language, in which the 'saying', *le dire*, or the basic directionality of language towards another, takes precedence over the 'said', *le dit*, the world disclosing language of being. This aspect of Levinas's reading of Celan is particularly pertinent for Valente, as it gives him a philosophical basis on which to challenge the common-sensical notion of poetry as a form of communication. Rather than containing a simple message, the poem reveals the possibility of communication as such. Using images from Celan's Bremen speech (2003), Valente describes the poem as an open gesture towards another, a message in a bottle:

> Mano, botella sin destino y cargada a la vez de destino como infinitamente multiplicada posibilidad. Hay otra mano que espera en una playa, en el límite móvil de las aguas, cuyo encuentro perfecciona el acto jeroglífico de la escritura. Raíz de la comunicabilidad, pero no comunicación como tan trivialmente se ha querido. (I: 646)

This does not mean that the poem is meaningless. The poem is significant and Celan's strange language — awkward compound neologisms and a lexicon borrowed from scientific manuals and encyclopaedias — has the aim of creating an 'objective' language capable of naming the real and creating a readership capable of comprehending it. From Levinas's point of view, however, its strangeness represents a fundamental and infinite responsibility to another that dislocates the subject.

In the Bremen speech (2003), Celan linked poetry not only to the notion of a 'reachable other', but also to memory, framing his discourse in the context of the disappearance of a 'landscape of both books and people' (2003: 33), the central European Jewish culture of his childhood. The assumption of the ethical duty to bear witness to the enormity of what was lost in the war years, and to create a public sphere in which an understanding of the ethical significance of this loss is possible, is a central aspect of Celan's work, as it is in that of Valente. In this chapter, I will explore the links between Valente and Celan, and argue that their work shares fundamental concerns: an ethical commitment to the memory of the victims of violence and a preoccupation with the difficulty of writing poetry in a language and poetic tradition — German, Spanish — that had been devalued through its implication in fascism. In doing so, I am not arguing that Valente gives a 'correct' account of Celan's work, or that his translations of Celan's poetry are exemplary. Rather, I am interested in the ways in which Valente's reading of Celan's work confirms his own intuitions as to the nature of poetry written in the aftermath of political disaster. I will examine these issues with regard to Valente's exploration of subjectivity and identity in his telling of the Narcissus myth, and conclude with a consideration of the significance of Valente's reading of Celan in the wider context of questions of cultural memory.

Narcissism and Irony

Valente's linking of Machado's notion of the 'heterogeneidad del ser' to Celan's poetry points to the ways that his reading of the German poet's work confirms his understanding of twentieth century Spanish poetry and, in a wider sense, European philosophy. It is precisely Machado's respect for the other that qualifies him, in Valente's eyes, as an ethical example. It is in this light that we can understand the distinction that Valente makes between the Sevillian poet and his contemporary Juan Ramón Jiménez in an essay from 1957, 'Juan Ramón Jiménez en la tradición poética del medio siglo'. Here, Valente argues that Jiménez is the inheritor of the egoism of certain aspects of the Romantic and Symbolist traditions, what Virgil Nemoianu describes as the High Romantic dream of a 'possible-impossible expansion of the self to a seamless identification with the universe' (1984: 27). In Valente's reading, this means that Jiménez maintains a 'sentimentalidad clausurada' (II: 108) that sees in the world only a reflection of the self, a 'visión radical y totalizadora de la irrealidad del mundo y de la suprema, solitaria y suficiente realidad del yo' (II: 112), an attitude that is distilled in the lines Valente quotes from *La estación total*: 'Yo todo: poniente y aurora; | amor, amistad, vida y sueno. | Yo solo | universo' (II: 111).

We can note here the coincidence of Valente's criticism of Jiménez with Jean Paul Sartre's criticism of Baudelaire in his study from 1946, *Baudelaire*, Aurora Bernárdez's Spanish translation of which, published in 1949, is held in Valente's library at the University of Santiago de Compostela. For Sartre, Baudelaire is a man who is defined by a downward stoop, a Narcissus, entranced by his own reflection rather than the surrounding world. In lines that Valente reproduces in a diary entry from 18 October 1959, Sartre claims that Baudelaire sees the objects of the world as 'pretextos, reflejos, pantallas, los objetos jamás valen por sí mismos y no tienen otra misión que la de darle la oportunidad de contemplarse mientras los ve' (qtd. in DA: 35). Baudelaire's fascination with the means through which he perceives the world, as opposed to the world itself, could be a metaphor for a philosophical modernity that, since Kant, has replaced claims as to the nature of being with claims as to the nature of the categories of understanding. Valente notes the similarity between Sartre's understanding of Baudelaire's attitude and his own understanding of that of Jiménez and makes claims for a 'nuevo realismo' in which the singularity of the object described would not be subsumed by an all-powerful consciousness. For Valente, Antonio Machado, though indebted to Romantic and Symbolist tradition, moves from a totalizing subjectivism to a poetry that is based on the existence of an unassimilable 'tú esencial' (II: 112). Valente quotes Machado's use of the image of the mirror, in his 'Reflexiones sobre la lírica', to describe this change of attitude:

> Se diría que Narciso ha perdido su espejo, con más exactitud que el espejo de Narciso ha perdido su azogue, quiero decir la fe en la impenetrable opacidad del otro, merced a la cual — y solo por ella — sería el mundo un puro fenómeno de reflexión que nos rindiese nuestro proprio sueño, en último término, la imagen de nuestro soñador. (qtd. in II: 108)

Whereas the Symbolist poet sees in the world evidence for his own mental and spiritual processes, the modern poet must comprehend his or her subjection to a universe that exceeds intention. Valente approves of Machado's break from forms of what he takes to be Romantic/Symbolist egoism, and of his conception of the 'incurable *otredad* de lo uno' (II: 115), the implication of the self in the surrounding world, relating this stance to irony. Irony here is understood as:

> movimiento de participación que complica al creador en las mismas leyes de la realidad que reconoce. El recinto de lo subjetivo queda abierto, se destruye en cierto modo al reconocerse como tal. [...] La ironía es un atisbarse o verse de lo uno, que toma así distancias de sí mismo y se descubre diversificable, alterable. (II: 117)

Irony, the trope that undermines a given truth claim is also apt for the structure of identity, in which a sense of continuous self is undermined by the perception of the fundamental instability of a self that is subject to time. The poem, in the disjunction it implies between lyrical and empirical self, is the fluid mirror in which this alterity of identity is played out. Thus, for Valente: 'La imagen de Machado tendríamos que reconstituirla con espejos de agua, donde lo por un instante reflejado se borrase luego para reaparecer después igual y distinto' (II: 115).

We can place Valente's writings on Machado and Jiménez in a wider critique of identity and self-reflection that is one aspect of the modern philosophical tradition. By 'reflection' I refer to the tradition in modern philosophy, exemplified in the philosophy of Descartes and Kant, in which the philosophical enterprise is based upon a reflexive relation of the self to the self that grounds our knowledge of the world. Rodolphe Gasché, in his influential study of the work of Jacques Derrida, *The Tain of the Mirror*, describes this concept of philosophical reflection as a 'name for philosophy's eternal aspiration for self-foundation' (1986: 13). Reflection, the semantic and etymological connotations of which suggest a schema in which the mind, a mirror, receives the light of the objects of the world, and also sees itself in this process, in effect a mirror looking upon itself, becomes, with the philosophy of Descartes, the unsurpassed principle of thought. For Descartes, it is impossible to derive knowledge from grounds that are outside mental processes; certainty can only be found through reflection, through a consideration of the experience through which the objects are apprehended. Gasché writes:

> By lifting the ego out of its immediate entanglement in the world and by thematizing the subject of thought itself, Descartes establishes the apodictic certainty of self as a result of the clarity and distinctness with which it perceives itself. Through self-reflection, the self — the ego, the subject — is put on its own feet, set free from all unmediated relation to being. In giving priority to the human being's determination as a thinking being, self-reflection marks the human being's rise to the rank of a subject. It makes the human being a subjectivity that has its center in itself, a self-consciousness certain of itself. This is the first epoch-making achievement of the concept of reflection, and it characterizes modern metaphysics as a metaphysics of subjectivity. (1986: 13–14)

Descartes's attempt to satisfy philosophy's 'eternal aspiration' for self-foundation fails, however, in terms of another of philosophy's fundamental drives — the desire to explain the totality of noumenal reality. Kant's critical project, which aims to uncover the conditions of possibility for our knowledge, recognizes that our metaphysical pretensions are necessarily inconsistent. We can only have knowledge of that which is given according to the transcendental categories of experience — the noumenal realm of things in themselves lies outside our knowledge. Furthermore, there seems to be a fundamental antinomy between the unity of the 'I' in identity, and its division, the mind looking back on mind, in the process of reflection. In Kant's thought this duality is characteristic of the faculty of understanding and is coeval with the opposition between subject and object. For Kant this opposition is insurmountable, and if unity can be thought, it is only as a necessary presupposition, in Gasché's terms 'a hypothetical necessity, or as an abstract and absolute beyond (*Jenseits*), that is, an object only of human faith and strife' (27). Hegel's revolution consists of radicalizing reflection towards what has been termed an 'absolute idealism', in which oppositions are subsumed in the unitary totality of the identical and the non-identical. Thus, according to Gasché, Hegel's system achieves the absolute that Kant's thought could only presuppose.

As Frederic Jameson notes, there is a certain 'narcissism' inherent to absolute idealism; alterity, in Hegel's scheme, can always be subsumed within the dialectical process of Reason — we 'search the whole world, and outer space, and end up only touching ourselves, only seeing our own face persist through multitudinous differences and forms of otherness' (2010: 131). The Romantic tradition that perhaps most resists this 'narcissism' is that which opposes the pretension to absolute knowledge with the recognition of the necessary incompleteness of understanding, which is defined by the trope of irony. Paul de Man, in a now classic text, 'The Rhetoric of Temporality' (1983), discusses irony in the context of the Romantic distinction between symbol and allegory. For the Romantics, at least according to then dominant interpretations, allegory was a formal, sterile representation of ideal entities; symbol, on the other hand, was intimately involved with what it represents, reflecting an essential monism in which mind and nature enter into a dialectical relationship according to what Samuel Taylor Coleridge described as the 'one life both within us and abroad' (1997: 87). The Romantic vision implies a specific understanding of self-identity. Wordsworth's description of the 'the stationary blasts of waterfalls' would seek to grant the constancy of nature to a self-identical subject that perdures over time. For de Man, this Romantic vision of self-identity is misleading, hiding the more disquieting nature of selfhood, which is temporal to the core. Irony, for de Man, is the trope that reveals the disjunctions of selfhood. In a reading of Baudelaire's *L'essence du rire*, de Man relates irony to the capacity for self-reflection, and, more specifically, the capacity to see one-self as another: 'It is a relationship, within consciousness, between two selves, but it is not an intersubjective relationship' (1983: 212). This type of self-reflection is available to those who, like poets, use language in a specific way. Rather than an unquestioned tool for communication, the poet, according to de Man, uses language as a material, in the same way a cobbler uses leather. Language defined by shape and form loses pragmatic immediacy — the self that speaks in the poem is removed from the self immersed in a life world. As de Man writes: 'Language thus conceived divides the subject into an empirical self, immersed in the world, and a self that becomes like a sign in its attempt at differentiation and self-definition' (1983: 213). This splitting allows us to see the true nature of the self, which rather than perduring as identity over time, is constantly reiterated in the subject's identification with and through language.

De Man's description of the structure of irony mirrors the Italian philosopher Giorgio Agamben's meditation on the difficulty of testimony in the aftermath of the Shoah, *Remnants of Auschwitz*. In this work, Agamben explores the difficulty of bearing witness to the extremity of suffering experienced by the camp prisoners. This extreme suffering is embodied in the fate of the *Musselmen*, those prisoners who were so maltreated as to lose the capacity to eat, speak, or defend themselves, and who invariably died in the camps. The *Musselmen* are the 'complete witnesses', in that they suffered the full brunt of the organized brutality of the camps, but are also, for that very reason, those who did not survive to bear witness. For Agamben, the *Musselmen*'s necessary incapacity to tell us directly of their suffering means that, in the context of Auschwitz, 'testimony contains a lacuna. The true witnesses cannot bear witness; the survivors, proxy witnesses, speak in their stead' (1983: 34).

For Agamben, the impossibility of bearing witness to the experience of the victim mirrors an essential lack in the constitution of the self. Drawing on Émile Benveniste's discussion of language shifters, Agamben claims that in saying the word 'I', we identify as an impersonal linguistic element, the word 'I', which has no external referent. The word 'I' is a language shifter the meaning of which is dependent on the time, place, and person of its enunciation. It refers to the person who is uttering the present instance of discourse containing the pronoun 'I'.[3] This means that our constitution as selves in language happens in the moment of enunciation, in our identification with an anonymous linguistic element. For Agamben, this constitution of the self is a process of both subjectification and desubjectification. We become subjects through a depersonalizing process in which the living being and the 'I' of enunciation are simultaneously separated and bound together. Agamben argues that Western metaphysics and thought of language is an attempt to reconcile the fundamental gap between the living and speaking subject, whether in the form of an 'I' before language or a silent voice of conscience. But for the Italian philosopher, outside 'theology and the incarnation of the Verb, there is no moment in which language is inscribed in the living voice, no place in which the living being is able to render itself linguistic, transforming itself into speech' (1998: 129). There is always a gap between the living human being and the linguistic enunciation of the self. Testimony is precisely that which occurs in this 'non-place of articulation' (1998: 129). At the site of this disjunction between voice and word, *phone* and *logos*, Agamben places the witness, the figure whose authority lies in his or her capacity to testify for another, to speak for someone who cannot speak for themselves. It is in this context that he can claim that 'perhaps every word, every writing is born in this sense, as testimony' (1998: 38).

For Agamben, the witness's relation to language is like that of the poet. Taking Keats description of the 'chameleon poet' who can take on all personalities but who has none of his own as exemplary, Agamben asserts that it is in poetic language, and the modern tradition of the impersonal poet — Pessoa, Machado, Yeats — that the gap between the enunciative voice and an imagined psychological interiority is made visible. In this way he can conflate the structure of witnessing and poetic enunciation: 'Poets — witnesses — found language as what remains, as what actually survives the possibility, or impossibility, of speaking' (1998: 161). To bear witness, or to write poetry, is to speak from this zone of survival between presence and absence that Agamben relates to what he terms the 'dark shadows' (1998: 162) of Celan's work.

The Mirror and the Witness

The problematization of identity through irony is a major aspect of modern poetry that is often, as Fernando Cabo Aseguinolaza notes, rendered through the figure of Narcissus:

> como sugerían agudamente las palabras de Machado, bajo la influencia de Narciso, habrá que situar sobre todo la misma problematización de esa identidad, no tan definida cuando el azogue del espejo falta o bien, por cualquier irregularidad, deja sentir patentemente su intermediación, como ocurre con el lenguaje en la escritura poética, animando lo que, con ceño platónico, podríamos tachar de fantasmagorías. Al fin y al cabo, el drama de Narciso no es otro que el de la extrañeza fatal ante la imagen propia. (1998: 20).

Valente's poetry, too, often alludes to this difficulty of identity, the Machadian recognition of our temporality, the fact that linguistic enunciation of the self implies a split between a self that identifies as 'I' and an empirical self that is silenced in this very enunciation. This gap or split implies a refusal of a closed identity, what Levinas would describe as the reduction of the other to the same. It is in this context that we can understand Valente's reading of Celan's work, and, in a wider sense, the tension in his poetry between the desire to recuperate and testify to experience on the one hand, and the recognition of irretrievable loss of the past and the absence that is constitutive of the self, on the other. We can trace this struggle in Valente's work in his exploration of the mythical figure of self-reflection, Narcissus.

Valente's employment of the figure of Narcissus, to which he refers in his essay on Machado, is repeated in his 'Pasmo de Narciso', an essay published in 1982 that describes what he sees as the 'soterrado' meaning of the myth. This hidden aspect of the Narcissus myth resists later understandings of it as an allegory of self-contemplation, of the self-reflective process of mind looking back on mind. Rather, for Valente the myth reveals an essential alterity in self-relation, in which what is seen in the water is not an echo, a confirmation of the self, but a vision of the self as other: 'En la mediación del espejo de las aguas, el sí mismo se descubre como otro y ambos quedan amorosamente unificados — pasmo de Narciso — en la visión' (II: 277). The image of Narcissus represents the survival of poetic language beyond the life or death of the subject: 'La imagen que Narciso ve está más allá de la muerte. El mito de Narciso es pues un mito de amor, de supervivencia o de resurrección' (II: 277). In a later short text, 'Boceta improbable', written in 1994 for the *ABC Cultural*, Valente takes up once more the themes discussed in 'Pasmo de Narciso'. Here, however, the relevance of the Narcissus myth to representation is made more obvious. The text is framed in terms of the difficulty of artistic self-representation: 'Para retratarse hay que mirarse a sí mismo. Pero cuando trato de mirar a un presunto mí mismo, siempre veo a otro y, por lo general, no suelo reconocerme' (II: 1497). The artistic representation of the self implies a fundamental paradox, as the represented self, the self that speaks in a poem, will always differ from the self that is depicted. This vision of the self as other, according to Valente, implies a profound destabilization of identity, and here he quotes from the Fernando Pessoa's heteronym, Bernardo Soares, who on looking at himself in the mirror comprehends 'en un relámpago íntimo que no soy nadie. Nadie, absolutamente nadie' (II: 1497). The process of self-reflection leads to a recognition of difference, in which the self recognizes its temporal character, and the gap that exists between the 'I' that speaks in the poem and the self for whom it speaks. To define oneself as 'nadie' is to recognize the ironic duality of linguistic enunciation, in which identity is simultaneously enacted and denied.

The problems of self-relation that I argue are central to Valente's poetry are evident from his early work, most obviously so in 'El espejo', from *A modo de esperanza*, which can be understood as a staging of the processes of subjectification and desubjectification that are inherent in linguistic enunciation. 'El espejo' turns precisely on the ironic disjunction between a speaker and the muted self, represented by an 'I' that addresses its own face in the mirror.

> Hoy he visto mi rostro tan ajeno,
> tan caído y sin par
> en este espejo.
>
> Está duro y tan otro con sus años,
> su palidez, sus pómulos agudos,

> su nariz afilada entre los dientes,
> sus cristales domésticos cansados,
> sus costumbres sin fe, sólo costumbre.
> He tocado sus sienes, aún latía
> un ser allí. Latía. ¡Oh vida, vida!
>
> Me he puesto a caminar. También fue niño
> este rostro, otra vez, con madre al fondo.
> De frágiles juguetes fue tan niño
> en la casa lluviosa y trajinada,
> en el parque infantil
>   — ángeles tontos —
> niño municipal con aro y árboles.
>
> Pero ahora me mira — mudo asombro,
> glacial asombro en este espejo solo —
> y ¿dónde estoy — me digo —
> y quién me mira
> desde este rostro, máscara de nadie? (I: 71)

The face is objectified, dehumanized in the description of its 'nariz afilada entre los dientes | su cristales domesticos cansados'. The physical changes wrought by time undermine the self's sense of identity; it becomes difficult to reconcile the 'I' that speaks with the face in the mirror: 'Pero ahora me mira — mudo asombro | glacial asombro en este espejo solo — | y donde estoy — me digo — | y quien me mira | desde este rostro, mascara de nadie?'. The irony of the poem lies in the fact that the voice we hear is that of the lyric subject, a voice that is petrified in the poem in the same way the face is petrified in the mirror. The language shifters that predominate in the poem — 'Hoy he visto,' 'este rostro,' 'ahora me mira' — mark this distance, telling us that language, not the subject, speaks, and that the poem is a 'mascara de nadie' that bears witness to a mute subject.

'El Crimen', from the same collection, again stages the disjunction between the enunciative act of language and the living human being. The enunciative position is that of a dead man who wakes 'como siempre, pero | con un cuchillo | en el pecho' (I: 97). The voice describes the investigation of his own murder but admits that he himself has 'nada que declarar' (98). 'El crimen' allows for what Agamben sees as the specific enunciative capacity of poetry, the ability 'to place oneself in one's own language in the place of those who have lost it' (161), a performance that is especially obvious in a poem which makes the dead speak. One of the many ironies in the poem is that the voice claims that his own murder 'carece de testigos' (98). In this case the poem speaks, bearing witness as remnant, that which survives the possibility and impossibility of speaking. The fragility of the remnant, its survival as the mere marking of non-coincidence between voice and subject, is rendered visible in the paradoxical Homeric accusation: 'No hay pruebas contra nadie. Nadie | ha consumado mi homicidio' (I: 98).

'Los olvidados y la noche', from *Poemas a Lázaro*, takes on the motifs of witnessing and reflection in the context of a confrontation with the dead and the forgotten. The poetic voice is confronted by the presence of dead loved ones, represented by 'los ojos de mi madre antes | de haberme concebido' (I: 118). The poem is defined by movement, a flowing river represents the 'implacable paso, | el terrible descenso' of time (I: 118) that sweeps the dead away in its path. If the passing of time makes a dialogue with the dead impossible, so too does it prevent an unproblematic revelation of the self: 'Mientras escribo sobre | la resistencia de mi propio cuerpo, | el mundo habrá pasado, | habrá cerrado el ciclo | completado el retorno | de su nada a su origen, | y yo seré antepasado pálido | de mi futuro olvido' (I: 119). The ironic self-distancing reaches a pitch here, as we are confronted with the performative contradiction of a voice that urgently tells us that it no longer exists. It is in this context that the poem is a remnant, a 'nada' that remains, which does not speak of the dead, but rather, testifies to a shared fragility: 'sé que no soy, | que no me pertenezco | Pasé por vuestros ojos | y creí desgarrarlos, arrastrarlos conmigo, | mas fue vuestra pupila la que hizo presa en mí' (I: 119). Memory, here, is not the power to recall the dead, but the power the dead exert upon the living. While conversation with the dead is impossible, we can address them in lyric apostrophe, sustaining a relation that survives absence: 'y a un lado y otro lado | permanecemos solos, | dando voces, llamandonos, | gesticulando, mientras | la corriente se ensancha y yace | consumido el crepúsculo' (I: 120).

The thematics of witnessing are central to the collection *La memoria y los signos*. In 'El autor en su treinta aniversario', the problems of self-relation are again explored in the context of the memory of the suffering of the victims of violence. The poem begins in the liminal space to which Valente's work obsessively returns — 'al borde de nacer o de morir' (I: 169). The poem is a meditation on the nature of self-representation, in which the lyric voice reflects on a self that offers itself up for depiction in the same way that a model poses for a painter: 'Como el modelo no es vida | en el pincel, sino material | que aún no imita la vida, inmóvil | permanezco dentro | de mi propia visión' (I: 169). It is implied that as a model is only such after it has been represented, so one becomes a writer only as an aftereffect of writing. The self that is registered in this self-portrait 'sobre un fondo gris' (I: 169) is necessarily absent. The contemplation of the other, past, selves from which the poetic voice is irreparably divorced leads to a recognition of the discontinuity of selfhood, of the separation from the past: 'Objeto | ciego de mi propia visión, petrificado | perfil de nino tenebroso, | el hombre que contemplo no desciende| de su memoria sino de su olvido' (I: 170). The irreparable distance from a past self, a child that can only be 'petrified' in the language of the poem, is linked to the absence of the dead of the civil war: 'Como podría pues reconocerlo | en la presencia opaca de otras vidas, | en los lentos cadáveres perdidos | bajo los puentes rotos | de otro país al que pertenecimos' (I: 170). The paradoxes of self-representation, the ways in which poetic enunciation shows an essential gap in all identity, means that the lyric poem is perhaps the cultural form most adequate to testifying to the dead, as its enunciative structure implies discontinuity, a voice that speaks despite absence.

It is in this context that we can understand a developing distrust in narration in the poems from *Interior con figuras* onwards. 'Criptomemorias', from the aforementioned collection, prefigures what will become a persistent theme:

> Debiéramos tal vez
> reescribir despacio nuestras vidas,
> hacer en ellas cambios de latitud y fechas,
> borrar de nuestros rostros en el álbum materno
> toda noticia de nosotros mismos.
>
> Debiéramos dejar falsos testigos,
> perfiles maquillados,
> huellas rotas,
> irredentas partidas bautismales.
>
> O por toda memoria,
> una ventana abierta,
> un bastidor vacío, un fondo
> irremediablemente blanco para el juego infinito
> del proyector de sombras.
> Nada.
> De ser posible, nada. (I:342–43)

Here, the images of memory, the faces in an album of family photographs, are to be replaced by an empty frame, a white background on which memories can be projected. There is a sense that the most effective way to witness absence is to make manifest the irrecuperability of all that has been lost. The verb 'borrar', reminiscent of Machado's 'fuente' that 'borrada la historia, | contaba la pena' (1964: 63), alludes to lyric as the discourse that communicates, but does not chronicle, events. It is significant, in this regard, that from this period onwards the mirrors in Valente's poems are often emptied of figures, as in 'Meditación sobre una imagen cóncova':

> Ahora cuanto fuimos
> no capaces de amar
> nos mira no engendrado.
> Espejo. (I: 357)

The mirror, the poem, is the concave space that reveals absence, that which has not been born, or that which might have been. In the same collection, the poem becomes the place of what Valente titles the 'Transparencia de la memoria':

> Como un gran salón desierto al cabo los espejos
> han absorbido todas las figuras,
> tal en el centro inmóvil bebe
> la luz desnuda todo lo visible (I: 365)

In *Mandorla*, the capacity of the poem/mirror to represent the self is again questioned:

> LA IMAGEN se desdobla en el espejo como si engendrase de sí el espacio de otro aparecer. Qué nombre darle al que aquí acude, al que es igual y no es igual a quién. Margen, lugar incierto de este pacto. Entre la imagen y su doble rostro algo ha podido morir. Alguien o algo como vacío o huella de un grito no emitido o caída sin término de un cuerpo en la no duración. Perfil, mirada, sesgo, espacio entre la imagen y la imagen que de la imagen se desprende. Lugar donde algo al cabo se hubiera consumado. Me mira: quién. Y una vez más

vivimos el adiós. Pero no queda en los espejos huella. No guardan, incruentos, testimonio ni amor. (I: 421)

In representation, something is lost, and between the speaker of the poem and the self to which it refers there is an unbridgeable gap. While in this piece the poetic voice claims that mirrors/poems are completely divorced from what they represent, the wider thrust of Valente's 'mirror' poems suggests that lyric can be a corrective to exclusionary epic narratives. In this sense, lyric has a fundamental kinship with melancholy, the emotion, as we have seen, that is bound up with memory and political defeat — we might recall here, with Jean Starobinski, the traditional pairing of melancholy and the mirror.[4] The following poem, from *Al dios del lugar*, explores the question as to whether lyric can oppose the grandiosity of epic:

> LA LENTITUD de la destrucción,
> sus prolongados hilos húmedos,
> el odio con retráctiles
> pupilas amarillas,
> la corrupción de la memoria y las figuras
> revestidas de cera muerta en los salones
> de derrumbada cal.
>
> Tanteas, tocas, palpas ciego
> los residuos de ti.
>
> Sombrío cae el año hacia su muerte,
> las conmemoraciones del difunto, el ácido
> reclamo de la noche.
> Imágenes
> de imágenes.
> Qué queda en los espejos,
> en los largos pasillos naufragados,
> en el recinto pálido del aire,
> en el testimonio del testigo de quién.
>
> Resuenan victoriosos los timbales
> sobre las sumergidas formas rotas,
> el viento y sus cenizas.
> Desaparición. (I: 478)

In the wake of disaster, the victors preside over the corruption of memory. Their triumphant narratives and commemorations obscure the suffering of the victims of history, those reduced to wind and ash. The poem, on the other hand, testifies to what has been lost, if only in the sense that it resists the images of the epic tale. The poem survives as the 'residuo' of a life that has been extinguished, or what Valente terms in a prose piece titled 'Antimemorias', the 'poso no legible' (I: 493) of vanquished political ideals.

Elements within the semantic field of remnants — 'ceniza', 'poso,' 'residuo', 'rastro' — intensify in frequency in the latter period of Valente's writing, symptoms of what Miguel Casado describes as a 'biografía de restos' (2012: 170). This writing of remains is explicitly framed in poems from the 1980s on in terms of inscription. In 'Elegía menor, 1980' Valente records the suicide of an anonymous woman:

> El viernes,
> Treinta y uno de octubre
> de este año cualquiera,
> una mujer saltó
> del puente de Vessy al río
> Arve.
> Su cuerpo fue recuperado
> por los hombres del puesto permanente.
> El otoño desciende en avenidas,
> procesional y enorme, hasta los bordes
> amarillos del aire.
> Salud hermana.
> En la noticia anónima
> no te acompañan deudos
> ni cercanos amigos.
> Sólo un rastro
> de soledad arrastran sin tu cuerpo
> los dolorosos ríos. (I: 434)

The poem implicitly refers to Paul Celan, who committed suicide by throwing himself into the river Seine on 20 April 1970. It begins with the certainty of the past simple (una mujer saltó) and the exactness of the date (El Viernes | treinta y uno de octubre).[5] But this specificity is undermined by the the adverb, 'cualquiera'. The singularity of the date is undermined by the adverb that implies its essential interchangeability. This is a time without inherent quality, the 'homogenous empty time' which for Benjamin defined the modern.[6] The woman's death is recorded in a 'noticia anónima,' in the absence of friends and mourners. This absence is perhaps an existential difficulty, reflective of that special loneliness that can only be found in great cities, but also a necessity of writing: the woman's existence is recorded in her absence, in the solitude of the letter.[7] We can read the final lines — 'Sólo un rastro | de soledad arrastran sin tu cuerpo | los dolorosos ríos' — as referring to the presence of the letter, a 'rastro' on paper that survives absence, in the same way that the song of the dismembered Orpheus survives in the waters into which he was cast.

The date and writing are also central to the following prose fragment from *No amanece el cantor*:

> Quería escribir *unter den Linden*. Escribir las palabras en el mismo lugar al que designan. Igual que los *graffiti*. Decir ante un simbólico público alemán *der Tod ist ein Meister aus Deutschland*. Como si yo mismo fuese un campesino de esa tierra. Decirlo con amor y con tristeza. El día dos de noviembre, un día de difuntos, de mil novecientos noventa, ya casi al término de siglo, el aire es tenue aquí y frío y luminoso. Una niña cruza en bicicleta, haciendo largas eses descuidadas, los vestigios del límite aún visibles. (*Berlín*) (I: 496)

The poem refers to the political relevance of literature, which, like graffiti, can intervene directly in the public sphere. This situation of the poem is affirmed in the second scene of inscription, in which, with 'amor y tristeza', the voice expresses the desire to pronounce the famous words from Celan's 'Todesfugue', *der Tod ist ein Meister aus Deutschland*, in front of an imagined German audience, a gesture that refers to the necessity of societal remembering of the genocide. Finally, a third type of inscription is invoked, a child drawing curves with the path of her bicycle on 2 November 1990. 2 November, the day in which the boundaries between the living and the dead are blurred, is marked by a pure inscription. Inscription, as Derrida reminds us in his 'Shibboleth for Paul Celan', is that aspect of writing that retains the historical singularity of the event, that which is transmitted but also effaced by the meaning of words. The recording of inscription in the poem is, then, a gesture that reminds us that the poem, as testimony, speaks for those who cannot speak for themselves, communicating a fundamental lack of communication. It is in this context that we might read this fragment from 'Tiempo', a poem included in *Fragmentos de un libro futuro*:

> Efímera
> construyo mi morada.
> Trazo un gran círculo en la arena
> de este desierto o tiempo donde espero
> y todo se detiene y yo soy sólo
> el punto o centro no visible o tenue
> que un leve viento arrastraría. (I: 581)

The poem refers to its own fragility, its solitude in the letter, but this fragility belies the strength of the written word, its capacity, despite absence, to survive and sustain a lyrical voice, to be read and reread. In *Paisaje con pájaros amarillos* this impossible survival in the written word is again enacted through the marking of sand: 'Sobre la arena trazo con mis dedos una doble línea interminable como señal de la infinita duración de este sueño' (I: 497). The gesture of inscription, the 'raíz de comunicabilidad', is for Valente that aspect of poetry which corresponds to Celan's handshake or message in a bottle. It is the fundamental opening to a 'tú invocable', the possibility of a world transformed.

Valente and Celan: The Politics of Memory

Valente's interpretation of Celan's work has been criticized. Arnau Pons, a disciple of the French philologist and interpreter of Celan, Jean Bollack, claims that Valente's Levinasian reading of Celan's work gives a misleading picture of the poet. In an interview with Bollack , published in *Quimera* No. 201, published in March 2001, Pons reproduces Bollack's contention that the philosophy of alterity, which for him includes the work of Martin Buber and Levinas, is not pertinent for an understanding of Celan's work:

> Hay que saber que el principio dialógico es lo más falso en la interpretación de Celan, ya que en su poesía el otro está dentro de la misma obra y nunca fuera de ella, mientras para Levinas y Buber el otro es siempre el Otro. Pero en Celan nunca. El otro es él mismo. De ahí que yo insista tanto sobre el 'tú,' ya que el 'yo' y el 'tú' están en diálogo permanente en su poesía. [...] Se trata, pues, de la exclusión de todo principio dialógico tal y como se lo encuentra expuesto en Levinas y Buber. Celan ha acabado con Buber, de una cierta manera'. (Pons 2001: 57)

It is true that Celan's relationship with Buber is a complex one. As Sonja Boos (2015) has shown, Celan's Meridian address can be read as an undermining of Buber's optimism regarding the possibility of dialogue between Germans and Jews. For Celan, it is not possible to maintain a dialogue with the German audiences to whom he speaks. It is also true that the relation between the 'du' and the 'ich' in Celan's poetry is often self-reflective, opposing the lyric 'I' of poetry to the 'You' of life. But to imagine that the play of identity and difference in Celan's poetry excludes the pertinence of Levinas's thought to his work is mistaken. The Levinasian relationship to the Other is not characterized by a face to face dialogue. It is, rather, a prelogical responsibility of the self to the other that undermines any sense of subjective mastery of either self or world. We can never master or recuperate in language the negativity of this self, subject as it is to the Other and characterized, in Levinas's terms, by the 'disjonction de l'identité où le même ne rejoint pas le même: nonsynthèse, lassitude' (1990: 67).

But beyond the specific issue of the validity of a Levinasian approach to Celan's work, Pons claims that Valente's approach to Celan is overdetermined by religious and philosophical elements, and as such is 'claramente ontológica, religiosa, gratamente oscura, cuando no apropriativa' (2001: 41). Pons's criticism here is, I believe, ungenerous. It ignores Valente's fundamental understanding of Celan's work, which is determined not by any sacralization of the Nazi murder of Jews, but by a shared determination to renew a language that has been corrupted through its use in fascism. It ignores too Valente and Celan's common preoccupation with the possibility, always questioned, of dialogue, in which the capacity for address retains, even in the most minimal sense, elements of hope. It ignores their shared distrust of the totalizing tendencies of modern political ideologies and a shared enthusiasm for figures within the revolutionary tradition, such as Rosa Luxemburg, most attentive to difference. Finally, it ignores Valente's immersion in a tradition of twentieth century Jewish thought — Benjamin, Scholem, Levinas — that is of great import to Celan and pertinent to the wider question of memory in the wake of the Second World War. This is a tradition that is precisely *not* ontological, as it is based on singularities that escape the concepts of philosophy. If there is a religious element in Valente's work, this has nothing to do with a transcendent sphere. Rather, the religious in Valente's poetry and thought should be understood in immanent terms, as an infinite responsibility to the other and a utopian faith in the possibility of entirely new social and political structures.

In a broader sense, however, there is a consensus among scholars interested in the reception of Celan's work in Spain, reflected in the essays of *Lecturas de Paul Celan*, that Valente's representation of Celan's work has led to a misleading or mystifying vision of the German poet, reducing its political import. José Luis Gómez Toré, who gives a sympathetic and insightful account of the relation between the two poets, even speaks of the need to '*desvalentizar* a Celan' (2017: 230). There is some truth to this. It should be remembered that despite Valente's position as the most distinguished interpreter of Celan's poetry in Spain, he translates only seventeen of Celan's poems, and dedicates just two short essays to his work. Given the brevity of Valente's published engagement with Celan, it is to be expected that important aspects of the German poet's work should be underrepresented. The absurd and comic elements of Celan's poetry, for example, which Andreas Lampert brilliantly evokes in his contribution to *Lecturas de Paul Celan* (2017), are missing in Valente's account. But perhaps the most damaging aspect of the association of the names Valente and Celan has to do with a mistaken view of Valente as a modern mystic poet whose purified 'poetry of silence' ultimately refers to the ineffable and the divine. To understand Valente's work, then, and his reading of Celan, it is necessary to *desvalentizar* Valente, making clear the political and social significance of his poetry.

The fundamental stakes at play in Valente's reading of Celan are evident in the long poem *Hibakusha*, which completes *El dios del lugar*. *Hibakusha* is a Japanese term that refers to those affected by the nuclear bombs dropped on Hiroshima and Nagasaki in 1945. Valente's poem is a meditation on the possibility of testifying to the experience of the victims of technologically advanced barbarity. Significantly, it has a similar structure to Celan's long poem, 'Einfahrung', the final poem of the collection *Sprachgitter* (1980), which is sometimes called 'Strette', referring to its fugue-like composition — a *stretto* is a type of fugue in which the subject is presented in one voice and then imitated in one or more other parts, with the imitation starting before the subject has finished. Celan's poem is divided into nine sections, with each section, as in the voices of a fugue, beginning with a modified version of the last words of the previous section. Peter Szondi identifies a movement in the poem — from present to past and from past to present — that coincides with pronoun positions that move from 'you' to 'they' to 'I' to 'we'. These elements, as well as the stuttering recapitulation of the subject at the beginning of each section, make the poem one of 'repetition, transformation, and contradiction' (2003: 8). *Einfahrung* explores, or is an enactment of, memory in the wake of disaster. In a movement that takes in the Nazi concentration camps and the atomic bomb, the poem arrives at an aftertime in which 'there are temples yet. A | star | probably still has light. | Nothing, | nothing is lost' (Celan 1980: 127). The line break between the first 'nothing' and the second means that we must consider the word in isolation. The word 'nothing' demonstrates the capacity of language to bring absence to presence, to make that which has no being — nothingness — appear in the word. This capacity of language to bring absence to presence in the word allows it to bear witness for what has been lost. At the same time, however, the enormity of the disasters of the camps and Hiroshima cast this capacity into doubt, and it is this redemptive aspect of language that is being called into question in the phrase 'nothing is lost'. What is being marked here is the necessary failure of language, which attempts and fails to recover the dead, who can only exist as the 'unmistakeable trace' left in the grass that grows around the tracks that lead to Auschwitz.

Valente's *Hikabusha* is also written in an aftertime. It responds, like Celan's poem, to Adorno's dictum that poetry is impossible after Auschwitz:

> ¿No habría que escribir precisamente
> Después de Auschwitz o después

> de Hiroshima, si ya fuésemos, dioses
> de un tiempo roto, en el después
> para que al fin se torne
> en nunca y nadie pueda
> hacer morir aún más los muertos?

We have an ethical responsibility to bear witness to the dead and to recall the historical circumstances of their destruction. To forget them is to consign them to a death without end. It is in this context that Valente strives, as he did in the collection *Presentación y memorial para un monumento*, to recreate the language of genocide. The collage technique used in the previous collection is also employed here in the insertion of phrases attributed to the scientists who worked on the Manhattan Project to build the first Atomic Bomb: 'We are all sons of a bitch' and 'Babies satisfactorily born' (I: 485).[8] The insertion of these phrases in the poem create an uncomfortable proximity to the architects of the bombing. There follows a description of the explosion and the question, '¿Quién llora aún? (I: 486), that reiterates the earlier '¿Quién llora | que no puede llorar | desde los cuencos secos?' (I: 484). After the disaster, death seeks to live in the voice: 'Lenta, | pronunciada, la voz, la muerte | quiso en ella vivir' (I: 487). Similar to *Einfahrung*, in Valente's poem to remember the dead is to make visible the impossibility of their recovery. In this context, day turns to night: 'Nocturno viene el día contra las abiertas | entrañas de la noche' (I: 487). There is no easy redemption of the dead, their suffering is not justified as a moment in a dialectical movement in which the obscurity of lived experience is brought to life in the light of the word. Rather, as in Celan's poem, the poet writes from a time that is marked not by triumph and reconciliation but by mere survival in desolation: 'Despertar. | ¿A qué? Morir. ¿A qué? | ¿Nacer al reino | de la calcinación?' (I: 488).

The idea that a poem can commemorate the absence of the dead, becoming a paradoxical witnessing of unimaginable loss and suffering, is reiterated in the poem 'Sonderaktion, 1943', from *Fragmentos de un libro futuro*:

> El humo aciago de las víctimas.
>
> Todo se deshacía en el aire.
> La historia como el viento dorado del otoño
> arrastraba a su paso los gemidos, las hojas, las cenizas,
> para que el llanto no tuviera fundamento.
> Disolución falaz de la memoria.
> Parecía
> como si todo hubiera sido para siempre borrado.
>
> Para jamás, me digo.
> Para nunca. (I: 545)

The title refers to the *Sonderaktion* units of the German army who attempted to destroy evidence of the massacres they had committed in central and eastern Europe during the Second World War. The 'humo aciago' is that of the cremated remains of the victims, whose memory, for the Nazis, would be dispersed on the winds of history. The Nazi attempt to destroy the evidence of their genocide failed, a failure that is proved by the poem, within which the memory of the victims survives, if only in the same structure of negation that we have seen in *Einfahrung* and 'Hibakusha', 'para jamás' and 'para nunca'.

Valente's approximation to Celan's work can be seen, then, in terms of his wider intellectual and biographical evolution from the 1960s onwards, which is characterized by a 'postmodern' scepticism with regard to historical metanarratives and a concern for the victims of history. Such a trajectory is common to many of his generation and forms part of the post-1968 distrust of traditional party structures and the development of what we now term identity politics. References to Jewish culture are central to this development. As we have seen, the trope of the deracinated Jew becomes an important element in the work of philosophers who want to develop ways of thinking community not bound to the structures of the nation state. Similarly, the murder of Jews in the Shoah becomes the touchstone for ethical thought that pays special attention to questions of difference. Valente, who had grown up in the suffocating atmosphere of Fascism, had grown disillusioned with the intellectual and political mediocrity of the Communist Party, who had imbibed a liberal Spanish discourse that emphasized Spain's ethnic plurality, and whose intellectual life was centred on authors writing in French, was, perhaps more than any other Spanish writer of his time, especially prepared to take on the then contemporary discourses on Jewish suffering, which in poetry were embodied in the work of Jabès and Celan. In the work of these poets, he found resources for understanding his own historical experiences as an exile from a country that had borne the brunt of decades of fascist violence and repression.

Enzo Traverso argues that the growth in the West of a memory culture that centres on the Shoah and the Second World War has had the effect of obscuring the political context of those events and the possibility of political structures other than increasingly hollow neoliberal democracies. This may be true, but for Valente, the need to remember the dead, exacerbated in the case of a country like Spain where public mourning of the Republican side in the Civil War had not taken place, does not negate the political import of his poetry. Valente's reading of Celan and the assimilation to his work of elements of discourses relating to the Shoah might better be thought of as an act of what Michael Rothberg (2015) calls 'multidirectional memory', a term that describes the way in which cultural memory of events such as the Shoah can be adapted and rearticulated in different contexts, allowing for new cultural understandings of historical events in the cultures that receive them. In his writings on, and translations of, Celan, as well as in his own poetry, Valente is one of the first writers in Spain to articulate the cultural memory of the Shoah in an Iberian context, a process that has quickened since the 1990s and has had significant, if unequal, results.[9] For Valente, however, the need to remember the dead never negates the political, nor does it negate the desire for alternative political and social arrangements — his acerbic contributions to the press regarding the Transition period and its optimistic social democratic ethos leave no doubt in this regard. In this way, Valente has much in common with Celan, whose responsibility to bear witness to the Jewish dead did not preclude a fierce political acumen nor a capacity to place the suffering of the Jews in the context of historical fascism and its enemies. It is significant, then, that Valente should translate Celan's 'Shibboleth', a poem that enacts the paradox of words — *no pasarán* — that are simultaneously untranslatable and mobile, that remain, beyond their time and place, a promise of memory and of resistance:

> Junto a mis piedras
> crecidas bajo el llanto
> tras las rejas,
> me arrastraron
> al medio del mercado,
> allá,
> donde se iza la bandera, a la que
> no he prestado nunca juramento.
> Flauta,
> flauta doble en la noche:
> piensa el sombrío
> y doble rojo
> en Viena y en Madrid.
> Pon tu bandera a media asta,
> recuerdo.
> A media asta
> hoy para siempre.
> Corazón:
> dalo también aquí a conocer,
> aquí, en medio del mercado.
> Haz que resuene, el shibboleth,
> en lo extranjero de la patria.
> Febrero. No pasarán.
> Unicornio:
> sabes de las piedras,
> sabes de las aguas,
> van,
> te llevo
> hacia las voces
> de Extremadura. (I: 651–52)

Notes to Chapter 5

1. Jaime Siles (2017) recounts reading Valente's translations of Celan in 1974, four years before their publication, and argues that Valente's 1971 collection, *Treinta y siete fragmentos*, shows the mark of the then contemporary understanding of Celan as the poet *par excellence* of linguistic economy and intensity.
2. Valente underlines this section of the essay in his copy of the collection *Noms propres* (1982), which that is held at his library in the University of Santiago de Compostela.
3. Valente was aware of both Benveniste's and Ramon Jakobson's work on linguistic shifters. In the entry for 5 July 1981 of the *Diario Anónimo*, he writes: 'Emile de Benveniste, "La natur des prenoms," en *Problemes de linguistique general*, París, Gallimard, 1966. Shifter es el término empleado por Jakobson para indicar una categoría del signo lingüistico que está "lleno de significación" sólo porque está "vacío." Esto...se espera la aparición del referente. *Yo y tú*: yo

soy el referente del "yo" sólo cuando el que habla soy yo. Cuando empiezas a hablar tú el yo te pertenece a ti' (DA: 213).
4. Starobinski explores the link between melancholy and the mirror in his *La mélancolie au miroir: trois lectures de Baudelaire* (1989).
5. Jacques Derrida discusses the importance of the date, which he links to the singularity of inscription, in Celan's work in his well-known essay, 'Shibboleth: For Paul Celan' (2005).
6. The life of the dead woman is recorded in an anonymous note in a newspaper. Benedict Anderson identifies the role of newspapers in reinforcing a modern sense of temporality in his *Imagined Communities* (1991: 22–36).
7. María Lopo, in *Valente Vital: Ginebra, Saboya, París*, records Valente's feelings of unhappiness on his moving to Paris in the early 1980s: 'En definitiva, esta primera etapa en París parece haber estado intensamente marcada por un profundo agotamiento y por la experiencia de la soledad en la gran urbe, quizá nunca antes experimentada tan radicalmente en la vivencia del poeta' (2014: 424).
8. Valente's source for these phrases is probably Robert Jungk's *Brighter than a Thousand Suns* (1960), a copy of which is held in his library at the University of Santiago de Compostela.
9. For a discussion of the adaptation of discourses about the Shoah in a Spanish context, see Alejandro Baer (2011, 2016).

CONCLUSION

In a diary entry from 6 September 1968, Valente quotes from Maurice Blanchot's well known essay, 'Le regard d'Orphée': 'Quand Orphée descend vers Eurydice, l'art est la puissance par laquelle s'ouvre la nuit' (DA: 132), and adds the following fragment, which he will later publish in the collection of aphorisms, *Notas de un simulador*:

> La visibilidad de lo invisible. La forma que lo invisible toma en la mirada es la de su perdida. Lo invisible queda así vista como tal, como en cierto modo queda lo indecible dicho en el lenguaje. Hay algo en la palabra poética vuelta hacia lo indecible que corresponde a la mirada de Orfeo vuelta hacia lo invisible. (DA: 132)

Blanchot's essay explores the paradoxes of the myth of Orpheus. Orpheus's desire is the desire of art — to approach the origin of night and, in turning away, draw it back towards the light. This is a version of the Hegelian dialectic, in which even the negativity of death can be recuperated for spirit. The Orphic legend is a refusal of the dialectic, as Orpheus sacrifices the law of art in his desire to gaze upon the face of the night, in the process losing both Eurydice and his work. For Blanchot, the moment of turning back to gaze into the face of Eurydice is the moment of inspiration. It is only in breaking the law of art that a work can surpass itself, and 's'unir à son origine et se consacrer dans l'impossibilité' (Blanchot 1955: 232). The writer sacrifices his self and his work in order to testify to an absence that resists artistic recuperation.

Blanchot's description of the poet's self-sacrificing desire to grasp death in itself, to bring absence as such into presence, defines the basic intuition that drives Valente's poetry, and which determines his reading of the Jewish tradition of philosophy and poetry that I have identified in this work. This is a tradition whose key thinkers — Scholem, Benjamin, Bloch, Levinas, Derrida — attempt to think beyond the basic categories of being and nothingness that define Western philosophy. Though these thinkers exhibit many differences, each attempts to think a paradoxical immanence of the transcendent, whether in terms of a relation of infinite responsibility to the Other or as a foreshadowing of utopia in the present, which constitutes an indivisible remainder that refuses dialectical appropriation. To conclude, therefore, is difficult, as this thought To conclude, therefore, is difficult, as this thought suggests the impossibility of ending, provoking what Levinas describes as pure questions, questions that seek no response. It is perhaps best, then, to explore in this inconclusive conclusion the presence within Valente's poetry of that which has always been understood as the marker of human finitude, death, and ask whether, at this limit, something remains to be said.

In an early poem from *A modo de esperanza*, 'Consiento', Valente writes:

> Debo morir. Y sin embargo, nada
> muere, porque nada
> tiene fe suficiente
> para poder morir.
>
> No muere el día,
> pasa;
> ni una rosa,
> se apaga
> resbala el sol,
> no muere.
>
> Sólo yo que he tocado
> el sol, la rosa, el día,
> y he creído,
> soy capaz de morir. (I: 79–80)

The rose, sun, and day recall a similar triad from Cernuda's 'El Poeta', from *Vivir sin estar viviendo*, which Valente cites in reference to Coleridge in his essay from 1962, 'Luis Cernuda y la poesía de la meditación':

> Cuando en ella un momento se unifican,
> Tal uno son amante, amor y amado,
> Los tres complementarios luego y antes dispersos:
> El deseo, la rosa y la mirada. (Qtd. in II: 373)

The *ella* in Cernuda's poem refers to the poetic work that would unify subject, desire, and object. 'Consiento', on the other hand, is more concerned with human finitude, the knowledge of which separates the human from the temporality of the sun and the rose. To be human, in this context, is to be capable of death. Here we can see the influence of Heideggerian thought. For the Heidegger of *Being and Time* (1962), death for *Dasein* must be 'distinguished from the going-out-of-the-world of that which merely has life' (284), which would be a mere perishing (*verenden*). Death is proper to man, the 'possibility of the impossibility of *Dasein*' (294), and thereby the 'possibility which is one's ownmost' (294), which cannot be related to the experience of another. It is in this sense that, for Heidegger, as for Valente, *Dasein* is uniquely capable of death.

Levinas, in a series of lectures from 1975 and 1976, published as *Dieu, la morte et le temps*, carries out a complex critique of Heidegger's rendering of death as the privileged capacity of *Dasein*. For Levinas, Heidegger's thought conforms to the philosophical tradition that conceives rationality as:

> [...] ce résultat saisissable, compréhensible, par rapport à quoi la durée nous inquiète par son pas-encore, par l'inaccompli. Idéal du sensé pour une conscience s'attachant au terrain inébranlable du monde, c'est-à-dire à la terre sous la voûte du ciel. Rationalité d'une penseé pensant à sa mesure, à son échelle, par rapport à laquelle toute recherche, tout désir, toute question sont devenir, constituent un pas-encore, un manque, sont le non-satisfaisant, représentent d'indigentes connaissances. (1993: 130)

For Levinas, Heidegger's approach leaves unexamined the sheer unknowability of death, the enigma that cannot be captured by what he terms, describing Heidegger's philosophy, the 'l'épopée de l'être' (Lévinas 1993: 67) . The alterity of death is not commensurable to human knowledge; it can only be thought of in terms of desire and questioning. These would be pure desires, and pure questions, that do not aim at anything that would be commensurate to them, remaining in a paradoxical relation without relation to the unknown. The disquiet provoked by these desires and questions is similar to the discomfort we feel in our absolute responsibility to the Other, a responsibility that is confirmed when we meet the gaze of the dying man or woman: 'La mort dans le visage de l'autre homme est la modalité selon laquelle l'altérité par laquelle le Même est affecté, fait éclater son identité de Même en guise de question qui se lève en lui' (Levinas 1993:133). Our responsibility in the face of the death of the other arises as an unanswerable question with regard to our own mortality. It is an experience that opens a fundamental aspect of our selves that is beyond our subjective intentionality. As opposed to the Heideggerian thinking of death as a fundamental property of *Dasein*, here death is a debt we owe to the Other that is beyond all recompense.

In Valente's later work, this sense of responsibility for the death of the other is marked in the many poems he writes on the tragic passing of his son, Antonio. 'Paisaje con pájaros amarillos', which forms part of the collection from 1992, 'No amanece el cantor' is dedicated entirely to recounting the suffering this event provoked. For Levinas, in lines from *Totalité et infini* that Valente marks in his edition of the work, the relation of the father and the son is emblematic of the structure of transcendence in immanence that informs his thought. The father is, in a sense, part of the son, with whom he shares genetic material, but yet at the same time is other: 'c'est moi étranger à soi (Lévinas 1961: 299). The relationship with the son, which need not be taken in a literal, biological sense, reflects the depth of affective relation to the death of the other. This paradoxical identity with the other is present in many of the fragments which seek to question beyond the knowable:

> YO CREÍ que sabía un nombre tuyo para hacerte venir. No sé o no lo encuentro. Soy yo quién está muerto y ha olvidado, me digo, tu secreto. (I: 498)
>
> AHORA ya sé que ambos tuvimos una infancia común o compartida, porque hemos muerto juntos. Y me mueve el deseo de ir hasta el lugar en donde estás para depositar junto a las tuyas, como flores tardías, mis cenizas. (I: 499)
>
> PARA cuán poco nos sirvió vivir. Qué corto el tiempo que tuvimos para saber que éramos el mismo. Mientras el pájaro sutil de aire incuba tus cenizas, apenas en el límite soy un tenue reborde de inexistente sombra. (I: 502)

It is, in a sense, possible to share the death of the other, as the relationship with the other is always a relation with an unknowable, a relation prior to knowledge and intention. This is not to take away the sting of death, the profound absence that it marks, but rather to restore within it, beyond nothingness, the enigma, the relation without relation that denies the absurdity of finitude, but does not provide the consolation, for Levinas in itself based on a limited thought of being, of eternal life. The poem remains as a question without answer: 'me dan la clave del enigma | en la pregunta misma sin respuesta | que hace nacer la luz de mis pupilas ciegas' (I: 580), testimony to the unknown that is less than nothing, the enigma of the absent other, the 'tenue reborde de inexistente sombra' (I: 502).

In a wider sense, Levinas's thought in respect of death here opens on to questions of temporality and the social. Reading the utopian philosophy of Ernst Bloch, Levinas argues that Bloch's thought allows for 'une dimension de sens où se pense un au-delà de l'être et du néant' (1993: 107). This is because the temporality of utopia exceeds the temporality defined by Heidegger as having no other meaning than the 'to-be-toward-death'. Rather, Bloch understands time in relation to a utopia that exceeds all predetermined being-towards. If men and women are alienated, their work incomplete, then their relation towards death takes on significance in terms of this incompletion. Their emotional state would not, in this case, be defined by a fundamental anxiety, the Heideggerean *angst*, rather, anxiety would be but one mode of a melancholy for the world undone, a history defined by suffering and defeat. This melancholy refusal of the given determines both Valente's commitment to the memory of the victims of totalitarian regimes and his resistance to a neoliberal politics of the spectacle. Time, in this context, is defined by hope, and this hope is nourished by the glimpse of a completed world, which Bloch argues can be attained in culture, in the astonishing moment when 'cet instant où la lumière de l'utopie pénètre dans l'obscurité de la subjectivité' (Lévinas 1993: 115).

Though Valente's writings are infused with a sense of profound loss, his poetry finds its power from the intuition that an unalienated life is possible. The 'remota luz' that invites the speaker of the first poem of his first collection, 'Serán ceniza', could stand for the ethical stance of a writer who refused, throughout his life, to renege on a vision of radical political change, despite the failures of twentieth century communism. For Valente, the hope that sustains this vision is provided by the infinite disponibilidad of a poetic language that is experienced as a 'preaparecer', or, in Bloch's terms, a *vor-schein*, of a world to come. It is fitting, then, that the last poem of Valente's posthumous *Fragmentos de un libro futuro* should refer to the moment of achieved utopia, the moment in which the song of the nightingale and the voice of the poem unite:

> Cima del canto.
> El ruiseñor y tú
> ya sois lo mismo.
> (*Anónimo: versión*) (I: 582)

Despite its claim to unity, the poem is written in time, and as such essentially incomplete, a fragment. And yet, it affords death a meaning that exceeds the categories of finitude, being, and nothingness – the hope of an enigmatic time to come. Valente's first poem describes the desert, a symbol of absence; his last, the Edenic language of birds, a symbol of presence. Between, or beyond, these lies the pure question that defines his poetry, the desire that remains desire, the language of hope.

BIBLIOGRAPHY

ADAMS, HAZARD. 1983. *Philosophy of the Literary Symbolic* (Tallahassee: Florida University Press)
ADORNO, THEODOR W. 1991. *Notes to Literature*. Vol. I (New York: Columbia University Press)
—— 2002. *Essays on Music: Theodor W. Adorno* (Berkeley, CA: University of California Press)
AGAMBEN, GIORGIO. 1993. *The Coming Community* (Minneapolis: University of Minnesota Press)
—— 1990. *La Communauté qui vient: théorie de la singularité quelconque* (Paris: Editions du Seuil)
—— 1996. 'No amanece el cantor', in *En torno a la obra de José Ángel Valente*, ed. by Jacques Ancet, Rosa Rossi and Americo Ferrari (Madrid: Alianza), pp. 47–57
—— 1999. *Potentialities: Collected Essays in Philosophy* (Stanford, CA: Stanford University Press)
—— 2000. *Remnants of Auschwitz: The Witness and the Archive* (New York: Zone)
AGUDO, MARTA, and JORDI DOCE (eds). 2010. *Pájaros raíces: En torno a José Ángel Valente* (Madrid: Abada)
ALEIXANDRE, VICENTE. 1955. *Algunas carácteres de la nueva poesía española* (Madrid: Instituto de España)
ALBERTI, RAFAEL. 1937. *De un momento a otro: (Poesía e historia) 1932–1937* (Madrid: Europa-América)
—— 1966. *El poeta en la calle: poesía civil, 1931–1965, con un poema de Pablo Neruda* (Paris: Librarie du Globe)
ALEGRIA, CLARIBEL, and OTHERS. 1971. 'La lettre des intellectuels à M. Fidel Castro', *Le Monde* <https://www.lemonde.fr/archives/article/1971/05/22/la-lettre-des-intellectuels-a-m-fidel-castro_2476142_1819218.html> [Accessed 6 February 2020]
ALEIXANDRE, VICENTE. 1987. *Pasión de la tierra*. (Madrid: Ediciones Cátedra)
—— 1993. *Espadas como labios; La destrucción y el amor* (Madrid: Ediciones Castalia)
ALTER, ROBERT. 1991. *Necessary Angels: Tradition and Modernity in Kafka, Benjamin, and Scholem* (Cambridge MA: Harvard University Press)
ANCET, JACQUES, ROSA ROSSI, and AMERICO FERRARI. 1996. *En torno a la obra de José Ángel Valente* (Madrid: Alianza)
ANDERSON, BENEDICT. 1991. *Imagined Communities* (London: Verso)
ARKINSTALL, CHRISTINE RETA. 1993. *El Sujeto en el exilio: Un estudio de la obra poética de Francisco Brines, José Ángel Valente y José Manuel Caballero Bonald* (Amsterdam: Rodopi)
ASEGUINOLAZA, FERNANDO CABO. 1998. 'Entre Narciso y Filomena', in *Teoría del poema: La enunciación lírica*, ed. by Fernando Cabo Aseguinolaza and Germán Gullón (Amsterdam: Rodopi), pp.11–39
ASSMANN, JAN. 1995. 'Collective Memory and Cultural Identity', *New German Critique*, 65: 125–33
ATTELL, KEVIN. 2015. *Giorgio Agamben: Beyond the Threshold of Deconstruction* (New York: Fordham University Press)
BACHELARD, GASTON. 1965. *Lautréamont* (Paris: Librairie José Corti)

BAER, ALEJANDRO. 2011. 'The Voids of Sepharad', *Journal of Spanish Cultural Studies*, 12, 1: 95–120
—— 2017. *Memory and Forgetting in the Post-Holocaust Era: The Ethics of Never Again* (London: Routledge)
BARJAU, EUSTAQUIO. 1975. *Antonio Machado, teoría y práctica del apócrifo: Tres ensayos de lectura* (Esplugues De Llobregat: Editorial Ariel)
BARRAL, CARLOS. 1953. 'Poesía no es Comunicación', *Laye*, 23: 23–26
BENJAMIN, WALTER. 1999. *Illuminations*, trad. by Harry Zorn (London: Pimlico)Bottom of Form
—— 2005. *Selected Writings 1927–1930*, 2 vols, 2 (Cambridge, Mass.: Belknap Press)
—— 2007. *Reflections: Essays, Aphorisms, Autobiographical Writings* (New York: Schocken)
BENLABBAH, FATIHA. 2008. *En el espacio de la mediación: José Ángel Valente y el discurso místico* (Santiago de Compostela: Universidade de Santiago de Compostela)
BIALE, DAVID. 2011. *Not in the Heavens: The Tradition of Jewish Secular Thought* (Princeton, NJ: Princeton University Press)
BLANCO DE SARACHO, TERA. 2010. 'La esclava y el ángel: correspondencia y dedicatorias entre María Zambrano y José Ángel Valente', *Moenia*, 16: 83–101
BLANCHOT, MAURICE. 1955. *L'espace littéraire* (Paris: Gallimard)
—— 1967. *Lautréamont et Sade* (Paris: Editions de Minuit)
BLOCH, ERNST. 1988. *The Utopian Function of Art and Literature*, trans. by Jack Zipes and Frank Mecklenberg (Cambridge, MA: MIT Press)
BOOS, SONJA. 2015. *Speaking the Unspeakable in Postwar Germany: Toward a Public Discourse on the Holocaust* (Ithaca, NY: Cornell University Press)
BOUNOURE, GABRIEL. 1985. *Edmond Jabès, la demeure et le livre* (Paris: Fata Morgana)
BOUSOÑO, CARLOS. 1952. *Teoría de la expresión poética* (Madrid: Gredos)
BUTLER, JUDITH. 2000. *Antigone's Claim: Kinship between Life and Death* (New York: Columbia University Press)
CAGE, JOHN. 1961. *Silence: Lectures and Writings* (Middletown, CT: Wesleyan University Press)
CASADO, MIGUEL. 2005. *Los artículos de la polémica y otros ensayos.* (Madrid: Biblioteca Nueva)
—— 2012. *La palabra sabe* (Madrid: Libros de la resistencia)
CASSIRER, ERNST. 1944. *An Essay on Man: An Introduction to a Philosophy of Human Culture* (New Haven: Yale University Press)
CEBREIRO RÁBADE VILLAR, MARÍA DO. 2010. 'Los límites del poema no son los límites del mundo. Una lectura de *Cántigas de alén*', in *Pájaros raíces: en torno a la obra de José Ángel Valente*, ed. by Marta Agudo and Jordi Doce (Madrid: Abada), pp. 471–84
CELAN, PAUL. 1980. *Paul Celan: Poems, a Bilingual Edition*, ed. and trans. by Michael Hamburger (Manchester: Carcanet)
—— 2003. 'Speech on the Occasion of Receiving the Literature Prize of the Free Hanseatic City of Bremen', in *Paul Celan: Collected Prose*, trans. by Rosemarie Waldrop (Manchester: Carcanet)
CERNUDA, LUIS. 2000. *La realidad y el deseo: (1924–1962): seguido de historia de un libro (La realidad y el deseo)* (Madrid: Alianza)
COLERIDGE, SAMUEL TAYLOR. 1997. *The Complete Poems of Samuel Taylor Coleridge*, ed. by William Keach (London: Penguin)
CONTE IMBERT, DAVID. 2006. 'La palabra de lo singular: figuraciones del origen entre lírica y filosofía (Martin Heidegger, Claudio Rodríguez, José Ángel Valente)' (unpublished doctoral thesis, Carlos III de Madrid)
CUESTA ABAD, JOSÉ M. 1996. 'La enajenación por la palabra (Reflexiones sobre el lenguaje poético en Valente)', in *En torno a la obra de José Ángel Valente*, ed. by Teresa Hernández Fernández (Madrid: Alianza), pp. 49–77

―― 1999. *Poema y Enigma* (Madrid: Huerga & Fierro)
―― 2010A. *La transparencia informe: filosofía y literatura de Schiller a Nietzsche* (Madrid: Abada Editores)
―― 2010B. 'Figuras en fantasma', in *Pájaros raíces: en torno a José Ángel Valente*, ed. by Marta Agudo and Jordi Doce (Madrid: Abada), pp. 203–38
DAYDÍ-TOLSON, SANTIAGO. 1984. *Voces y ecos en la poesía de José Ángel Valente* (Lincoln, Nebraska: Society of Spanish and Spanish-American Studies)
DE CERTEAU, MICHEL. 1982. *La fable mystique: XVIe–XVIIe siècle* (Paris: Gallimard)
DE MAN, PAUL. 1983. 'The Rhetoric of Temporality', in *Blindness and Insight: Essays in the Rhetoric of Contemporary Criticism*, 2nd ed. (London: Routledge), pp. 187–228
―― 1984. 'The Intentional Structure of the Romantic Image', *The Rhetoric of Romanticism* (New York: Columbia University Press), pp. 1–18
DE OTERO, BLAS. 1955. *Pido la paz y la palabra: poema* (Torrelavega: Cantalapiedra)
DERRIDA, JACQUES. 1967. *De la grammatologie* (Paris: Les éditions de Minuit)
―― 1996. *Le monolinguisme de l'autre* (Paris: Galilée)
―― 2005. 'Shibboleth: For Paul Celan', in *Sovereignties in Question: The Poetics of Paul Celan*, ed. by Thomas Dutoit and Outi Pasanen, trans. by Joshua Wilner (New York: Fordham University Press)
DOCE, JORDI. 2005. *Imán y desafío: Presencia del romanticismo inglés en la poesía española contemporánea* (Barcelona: Ediciones Península)
DONAHUE, LUKE. 2013. 'Erasing Differences between Derrida and Agamben', *Oxford Literary Review*, 35.1: 25–45
DONNE, JOHN. 1953. *The Sermons of John Donne*, ed. by George R. Potter and Evelyn M. Simpson (Berkeley: University of California Press)
ENGELSON MARSON, ELLEN. 1978. *Poesía y poética de José Ángel Valente.* (New York: E. Torres)
ELIOT, T. S. 1948. *Selected Essays, 1917–1932.* 2nd ed. (London: Faber and Faber)
―― 1955. *The Use of Poetry and the Use of Criticism* (London: Faber and Faber)
―― 1963. *T. S. Eliot Collected Poems* (New York: Harcourt, Brace and World)
ESPOSITO, ROBERTO. 2009. 'Community and Nihilism', *Cosmos and History: The Journal of Natural and Social Philosophy* 5. 1: 24–36
―― 2010. *Communitas: The Origin and Destiny of Community* (Stanford, CA: Stanford University Press)
FABER, SEBASTIAAN. 2018. *Memory Battles of the Spanish Civil War: History, Fiction, Photography* (Nashville: Vanderbilt University Press)
FERNÁNDEZ CASTILLO, JOSÉ LUIS. 2008. 'El ídolo y el vacío. La crisis de la divinidad en la tradición poética moderna: Octavio Paz y José Ángel Valente' (unpublished doctoral thesis, Universidad Autónoma de Madrid)
FERNÁNDEZ QUESADA, NURIA, ed. 2000. *Anatomía de la palabra* (Valencia: Pre-Textos)
FERNÁNDEZ RODRÍGUEZ, MANUEL. 2001. 'Análisis integral de la narrativa de José Ángel Valente' (Unpublished doctoral thesis, Universidade de Santiago de Compostela)
FERNÁNDEZ RODRÍGUEZ, MANUEL and OTHERS. 2007. *Referentes europeos en la obra de Valente* (Santiago de Compostela: Universidad de Santiago de Compostela)
FERNÁNDEZ RODRÍGUEZ, MANUEL, FERNANDO GARCÍA LARA and CLAUDIO RODRÍGUEZ FER (eds). 2017. *Valente Vital (Magreb, Israel, Almería)* (Santiago de Compostela. Universidade de Santiago de Compostela)
FLAUBERT, GUSTAVE. 1954. *La tentation de Saint Antoine* (Paris: Éditions Garnier Frères)
FLETCHER, RICHARD. 2000. 'The Early Middle Ages: 700–1250', in *Spain: A History*, ed. by Raymond Carr (New York: Oxford University Press), pp. 63–89
FOUCAULT, MICHEL. 1966. *Les mots et les choses: Une archéologie des sciences humaines* (Paris: Gallimard)

FREUD, SIGMUND. 'Mourning and Melancholia'. *The Standard Edition of the Complete Works of Sigmund Freud 1953–1974*, trans. by James Strachy (London: Hogarth Press: Institute of Psycho-analysis), vol. 14, pp. 243–58.

FRITZSCHE, PETER. 2004. *Stranded in the Present: Modern Time and the Melancholy of History* (Cambridge, Mass.: Harvard University Press)

GARCÍA CANDEIRA, MARGARITA. 2013. 'Eterno inretorno: Melancolía e desterritorialización nas Cántigas de alén de José Ángel Valente' *Abriu*, 2: 109–22

GARCÍA MONTERO, LUIS. 1998. 'Poética', in *El último tercio del siglo (1968–1998): Antología consultada de la poesía española*, ed. by Jesús García Visor (Madrid: Visor)

GASCHÉ, RODOLPHE. 1986. *The Tain of the Mirror: Derrida and the Philosophy of Reflection*. (Cambridge, MA: Harvard University Press)

GIL DE BIEDMA, JAIME. 2017. *Las Personas del Verbo* (Barcelona: Debolsillo)

GOLDMANN, LUCIEN. 1964. *The Hidden God: A Study of Tragic Vision in the Pensees of Pascal and the Tragedies of Racine*. Trans. Philip Thody (London: Routledge)

GOMEZ TORE, JOSÉ LUIS. 2017. 'Después de Auschwitz, después de Hiroshima: Celan leído por José Ángel Valente' in *Lecturas de Paul Celan*, ed. by Mario Martín Gijón and Rosa Benéitez Andrés (Madrid: Abada), pp. 229–47

GOSETTI-FERENCEI, JENNIFER ANNA. 2010. 'Immanent Transcendence in Rilke and Stevens', *The German Quarterly*, 83.3: 275–96

GUÉNON, RENÉ. 1962. *Symboles fondamentaux de la science sacrée* (Paris: Gallimard)

GUICHOT REINA, VIRGINIA. 2010. 'La cultura escolar del franquismo a través de la historia oral', *Cuestiones pedagógicas*, 20: 215–45

HAMMERSCHLAG, SARAH. 2010. *The Figural Jew: Politics and Identity in Postwar French Thought* (Chicago: University of Chicago Press)

HEGEL, GEORG W. F., FRIEDRICH HÖLDERLIN, and FRIEDRICH W. J. SCHELLING. 1997. 'The Earliest Program for a System of German Idealism', in *Theory as Practice: A Critical Anthology of Early German Romantic Writings*, ed. by Jochen Schulte-Sasse (Minneapolis: University of Minnesota) pp. 72–73.

HEIDEGGER, MARTIN. 1962. *Being and Time*, trans. by John Macquarrie and Edward Robinson (New York: Harper & Row)

HELGERSON, RICHARD. 2007. *A Sonnet from Carthage: Garcilaso de la Vega and the New Poetry of Sixteenth-Century Spain* (Philadelphia: University of Pennsylvania Press)

HERNÁNDEZ FERNÁNDEZ, TERESA (ed.). 1995. *El silencio y la escucha: José Ángel Valente*. (Madrid: Ediciones Cátedra/Ministerio de Cultura)

IDEL, MOSHE. 1988. *Kabbalah: New Perspectives* (New Haven: Yale University Press)

——— 2002. *Absorbing Perfections, Kabbalah and Interpretation* (New Haven: Yale University Press)

IRIGARAY, LUCE. 1995. *Speculum of the Other Woman*, trans. by Gillian C. Gill (Ithaca, NY: Cornell University Press)

JABÈS, EDMOND. 1963. *Le livre des questions* (Paris: Gallimard)

——— 1976. *Le livre des ressemblances* (Paris: Gallimard)

——— 1978. *Le soupçon, le désert* (Paris: Gallimard)

——— 1989. *Un étranger avec, sous le bras, un livre de petit format* (Paris: Gallimard)

JABÈS, EDMOND, and MARCEL COHEN. 1980. *Du désert au livre: Entretiens avec Marcel Cohen* (Paris: P. Belfond)

JAMESON, FREDERIC. 2010. *The Hegel Variations: On the Phenomenology of Spirit* (London: Verso)

JIMÉNEZ, JOSÉ OLIVIO. 1972. *Diez años de poesía española: 1960–1970* (Madrid: Insula)

——— 1996. 'El vuelo de la imagen', in *En torno a la obra de José Ángel Valente*, ed. by Jacques Ancet (Madrid: Alianza) pp. 59–74

JIMÉNEZ HEFFERNAN, JULIÁN. 1998. *La palabra emplazada: meditación y contemplación de Herbert a Valente* (Córdoba: Servicio de Publicaciones de la Universidad de Córdoba)
—— 2004A. 'Literatura en España (1939–2000)', in *Akal Historia de la literatura*, ed. by Erika Wischer (Madrid: Akal), pp. 426–505
—— 2004B. *Los papeles rotos: Ensayos sobre poesía española contemporánea* (Madrid: Abada)
JUDT, TONY. 2005. *Postwar: A History of Europe Since 1945* (New York: Penguin)
JUNGK, ROBERT. 1960. *Brighter than a Thousand Suns* (London: Penguin Books)
KRÄMER, GUDRUN. 1989. *The Jews in Modern Egypt: 1914–1952* (Seattle: Washington University Press)
LABANYI, J. 2007. 'Memory and Modernity in Democratic Spain: The Difficulty of Coming to Terms with the Spanish Civil War', *Poetics Today*, 28.1: 89–116
LACALLE CIORDIA, MARÍA DE LOS ÁNGELES. 2001. 'La presencia del ángel en la poesía de José Ángel Valente', *Cuadernos del Marqués de Sán Adrián*, 1: 27–45
LAMPERT, ANDREAS. 2017. 'Algunas observaciones sobre el humor y lo serio en la obra de Paul Celan', in *Lecturas de Paul Celan*, ed. by Mario Martín Gijón and Rosa Benéitez Andrés (Madrid: Abada Editores), pp. 163–74
LANGBAUM, ROBERT. 1957. *The Poetry of Experience; the Dramatic Monologue in Modern Literary Tradition* (London: Chatto & Windus)
LANGER, SUSAN K. 1962. *Philosophy in a New Key: A Study in the Symbolism of Reason, Rite, and Art* (New York: New American Library)
LANZ RIVERA, JUAN JOSÉ. 2009. *Las palabras gastadas. Poesía y poetas del medio siglo* (Sevilla: Renacimiento)
LAUTRÉAMONT, ISIDORE DUCASSE, COMTE DE. 1967. *Les chants de Maldoror.* (Paris: Editions de la Renaissance)
LEAVIS, F. R. 1954. *New Bearings in English Poetry; a Study of the Contemporary Situation* (London: Chatto and Windus)
LEFEBVRE, HENRI. 1966. *Le langage et la société* (Paris: Gallimard)
LÉVINAS EMMANUEL. 1961. *Totalité et infini; Essai sur l'extériorité* (La Haye: M. Nijhoff)
—— 1982. *Noms propres* (Paris: Fata Morgana)
—— 1990. *Autrement qu'être ou Au-delà de l'essence* (Dordrecht: Kluwer Academic)
—— 1993. *Dieu, la mort et le temps* (Paris: Grasset)
—— 1996. 'Paul Celan: From Being to the Other', in *Proper Names*, trans. by Michael B. Smith (Stanford, Cal.: Stanford University Press), pp. 40–46
LÉVINAS, EMMANUEL, and PHILIPPE NEMO. 1982. *Ethique et infini: Dialogues avec Philippe Nemo* (Paris: Fayard)
LLERA, JOSÉ ANTONIO. 2019. 'Poesía y Censura Previa. A Propósito de José Ángel Valente', *Cuadernos Hispanoamericanos*, 826: 108–17
LÓPEZ CASTRO, ARMANDO. 2002. *En el límite de la escritura: poesía última de José Ángel Valente* (Ourense: Abano)
LOPO, MARÍA. 2007. 'José Ángel Valente y Edmond Jabès. Reconocerse en la palabra', in *Referentes europeos en la obra de José Ángel Valente*, ed. by Manuel Fernández Rodríguez (Santiago De Compostela: Universidade de Santiago de Compostela), pp. 149–84
—— 2013. 'Valente e Lautréamont', in *José Ángel Valente: Memoria sonora*, ed. by Raquel Rivera Fernández (Santiago De Compostela: Universidade de Santiago de Compostela), pp. 81–89
LOPO, MARÍA, TERA BLANCO DE SARACHO and CLAUDIO RODRÍGUEZ FER (eds). 2014. *Valente Vital (Ginebra, Saboya, París)* (Santiago de Compostela: Universidade de Santiago de Compostela)
LUCAS, JORGE MACHÍN. 2010. *José Ángel Valente y la intertextualidad mística postmoderna: Del presente agónico al presente eterno.* (Santiago de Compostela: Universidade de Santiago de Compostela)

FERNÁNDEZ RODRÍGUEZ, MANUEL (ed.). 2007. *Referentes europeos en la obra de José Ángel Valente* (Santiago de Compostela: Universidade de Santiago de Compostela)

MACHADO, ANTONIO. 1964. *Obras: poesía y prosa* (Buenos Aires: Editorial Losada)

MARCHAL, BERTRAND. 1988. *La religion de Mallarmé: Poésie, mythologie et religion* (Paris : J. Corti)

MARTZ, LOUIS LOHR. 1954. *The Poetry of Meditation: A Study in English Religious Literature of the Seventeenth Century* (New Haven: Yale University Press)

MAS, MIGUEL. 1986. *La escritura material de José Ángel Valente* (Madrid: Hiperion)

MAYHEW, JONATHAN. 1994. *The Poetics of Self-Consciousness: Twentieth-Century Spanish Poetry* (Lewisburg: Bucknell University Press)

—— 1999. 'The Avant-Garde and Its Discontents: Aesthetic Conservatism in Recent Spanish Poetry', *Hispanic Review*, 67.3: 347–63

—— 2004. 'Valente's Lectura de Paul Celan: Translation and the Heideggerian Tradition in Spain', *Diacritics*, 34.3–4: 73–89.

—— 2009. *The Twilight of the Avant-Garde* (Liverpool: Liverpool University Press)

—— 2012. 'The Genealogy of Late Modernism in Spain: Unamuno, Lorca, Zambrano, and Valente', *Modernist Cultures*, 7.1: 77–97

MILLS, PATRICIA JAGENTOWICZ. 1986. 'Hegel's Antigone', *The Owl of Minerva*, 17.2: 131–52

MORA, VICENTE LUIS. 2010. 'Desierto contra espejo', in *Pájaros raíces: en torno a la obra de José Ángel Valente*, ed. by Marta Agudo and Jordi Doce (Madrid: Abada), pp. 421–36

MORETTI, FRANCO, and DOMINIQUE PESTRE. 2015. 'Bankspeak', *New Left Review*, 92: 75–99

MOSÈS, STEPHÁNE. 2009. *The Angel of History: Rosenzweig, Benjamin, Scholem* (Stanford: Stanford University Press)

MOYN, SAMUEL. 2005. *Origins of the Other* (New York: Cornell University Press)

NANCY, JEAN LUC. 1986. *La communauté désouvrée* (Paris: C. Bourgois)

—— 1991. *The Inoperative Community*, ed. by Peter Conner, trans. by Peter Conner, Lisa Garbus, Michael Holland, and Simona Sawhney (Minneapolis, MN: Minnesota University Press)

NAVARRETE, IGNACIO ENRIQUE. 1994. *Orphans of Petrarch: Poetry and Theory in the Spanish Renaissance* (Berkeley: University of California Press)

NELIS, JAN. 2007. 'Constructing Fascist Identity: Benito Mussolini and the Myth of Romanità,' *Classical World*, 100.4: 391–415

NEMOIANU, VIRGIL. 1984. *The Taming of Romanticism: European Literature and the Age of Biedermeier* (Cambridge, Mass.: Harvard University Press)

PALLEY, JULIAN. 1992. 'El ángel y el yo en la poesía de José Ángel Valente', in *José Ángel Valente. El escritor y la crítica*, ed. by Claudio Rodriguez Fer (Madrid: Taurus), pp. 312–30

—— 1994. 'José Ángel Valente, poeta de la inminencia', in *Material Valente*, ed. by Claudio Rodriguez Fer (Barcelona: Jucar), pp. 43–55

PEINADO ELLIOT, CARLOS. 2002. *Unidad y trascendencia. Estudios sobre la obra de José Ángel Valente* (Sevilla: Alfar)

—— 2010. 'La influencia de Böhme en *Tres lecciones de tinieblas*: "Alef" y "Bet"', in *Pájaros Raíces. En Torno a José Ángel Valente*, ed. by Marta Aguda and Jordi Doce (Madrid: Abada Editores)

—— 2011. 'El simbolismo religioso en *Tres lecciones de tinieblas*: la cruz y la rueda', in *El guardián del fin de los desiertos: perspectivas sobre Valente*, ed. by José Andujar Almansa and Antonio Lafarque (Valencia: Pre-Textos)

POLO, MILAGROS. 1983. *José Ángel Valente: Poesía y poemas* (Madrid: Narcea)

PONS, ARNAU and PATRICK LLORED. 2001. 'Conversación con Jean Bollack', *Quimera*, 201: 34–57

PRADEL, STEFANO. 2018. *Vértigo de las cenizas: estética del fragmento en José Ángel Valente* (Valencia: Pre-Textos)

QUEVEDO, FRANCISCO DE. 2009. *Selected Poetry of Francisco de Quevedo*, ed. and trans. by Christopher Johnson (Chicago: University of Chicago Press)
RAMOS ABREU JOSÉ A. DE. 2008. *La fascinación del enigma: La poética de José Ángel Valente en sus ensayos* (Madrid: Fundación Universitaria Española)
RAMÓN, ESTHER. 2014. 'Tres Lecturas de Tinieblas', *Cuadernos Hispanoamericanos*, 763: 26–39
RANCIÈRE, JACQUES. 2011. *Mallarmé: La politique de la sirène* (Paris: Hachette)
RESINA, JOAN. 2000. *Disremembering the Dictatorship: The Politics of Memory in the Spanish Transition to Democracy* (Amsterdam: Rodopi)
—— 2017. *The Ghost in the Constitution: Historical Memory and Denial in Spanish Culture* (Liverpool: Liverpool University Press)
RIBEIRO DE MENEZES, ALISON. 2014. *Embodying Memory in Contemporary Spain*. (New York: Palgrave Macmillan)
RICHARDS, MICHAEL. 2013. *After the Civil War: Making Memory and Re-Making Spain since 1936* (Cambridge: Cambridge University Press)
RIVERA FERNÁNDEZ, RAQUEL, ed. 2013. *José Ángel Valente. Memoria sonora* (Ourense: Deputación Provincial de Ourense)
RODRÍGUEZ FER, CLAUDIO, ed. 1992. *José Ángel Valente: El escritor y la crítica*. (Madrid: Taurus)
—— 1994. *Material Valente* (Madrid: Júcar)
—— 1995. 'Valente en la lengua del origen', in *El silencio y la escucha*, ed. by Teresa Hernández Fernández (Madrid: Ediciones Cátedra), pp. 119–41
—— 1998. 'Entrevista vital a José Ángel Valente: de Ourense a Oxford'. *Moenia* 4: 451–64
—— 2000. 'Entrevista vital a José Ángel Valente: de Xenebra a Almería'. *Moenia* 6: 185–210
—— 2010. 'Valente dende as cartas de alén'. *Moenia* 10: 125–31
RODRÍGUEZ FER, CLAUDIO, MARTA AGUDO RAMÍREZ and MANUEL FERNÁNDEZ RODRÍGUEZ (eds). 2012. *Valente Vital (Galicia, Madrid, Oxford)* (Santiago de Compostela: Universidade de Santiago de Compostela)
ROMANO, MARCELA. 2002. *Imaginarios re-(des)-encontrados: Poéticas de José Ángel Valente* (Mar de Plata: Martin)
ROTHBERG, MICHAEL. 2006. *Multidirectional Memory: Remembering the Holocaust in the Age of Decolonization* (Stanford, Ca: Stanford University Press)
RUXANDRA GENIA, IOANA. 2008. *Escribir el tiempo. La huella de T. S. Eliot en Jaime Gil de Biedma y José Ángel Valente* (Granada: Editorial Universitaria de Granada)
SARTRE, JEAN PAUL. 1949. *Baudelaire*, trans. by Aurora Bernárdez (Buenos Aires: Losada)
—— 1964. *Qu'est-ce que la littérature?* (Paris: Gallimard)
SARTRE, JEAN-PAUL, and BENNY LÉVY. 1980. *L'espoir Maintenant* (Paris: Editions Verdier)
SAVELSBERG, FRANK. 2000. 'Aproximación a tres lecciones de tinieblas de José Ángel Valente'. *Moenia*, 6: 51–125
SCHOLEM, GERSHOM. 1969. *On the Kaballah and its Symbolism* (New York: Schocken)
—— 1972. 'The Name of God and the Linguistic Theory of the Kabbala', *Diogenes*, 20.79: 59–80
—— 1995. *Major Trends in Jewish Mysticism* (New York: Schocken)
SCHULTE-SASSE, JOCHEN. 1997. *Theory as Practice: A Critical Anthology of Early German Romantic Writings* (Minneapolis: University of Minnesota)
SZONDI, PETER. 2003. *Celan Studies*, ed. by Jean Bollack, Henriette Beese, Wolfgang Fietkau, Hans-Hagen Hildebrandt, Gert Mattenklott, and others, trans. by Susan Bernofsky and Harvey Mendelsohn (Stanford: Stanford University Press)
SILES, JAIME. 2017. 'Lecturas de Celan', in *Lecturas de Paul Celan*, ed. by Mario Martín Gijón and Rosa Benéitez Andrés (Madrid: Abada Editores), pp. 83–109
SIMHON, ARI. 2006. *Levinas critique de Hegel* (Brussels: Ousia)
SNARRENBERG, FRANK. 1994. 'Competing Myths: The American Abandonment of

Schenker's Organicism', in *Theory, Analysis and Meaning in Music*, ed. by Anthony Pople (Cambridge University Press), 29–56.

SÖDERBÄCK, FANNY (ed.) 2010. *Feminist Readings of Antigone.* (Albany: State University of New York)

STAMELMAN, RICHARD HOWARD, and MARY ANN CAWS (eds). 1989. *Ecrire le livre: Autour d'Edmond Jabès: Colloque de Cerisy-la-Salle* (Seyssel: Champ Vallon)

STAROBINSKI, JEAN.1989. *La mélancolie au miroir: trois lectures de Baudelaire* (Paris: Julliard)

STEINER, GEORGE. 1984. *Antigones* (New York: Oxford University Press)

STEVENS, WALLACE. 1997. *Collected Poetry and Prose* (New York: Literary Classics of the United States)

TRAVERSO, ENZO. 2016. *Left-wing Melancholia* (New York: Colombia University Press)

UGARTE, MICHAEL. 1979. 'Juan Goytisolo: Unruly Disciple of Américo Castro', *Journal of Spanish Studies: Twentieth Century*, 7: 353–64

UNAMUNO, MIGUEL DE. 1986. *Del sentimiento trágico de la vida* (Madrid: Alianza Editorial)

VALCÁRCEL, EVA. 2009. *El fulgor o la palabra encarnada. Imágenes y símbolos de la poesía última de José Ángel Valente* (Barcelona: Promociones y Publicaciones Universitarias)

VALENTE, JOSÉ ÁNGEL. 2001. *Punto Cero: (1953–1976)* (Madrid: Alianza)

—— 2006. *Obras Completas*, ed. by Andrés Sánchez Robayna, vol. I (Barcelona: Galaxia Gutenberg)

—— 2008. *Obras Completas*, ed. by Andrés Sánchez Robayna, comp. by Claudio Rodríguez Fer, vol. II (Barcelona: Galaxia Gutenberg)

—— 2011. *Diario Anónimo: 1959–2000*, ed. by Andrés Sánchez Robayna (Barcelona: Galaxia Gutenberg)

—— 2014. *Palais de justice* (Barcelona: Galaxia Gutenberg)

VALENTE, JOSÉ ÁNGEL, and IMA SANCHÍS. 3 May 2000. 'He vivido esperando la revelación', *La Vanguardia*, p. 100

VALLADARES, SATURNINO. 2017. *Retrato de grupo con figura ausente* (Ourense: Deputación Provincial de Ourense)

VILLON, FRANÇOIS. 1994. *Complete Poems*, ed. by Barbara N. Sargent-Baur, trans. by Barbara N. Sargent-Baur (Toronto: Univ. Of Toronto Press)

VIVAS, ELISEO. 1955. *Creation and Discovery: Essays in Criticism and Aesthetics* (New York: Noonday)

WACHSMASS, NIKOLAUS. 2015. *KL: A History of the Nazi Concentration Camps* (New York: Farrar, Strauss, and Giroux)

WALDROP, ROSEMARIE. 2002. *Lavish Absence: Recalling and Rereading Edmond Jabès* (Middletown: Wesleyan University Press)

WOLFSON, ELLIOT R. 1999. *Rending the Veil: Concealment and Secrecy in the History of Religions* (New York: Seven Bridges)

YILDIZ, YASEMIN. 2012. *Beyond the Mother Tongue: The Postmonolingual Condition* (New York: Fordham University Press)

INDEX

Adams, Hazard 17
Adorno, Theodor 14, 16, 87, 110
Agamben, Giorgio 22, 24 n. 11 & 13, 25 n. 14, 29–32, 64, 70–71, 72 n. 11, 92 n. 22 & 23, 100–01, 103
   The Coming Community 70–71, 72 n. 11
   'The Idea of Language' 22–25
   Remnants of Auschwitz 100–01
   Stanzas: Word and Phantasm in Western Culture 29–32
Alberti, Rafael 13–14, 53 n. 11
Aleixandre, Vicente 4–5, 11, 15–16, 24 n. 3
Aristotle 85
Arkinstall, Christine 72
Assmann, Jan 4

Barral, Carlos 12, 24 n. 4
Bataille, Georges 66
Baudelaire, Charles 46, 50, 53 n. 5, 97–98, 100, 114 n. 4
   and Benjamin 46
   L'essence du rire 100
   and Sartre 97–98
   'Le voyage' 53 n. 5
Beethoven, Ludwig van 86–87
   Piano Sonata no. 32 in C Minor, Op. 111: 86–87
Benjamin, Walter 3–4, 9, 14, 16, 23, 40, 43, 46–48, 50–51, 53 n. 13, 74–75, 94–95, 107, 109, 115
   'On some Motifs in Baudelaire' 46–47
   'An Outsider Makes his Mark' 43
   'Theses on the Philosophy of History' 3–4, 40, 94–95
Benveniste, Émile 100, 113 n. 3
Bergson, Henri 46, 53 n. 13
Bernárdez, Aurora 97
Blanchot, Maurice 36, 64, 71 n. 5, 75, 79, 95, 115
   'Le regard de l'Orphée' 36, 115
Blanco de Saracho, Tera 8, 24 n. 9 & 12, 53 n. 11
Bloch, Ernst 4, 18, 22–23, 28, 48, 74–75, 89, 95, 115, 118
   vor-schein 18, 22, 28, 48, 118
Bollack, Jean 108
Bounoure, Gabriel 78
Bousoño, Carlos 11, 24 n. 3
Brecht, Berthold 14, 16
Buber, Martin 108–09
Butler, Judith 56–57
   Antigone's Claim 56–57

Caballero Bonald, José Manuel 5

Cabo Aseguinolaza, Fernando 101
Cage, John 85, 91 n. 17
Canetti, Elias 3, 23, 75
Casado, Miguel 8–9, 11, 27, 53 n. 7, 106
Casey, Calvert 15, 48–52, 55
Cassirer, Ernst 17–18
Castro, Américo 73, 90 n. 1
Celan, Paul 4, 7, 9, 23, 55, 75, 93–112, 113 n. 1, 114 n. 5
Celaya, Gabriel 11, 24 n. 4, 39, 53 n. 10
Cernuda, Luis 12, 24 n. 6, 77, 83, 116
Certeau, Michel de 19, 24 n. 11
Cohen, Marcel 78
Cohn Bendit, Daniel 39
Coleridge, Samuel Taylor 91 n. 21, 100, 116
community, theories of 64–71
Cornford, John 39, 45, 51
Costa, Uriel da 89
Costafreda, Alberto 5
Couperin, François 88
Cuesta Abad, José Manuel 7, 8, 21–22, 28
Culler, Jonathan 29

De Beauvoir, Simone 15
De la Cruz, San Juan 19, 69, 72 n. 10
De Man, Paul 7, 99–100
De Otero, Blas 11, 24
Derrida, Jacques 22, 23, 24 n. 13, 75, 79, 82–83, 91 n. 13, 95, 98, 108, 114 n. 5
   "Monolinguisme de l'autre" 82–83
   and Scholem 91 n. 13
Do Cebreiro Rábade Villar, María 80, 90 n. 10
Doce, Jordi 7, 52 n. 2
Donne, John 32, 53 n. 3

Eliot, T. S. 7, 12–14, 16–17, 24 n. 5 & 7, 33, 52 n. 2, 53 n. 5, 61
   and Valente's poetics 12–14
Enzensberger, Hans Magnus 94
Esposito, Roberto 67–68

Fernández Castillo, José Luis 7, 91 n. 16
Fernández Quesada, Nuria 7
Fernández Rodríguez, Manuel 7, 24 n. 5
Ferrán, Jaime 5
Flaubert, Gustave 23, 49
Fletcher, Richard 3
Foucault, Michel 20

Freud, Sigmund 29–30
  'Mourning and Melancholy' 29–30
Fritzsche, Peter 2
Fukuyama, Francis 89

García Candeira, Margarita 90 n. 10 & 11
Garcilaso de la Vega 2–3
Gasché, Rodolphe 98–99
Gil de Biedma, Jaime 7–8, 10 n. 3, 24 n. 4 & 5
Goldmann, Lucien 32
Gómez Toré, José Luis 93–94, 109
Gomis, Lorenzo 5
González, Ángel 5
Goytisolo, José Agustín, 5
Goytisolo, Juan 10 n. 6, 15, 73, 90 n. 1
Guénon, René 91 n. 19

Hammerschlag, Sarah 73–75, 79
  Postmodern trope of the Jew 73–75, 79
Helgerson, Richard 2
Hegel, G. W. H. 24 n. 7, 56, 65–66, 71 n. 1, 74, 79, 90 n. 3, 93, 99, 115
Heidegger, Martin 7, 9, 59, 74, 78, 90 n. 4, 93, 95, 116–18
Herder, J. G. 17
Hernández, Miguel 14
Hernández Fernández, Teresa 6
Hierro, José 11
Hölderlin, Friedrich 93
Humboldt, Wilhelm von 17

Idel, Moshe 91 n. 13
Irigary, Luce 71 n. 1

Jabès, Edmond 4. 9, 23, 73–90, 90 n. 7 & 8, 91 n. 15, 95, 112
Jakobson, Roman 113 n. 3
Jameson, Frederic 99
Jiménez, Juan Ramón 24 n. 4, 91 n. 16, 97–98
  and Antonio Machado 97–98
Jiménez Heffernan, Julian 6–9, 10 n. 9, 27, 32, 82–83

Kafka, Franz 13, 75, 84
Kant, Immanuel 79, 93, 98–99

Lacan, Jacques 56
Langbaum, Robert 24 n. 7
Langer, Susanne K. 17–18
  presentational form 18
Lautréamont, Comte de 16, 24 n. 10, 71 n. 5
Leavis, F. R. 13–14, 16
Lefebvre, Henri 14, 16, 56, 71 n. 2
Levinas, Emmanuel 4, 7, 23, 65, 74–75, 79, 95–96, 101, 108–09, 115–18
  Dieu, la mort et le temps 115–18
  Jewish identity 74–75
  and Paul Celan 95–96, 108–09

Lévy, Benny 74
Lezama Lima, José 5, 8, 15
Lopo, María 7
Lorca, Federico García 57
Lukacs, Georg 14, 24 n. 8
Luria, Isaac 75–76, 85, 90 n. 5
  doctrine of the *Tsimtsum* 75–76

Machado, Antonio 12, 45–46, 95, 97–98, 101–02, 105
  Collioure commemoration, 1959: 12
  heterogeneidad del ser 95, 97–98, 101–02
  'Si supieras' 45–46
Mallarmé, Stephane 7, 28, 68, 71 n. 7, 91 n. 16
Mann, Thomas 87
Marchal, Bertrand 71 n. 7
Martz, Louis J. 12, 24 n. 6
  The Poetry of Meditation 12, 24 n. 6
Mayhew, Jonathan 7–9, 10 n. 8, 92 n. 24, 95
melancholy 9, 23, 29–31, 39–52, 82, 90 n. 11, 106, 114 n. 4, 118
memory 1–2, 4, 9, 10 n. 5, 11, 16, 18–20, 23, 27–53, 58, 62–64, 96–97, 104–13, 118
  cultural 4, 9, 11, 50, 58, 97, 112
  and victims of violence 104–13
Molinos, Miguel de 48, 51–52
Montero, Luis García 5–6, 10 n. 8, 92 n. 24
  criticism of Valente 5–6
Mora, Vicente Luis 79
Mosès, Stepháne 23

Nahman of Braslaw 83, 90
Nancy, Jean Luc 23, 64–67, 70
  The Inoperative Community 64–67, 70
narcissism 97–102
Nemo, Philippe 74
Nemoianu, Virgil 97
Novalis 93

Ouaknin, Marc Alain 90
Olivio Jiménez, José 22, 36
Orpheus myth 36, 107, 118

Padilla, Heberto 15
Peinado Elliot, Carlos 7
Petere Herrera, José 53 n. 11
Pessoa, Fernando 101–02
Pimentel, Luis 80
Pons, Arnau 108–09
Proust, Marcel 47, 53 n. 13

Quevedo, Francisco de, 'Amor constante más allá de la muerte' 27

Richards, Michael 1, 53 n. 6
Rilke, Rainer Maria 91 n. 18, 93
Risco, Vicente 4
Rodríguez Feo, José 15

Rodríguez, Claudio 5
Rodríguez Fer, Claudio 6, 8, 24 n. 9 & 12, 53 n. 8 & 11, 90 n. 10
Romano, Marcela 5
Rosensweig, Franz 23, 74
Rothberg, Michael 112
  multi-directional memory 112
Ruxandra Gruia, Ioana 7, 24 n. 5

Sartre, Jean Paul 11, 15–16, 74–75, 97–98
  and Baudelaire 97–98
  Hope now 74
  Padilla affair 15
  Jewish identity 74–75
  Qu'est-ce que la littérature 11
Schelling, Friedrich W.J. 24 n. 7, 91 n. 21, 93
Schenker, Heinrich 91 n. 21
Scholem, Gershom 4, 20–21, 23, 75–76, 79–80, 84, 87, 89, 90 n. 5, 91 n. 13 & 15, 109, 115
  doctrine of the *Tsimtsum* 74–75
  and Edmond Jabès 91 n. 13
  hermeneutics 20–21
Semprún, Jorge 15
Siles, Jaime 113 n. 1
Sophocles 14, 55, 71 n. 1
  Antigone 14–15, 55–58, 61, 63, 71 n. 1
Spinoza, Benedict 89, 92 n. 23
Starobinski, Jean 106, 114 n. 4
Steiner, George 71 n. 1
Suarès, Carlo 20, 75
Szondi, Peter 110

Tapiès, Antoni 76
Traverso, Enzo 39–40, 42, 112
  left-wing melancholy 39–40, 42
  memory cultures 112

Ugarte, Michael 90 n. 1
Unamuno, Miguel de 12, 71 n. 4

Valente, José Ángel:
  censorship of 90 n. 2
  childhood 1, 4
  critical reception of 5–9, 108–10
  Cuba 15, 39, 48, 53 n. 10
  education 4
  Geneva 20–39, 45, 48, 53 n. 8 & 11, 75, 90 n. 2
  and Judaism 3–4, 7, 19–21, 23, 27, 75–79, 83, 88–90, 94–97, 109–13, 115
  Madrid 4, 6, 10 n. 6
  Oxford 4, 10 n. 6, 12–13, 24 n. 5, 31, 39, 52 n. 2
  political stance 15, 39, 73, 109, 112, 118
  and Republican exiles 44–45, 53 n. 11
  works:
    'Acuérdate del hombre que suspira...' (poem) 58
    Al dios del lugar 70–71, 106, 110–11
    'Alef' (poem) 89

A modo de esperanza 27–31, 58, 64, 78–79, 102–03, 116
'Aniversario' (poem) 28–29
'Anónimo: versión' (poem) 118
'Antimemorias' (poem) 106
'Berlín' (poem) 93, 107
'Boceta improbable' (prose) 102
'Borde' (poem) 70
Breve son 10 n. 1, 58, 64, 77
'Canción de cuna' (poem) 64
'Cántiga de eterno irretorno' (poem) 83
Cántigas de alén 79–83, 90 n. 11
'Centro' (poem) 118
'César Vallejo' (poem) 46
'Cinco fragmentos' (prose) 76
'Como una invitación o una súplica' (poem) 47–48, 61
'Conocimiento y comunicación' (essay) 12–13, 17–19, 24 n. 4
'Con palabras distintas' (poem) 61
'Consiento' (poem) 116
'Criptomemorias' (poem) 104–05
'Crónica, 1968' (poem) 63
'Cuba: Dogma y ritual' (newspaper article) 15
Diario anónimo 8, 13, 15, 52 n. 2, 53 n. 5, 10 & 11, 91 n. 18, 94, 98, 113 n. 3, 114 n. 3, 115
'Edmond Jabès: judaísmo e incertidumbre' (essay) 78, 90
'El alma' (poem) 32
'El ángel' (poem) 87–88
'El ángel de la historia' (newspaper article) 1
'El autor en su treinta aniversario' (poem) 104
'El corazón' (poem) 30
'El crimen' (poem) 103
'El deseo era un punto inmóvil' (poem) 69
'Elegía menor, 1980' (poem) 106–07
'El emplazado' (poem) 31–32
'El espejo' (poem) 102–03
El fulgor
El inocente 31, 48–52, 58, 62–64
Elogio del calígrafo
'El poder de la serpiente' (essay) 15–16
'El poema' (poem) 63–64
'El signo' (poem) 46–47
'El testigo' (poem) 41
'El uniforme del general' (prose) 90 n. 2
'El viento trae sobre todas las cosas' (poem) 49
'El visitante' (poem) 45
'Entrada al sentido' (poem) 32–33
'Epitafio' (poem) 28
'Extramuros' (poem) 43–44
'Figura de home en dous espellos' (prose) 81
Fragmentos de un libro futuro 57, 68, 93, 108, 111, 118
'Hablábamos de cosas muertas' (poem) 42–43
'Hibakusha' (poem) 110–11
'He' (poem) 89

'Ideología y lenguaje' (essay) 14–15, 55–57, 63
Interior con figuras 58, 68–70, 85–87, 104–05
'Intervenciones en el congreso '40 anni di poesía in Spagna' (conference presentation) 5, 57
'John Cornford, 1936' (poem) 45–46
'Juan Ramón en la tradición poética del medio siglo' (essay) 97–98
La experiencia abisal 3, 70, 73, 77–78, 90, 93
'La experiencia abisal' (essay) 70
'La hermenéutica y la cortedad del decir' (essay) 19–21, 91 n. 13
'La lentitud de la destrucción' (poem) 106
'La memoria del fuego' (essay) 79, 83–84
La memoria y los signos 31, 39–51, 53 n. 10, 58, 61–62, 64, 104
'La mentira' (poem) 60
'La necesidad y la musa' (essay) 13
'La noche' (poem) 69–70
La piedra y el centro 11, 24 n. 6, 102
'La plaza' (poem) 60
'La respuesta de Antígona' (essay) 55
'La rosa necesaria' (poem) 58–60, 64
'La salida' (poem) 36–38
'La señal' (poem) 40–41
Las palabras de la tribu 11–14, 16–21, 24 n. 4, 6 & 8, 55–57, 63, 91 n. 3
'Lautréamont o la experiencia de la anterioridad' (essay) 16
Lectura de Celan: Fragmentos 93–96
'Literatura e ideología. Un ejemplo de Berthold Brecht' (essay) 14
'Los olvidados y la noche' (poem) 34–36, 103–04
'Lucila Valente' (poem) 28
'Lugar vacío en la celebración' (poem) 49–50
'Luis Cernuda y la poesía de la meditación' (essay) 24 n. 6
Mandorla 70, 93, 105–07
'Materia' (poem) 71
Material memoria 76, 87–88
'Meditación sobre una imágen cóncova' (poem) 105
'Melancolía del destierro' (poem) 44
'Memoria de Paul Celan, en la muerte de Gisèle Celan-Lestrange' (poem) 93
'Modernidad y postmodernidad: el ángel de la historia' (essay) 94
No amanece el cantor 93, 106–07
'Noche primera' (poem) 30–31
'No inútilmente' (poem) 48
'No puede a veces' (poem) 61
Notas de un simulador 115
'Objeto del poema' (poem) 60

"Oxford, 1956" (essay) 13
Paisaje con pájaros amarillos 117
'Palabra, linde de lo oscuro: Paul Celan (essay) 93
Palais de justice 8
'Para oprobio del tiempo' (poem) 62
'Pasmo de Narciso' (essay) 102
'Paxaro de prata morta' (prose) 80
'Perdimos las palabras' (poem) 77
Poemas a Lázaro 29, 31–38, 52 n. 2, 58–59, 60, 64, 67, 103–04
'Poesía y exilio' (essay) 3, 73, 77
Presentación y memorial para un monumento 58, 64, 111
'Primer poema' (poem) 59, 67
Punto cero 94
'Ramblas de julio, 1964' (poem) 44
'Serán ceniza...' (poem) 27, 78–79
'Si supieras' (poem) 46
'Sobre el lugar del canto' (poem) 60
'Sobre el tiempo presente' (poem) 50, 62–63
'Sobre la unidad de la palabra escindida' (essay) 78
'Sonderaktion 1943' (poem) 115
'Son los ríos' (poem) 36
SOS (poem) 93
'Sub nocte' (poem) 82
'Tendencia y estilo' (essay) 14, 24 n. 8
'Tiempo' (poem) 108
Treinta y siete fragmentos 113 n. 1
Tres lecciones de tinieblas 88–90, 91 n. 20
'Tres lecciones de tinieblas, una autolectura' (prose) 88
'Tubinga, otoño tardía' (poem) 93
'Una encuesta de 2000' (newspaper interview) 6
'Un canto' (poem) 61
'Una oscura noticia' (poem) 51–52
Variaciones sobre el pájaro y la red 11, 79, 83–84
'Viznar, 1988' (poem) 57

utopianism 2, 9, 18, 23, 27, 39, 41, 48, 51–52, 56, 61, 74–75, 77, 83, 89, 95, 109, 118

Vivas, Eliseo 12

Waldrop, Rosemarie 84, 91 n. 15
Wolfson, Elliot R. 91 n. 14

Yeats, William Butler 101
Yevtushenko, Yevgeyney 39, 53 n. 10
Yildiz, Yasemin 81

Zambrano, María 5, 7, 29, 53 n. 11, 53 n. 8

www.ingramcontent.com/pod-product-compliance
Lightning Source LLC
LaVergne TN
LVHW061253060426
835507LV00017B/2047